1980

Emergent African States

Topics in Twentieth Century
African History

by
S. A. Akintoye
Professor of History,
University of Ife

Longman Group Limited
London

Associated companies, branches and
representatives in Africa and throughout
the world

First published 1976
Second impression 1977

ISBN 0 582 60127 4

Printed in Hong Kong by
Yu Luen Offset Printing Factory Limited

Contents

To my son, Ademola.

Preface

Late in 1970, I was invited by the Ministry of Education, Western State of Nigeria, to prepare scripts and teachers' notes for a series of thirty-minute radio talks on the subject 'Emergent States of Africa' for Nigerian secondary schools and teacher-training colleges during the 1971 school year. At the time there was no thought of doing anything beyond the broadcasts. But during 1971, demand steadily grew for a book on the subject – especially from the teachers and students who were using the necessarily sketchy broadcasts for their history lessons. I have written this book in response to those demands.

A book like this is bound to suffer certain obvious limitations. The most important of these is that, because of the period of history with which it is concerned, most of its chapters deal with themes that are still unfolding. Moreover, as it is a book of selected topics, it does not present a continuous account of the period. Nevertheless, it is hoped that this book may prove useful not only to the students of secondary schools and teacher-training colleges but also to the general reader who wishes to be informed about developments in the recent history of Africa.

Ile-Ife, January, 1975   *S. A. Akintoye*

The colonial experience

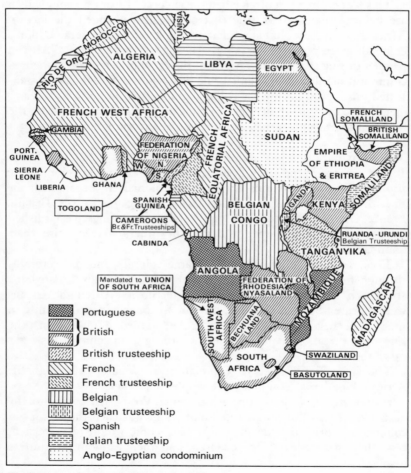

Portuguese

} British

British trusteeship
French
French trusteeship
Belgian
Belgian trusteeship
Spanish
Italian trusteeship
Anglo-Egyptian condominium

The European division of Africa into colonies

1 The colonial era and its heritage

Only a few scattered areas of Africa were under European rule before the middle of the nineteenth century. For almost all the rest of Africa, the colonial era began only in the years between 1885 and 1906. Furthermore, except for the Portuguese colonies and a few countries (like South Africa and Rhodesia) still under white minority regimes, practically all of Africa became independent during the 1950s and 1960s. For most of Africa, therefore, colonial rule lasted only between six and eight decades; in some places, indeed, not more than five.

This fact is often forgotten when the effects of European colonialism are being assessed. It is true that colonialism changed the face of Africa in many ways, but such changes must not be exaggerated, nor is colonialism responsible for all the changes in the lives of African peoples during this century. Many of the economic and social changes commonly attributed to colonial rule had begun before this was established; also, even during the colonial era, certain important developments (like the growth of Western education) resulted more from the work of other agencies than of the colonial governments.

The political effects of colonialism

It was perhaps in the area of political life that European colonial rule produced the most serious effects. The colonial era began with the main European countries sharing Africa among themselves. Britain, France, Germany, Portugal, Belgium, Italy and Spain each established its own areas of influence and got the others to recognise their boundaries.

These areas of influence then became colonies and protectorates through force of arms mostly, since Africans generally resisted the attempts of Europeans to take over their territories. Although Africans were defeated because they had inferior weapons and also because in most places neighbouring states and peoples failed to unite against the European threat, they put up a long, hard fight, in some places right up to the 1920s.

The immediate effect of colonialism, therefore, was that the African kingdoms, empires and peoples lost their freedom. Some African states, in fact, as in parts of French West Africa, were totally destroyed. In all the conquered countries, it was then the European colonial authority that decided how the people would be governed, how their society would be ordered, and their economic resources disposed of.

The creation of new states in Africa

The colonial authorities gave each colony or protectorate common national boundaries, a common national name, a common national capital city, a common central government, a common official language and certain other common institutions. In this way, they laid the foundations of the modern states of Africa. This is perhaps the most important development resulting from European colonial rule.

One must not overrate its significance however. It is wrong to see the new countries as the first successful attempts in Africa to build large centralised states with well organised machineries of government, judiciaries, civil services and armies. It is true that there were, by the nineteenth century, some African peoples who could be described as 'stateless' societies, but in most parts of Africa long before the Europeans arrived large kingdoms and empires had been built. In West Africa, for instance, there had been the empires of Ghana, Mali, Songhai, Kanem-Bornu and Old Oyo. When the European powers began to invade Africa in the nineteenth century, they encountered many large powerful states, such as, in West Africa, the Sokoto Caliphate, the Tukolor Empire, the Ashanti Kingdom, the Mandinka Empire, and others. What happened at the beginning of the colonial era was that the Europeans defeated and, in many cases, destroyed the existing African states and then went on to build new states (called colonies or protectorates) in their place, usually ignoring the boundaries of the old states. Each colony or protectorate was, therefore, a collection of peoples and old states, or fragments of these, brought together within the same boundaries.

Before a country created in this way could develop internal unity, before its various peoples could begin to feel a common loyalty to their new country, much needed to be done. How much did the colonial powers do? They gave each new country a number of common institutions, which united the peoples in many common activities. The common activities laid the foundations for the growth of common loyalties, and gradually, each country developed its own 'nationalism' above the smaller nationalisms of its component peoples.

However, the colonial authorities did not deliberately seek such a result. No colonial power pursued policies consciously aimed at encouraging national unity and national loyalty in any of its colonies, although the general attitudes of some might have tended to do so. The French usually paid little attention to the ethnic origins of their West African subjects, regarding them as Dahomeans or Togolese or Senegalese, rather than as Ewes, Fon, Mandinka or Bambara. The British, on the other hand, tended to regard their African subjects as Yorubas

3

or Hausas or Kikuyus, rather than as Nigerians or Kenyans. Loyalty to the ethnic group or to the old state therefore tended to survive more strongly in the British than in the French colonies.

More often, colonial policies were deliberately aimed at preventing the growth of national unity. The best examples are to be found in colonies in which the colonial powers were trying to crush or cripple the independence movement. For instance, from the outbreak of the liberation wars in the Portuguese colonies at the beginning of the 1960s, the Portuguese caused or encouraged disunity and even hostilities among the peoples of their colonies to weaken the freedom fighters. In the early 1950s when Britain was confronted with armed revolt in Kenya, the British encouraged suspicions among the peoples of Kenya to weaken the revolt. Probably in most colonies in the last years of the independence struggles, the colonial powers subtly encouraged disunity or took advantage of existing signs of disunity in order to hold on to their colonies longer or to obtain independence settlements favourable to themselves.

In short, whenever colonial control was faced with a serious threat, the colonial powers tended to adopt, among other measures, the tactics of divide and rule. Such tactics often worsened the problems of national unity which the African countries had to face; sometimes, indeed, they set the patterns of future hostilities. For instance, British manoeuvres contributed immensely to the growing fear which the smaller (minority) ethnic groups developed towards the larger (majority) ethnic groups in most British colonies in the last years of the colonial era.

Because of the way the colonies were created, their boundaries usually did not follow the old boundaries between African states and peoples. For instance, the Ewes were split between the Gold Coast (now Ghana) and Togoland, and the Yorubas between Nigeria and Dahomey (now Benin). Such boundaries were merely artificial, without foundation in the geography or history of Africa. Eventually, most Africans came to accept them as part of their national institutions, but, in many places, local inhabitants along the boundaries did not pay much attention to them, in spite of official efforts to make them do so. In at least a few areas, a people split between two neighbouring colonies continued to wish to be reunited, and border conflicts between neighbouring African countries have been common after independence.

Colonialism and African political institutions
In every colony, colonial administration had two levels. First, there was the central administration with its seat in the capital city. At the

top was the Governor (or Governor-General in some cases) surrounded by his top advisers, the top police and military officers and the top colonial judges. This central government was served by a central civil service. In larger colonies like Nigeria and Zaire, there were regional commissioners who acted as assistants to the Governor and were part of the central government. The central government received orders and instructions from Europe (London, Paris or Brussels); it interpreted the instructions and was responsible to the imperial government in Europe for the conduct of the affairs of the colony. In this set-up, all ultimate authority and responsibility within the colony belonged to the Governor (or Governor-General).

Below the central government was the local administration. Each colony was usually divided into small administrative units, called districts or divisions in the British colonies and *cantons* in the French colonies. Sometimes, a few neighbouring districts or divisions were grouped together to form provinces.

It was in this local administration that the colonial governments made use of the indigenous African political institutions – kings, chiefs, etc. There were two reasons why they did so. Firstly, it would have been impossible, and far too expensive, for each colonial power to bring from Europe the vast numbers of officials necessary to man and administer every district, village and town in each colony. Secondly, the colonial authorities found that, no matter what they thought about African political institutions, they could not easily do away with them. They were too well established among the people and an intrinsic part of their lives. For the purpose of local government, therefore, each colonial power began to make use of the influence of the African king or chief among his people. In each unit of local administration the indigenous African rulers were made to exercise some authority under the supervision of the European resident official. This system is generally referred to as 'native administration'.

The way in which the African ruler was used and treated in the local government set-up varies from one colonial master to another. On the whole, the British treated the local African rulers with some respect and allowed them a certain measure of initiative. Indeed, ideally, the British local official was supposed to be an adviser to the African chief, although he was more often a supervisor. In most places, the British preserved for each ruler the territory he had ruled in pre-colonial times; they did not usually interfere with the people's selection and installation of their rulers, although after selection by his people, a king or chief had to be approved by the central colonial administration. The African ruler was usually appointed as 'native authority' over his pre-colonial state. Local taxes were collected, a 'native treasury' was established and also 'native courts' in which the African rulers were made to administer modified forms of traditional law. Often, a 'native authority police force' was also set up and placed at the service of the native authority.

However, even when the British district officer was willing to act as adviser and interfere as little as possible, the actions of the native authority were always expected to meet standards and principles laid down by the colonial authorities and to win the approval of the district officer. The district officer was the court of appeal to all the native authority courts in his area, and the power to execute the decisions of the courts lay with him. The ultimate purpose of the native authority was to help the colonial government in carrying out its policies, like the building of roads to make trade move freely, the collection of taxes, or the maintenance of law and order in rural areas, etc.

Nevertheless, African rulers in British colonies enjoyed more freedom of action and more personal respect than under any other colonial power. The British called their system 'indirect rule'. All the other colonial powers attempted to rule their colonies more directly and used larger numbers of white officials in their local government systems. We shall take a look at Belgian and French systems to illustrate this.

Belgian local administration in the major Belgian colony, Congo (now Zaire), developed in three stages – 1885 to 1908, 1908 to about 1919, 1919 to 1960. Between 1885 and 1908, Zaire was the personal possession of King Leopold II of Belgium and the Belgian Government (cabinet and parliament) had nothing to do with the colony. During these years, the main objective of King Leopold was to extract as much rubber and ivory as possible from the country, and he used very harsh methods to achieve this. The chiefs were forced to recruit people, who were treated almost like slave gangs, to collect rubber and ivory. This led to many revolts against King Leopold's administration, and each revolt was crushed with military force. In this way practically all the major chiefdoms of Zaire were destroyed and broken up.

In 1908, as a result of world criticisms of King Leopold's administration, the Belgian Government took over Zaire. The new administration stopped some of Leopold's excesses and gave some recognition to African chiefs. However, to make sure that no chief would be powerful enough to start trouble, each chiefdom was kept very small. Thus, the old states and political boundaries within Zaire were ignored and large numbers of ridiculously small chiefdoms were created. Between 1914 and 1919, the number of chiefdoms rose from 3,653 to about 6,095. In Manyema district alone, with a population of 185,000 people, there

6

were 530 chiefdoms by 1919, i.e., one chief to about 350 people. Moreover, the administration ignored traditional rights of succession and appointed as chiefs only persons who were slightly literate and loyal to the Belgian administration. Some Belgian officials even appointed their own house-boys as chiefs. Finally, it was common for chiefs to be arrested and punished in front of their people.

This policy led to the almost total collapse of local government in Zaire by 1919. To prevent chaos, attempts were made to revive the traditional political order. Some former chiefdoms were revived and made units of local administration; elsewhere, smaller chiefdoms were combined to form larger units. From then on, the Belgians began to talk of 'indirect rule' in their Zaire colony. As in the British colonies, local taxes were levied to support the chiefs' local authority, and 'native courts' and 'native treasuries' were established. However, the chiefs were never allowed as much initiative nor given as much respect as their counterparts in the British colonies. The local Belgian officials preferred to act on their own initiative and give orders to the chiefs. They were so many – more than 10,000 by 1960 – that they could more or less directly control even the most remote parts of the country.

In the French colonies of sub-Saharan Africa, the African chiefs were made agents of the colonial administration, and their duties were clearly defined. The French ignored the traditional boundaries of the chiefdoms and divided each colony into *cantons*. Usually a chief was put over one of the new *cantons* rather than his own former chiefdom. Like the Belgians, the French appointed as chiefs not necessarily those who qualified by birth, but men who had some French education and showed loyalty to the French. The chiefs were subordinate to the French officials, and this point was emphasised in every possible way, both to the chiefs and to their people. The French officials showed very little respect to the chiefs, who were not recognised as 'native authority'. The chiefs were simply civil servants acting as a mouthpiece for the colonial administration and their principal duties were to collect taxes and to help recruit people for labour on government works like building railways and roads.

No matter whom he served, therefore, the traditional African ruler was no longer his own master. The colonial government had final authority for his actions. Moreover, many of the things which the chief had to make his people do – like payment of tax or submission to forced labour – were alien to, and unpopular with, the people. Finally, the colonial officials usually attempted to simplify the traditional political situation to make it easier to manage. Thus, in some areas where a single traditional authority had held sway over a very large territory, they would try to create smaller local authorities or units by breaking the one large kingdom or chiefdom into smaller ones. In places where the colonial officials felt there were too many traditional rulers sharing a territory, they would try to raise up one or two of the rulers over the rest so as to reduce the number of chiefs they had to deal directly with. Where there were no traditional chiefs, the colonial officials would sometimes create some of their own.

All these things had tremendous effects on traditional African political institutions. Firstly, some of the chieftaincies which existed at the time of independence had no traditional foundations at all, being merely the creations of the colonial administrators. Secondly, some traditional kings and chiefs survived into independence with influence over areas beyond the territories which they had ruled before colonialism. Thirdly, those traditional institutions (like councils of lower chiefs in a kingdom, assemblies of family heads, secret societies, age-groups, professional associations) which had been very important in the traditional political systems of Africa had lost their importance or even died out by the time of independence because the colonial administrators had ignored or suppressed them. Fourthly, because of their loss of independent authority under colonialism, many African traditional chieftaincies and kingships had lost their skills for managing their peoples. Fifthly, by the time of independence some traditional kingships and chieftaincies had lost favour with the people partly because they had become associated in the peoples' minds with the unpopular measures which they had been made to carry out during the colonial era, and partly because many chiefs and kings had acted as allies of the colonial masters during the independence struggles.

Moreover, in the last years of the colonial era, a new system of government – by the elective principle – was gradually introduced into many of the colonies. This meant that literate African commoners were now being allowed to take some part in the government of their countries as local government councillors or members of the legislative councils or national assemblies. An important step in the progress towards independence, this also represented an important historical change. It meant that as the European colonial masters gradually withdrew under nationalist pressure, they were leaving the running of the African countries not in the hands of the African kings and chiefs but in the hands of the educated commoners, for it was the educated men, not the chiefs, who had the requisite knowledge. In the new political order of the emerging African countries, kings and chiefs and other traditional institutions became less and less important.

However, the chiefs still enjoyed some influence. Before colonial times, the African ruler or chief had not been just a political leader, and until the end of the colonial era he remained important in the religious life of the people; he was still the centre of important rituals and ceremonies. For some people the king or chief remained 'God's lieutenant on earth', the great commander and judge. In spite of the emerging new order, most of the illiterate people in the remote districts would rather take their disputes to the king or chief for settlement in the traditional way than go to the new courts. In short, in spite of all the changes which traditional African institutions underwent during the colonial era, these institutions continued to command the allegiance of many people, even after independence in some places.

In practical terms, however, the colonial experience destroyed the systems of government represented by the African kings and chiefs. What did colonialism put in its place? European writers often claim that Europe introduced democracy to Africa by freeing the Africans from the brutal oppression which had characterised pre-colonial African governments. Usually they go on to lament that democracy has failed to take root in Africa, as shown by the events since independence.

However, although most parts of Europe enjoyed the main features of democratic government (adult suffrage, elected parliaments and governments, freedom of political association and press) by the beginning of the twentieth century, Europe did not bestow democracy upon its African subjects. Almost throughout the colonial era, European rule in Africa used a system of government in which the same small group (the European officials) took the decisions, executed them, and acted as the police officers and military commanders as well as the judges. It was a government responsible in no way to the people and resting, ultimately, on military and police force. It is true that in most African countries, the colonial masters introduced elections and certain aspects of responsible government in the years before independence. But the ultimate right and practice of self-determination and fully responsible government, such as most of Europe itself enjoyed, were not introduced until the very day of independence. In fact, traditional African governments, which colonial governments replaced, were far more democratic in many respects. Every traditional African state had its own checks and controls on the powers and actions of the king or chief.

Colonial rule was not subject to any such control. In most colonies, any criticism of the government earned terrible punishments. In Zaire, for instance, no political parties or newspapers were allowed until a couple of years before independence. The isolation of the government from the governed, the refusal to tolerate opposition or

9

criticisms, the fear of delegating authority, the branding of all virile opposition as treasonable action – all these were learned from Africa's colonial masters by the Africans who took over African governments at independence.

Economic effects of colonialism
Economically, Africa by the 1960s was very different from what it had been at the beginning of the colonial era. In parts of every country there had occurred a change-over from an economy based mainly on subsistence crop farming to one depending increasingly on cash-crop farming for export. For the masses of African peasants, this was an important development bringing with it new methods of organising farming, increased incomes, and improved standards of living. Every colonial power built roads and railways, harbours and airports. Such improvements opened up many parts of Africa, thereby putting agricultural, mineral and forest resources more easily within reach. Vastly increased trade with Europe and the rest of the world introduced new imports and led to the expansion of the people's economic desires and demands. European demands for African raw materials, the introduction of new ideas of economic organisation, the promotion of the European type of education and the introduction of health services – all these improved the economic performance of large sections of the African population.

Not all these changes, however, were brought about by the colonial governments. The change from subsistence to cash-crop farming had begun in the nineteenth century in many parts of Africa, due to European demands for African raw materials owing to the Industrial Revolution in Europe. By the middle of the nineteenth century European markets were already buying large quantities of palm oil from Eastern Nigeria, cotton and some palm oil from Western Nigeria and groundnuts from Senegal and the Gambia. Cocoa, the most valuable cash-crop in colonial West Africa, was introduced into West Africa from South America in the late nineteenth century by Africans returning from slavery in the Americas. Of the major cash-crops which became important in the lives of the peasants of colonial Africa, only a few – notably coffee – were introduced after the establishment of colonial rule. During the colonial era, the colonial authorities encouraged the growth of the cash-crop economy, but it was the Africans themselves that had initiated it.

The spread of the European type of education owed more to the Christian missionary bodies than to the colonial governments. The missionaries had introduced schools into many parts of Africa before the imposition of colonial rule. Even afterwards the missionaries continued to mobilise their converts to build schools and send their children to those schools. Most future leaders of Africa were products of the mission schools, and purely government schools were scarce. Government hospitals were also few and they were to be found mostly in the major towns where the colonial administrations were based. Beyond these, most of the hospitals, health centres and maternity centres were missionary institutions.

Indeed, in comparison with the immense wealth they derived from the exploitation of the resources of Africa, the colonial powers did very little for their colonies' improvement and welfare. For instance, educational facilities, when viewed against the population, were very inadequate. In Nigeria and Ghana, the two most educationally advanced colonies in British West Africa, only 21·4 and 43·6 per cent respectively of children of school age were enrolled in primary schools in 1947. In Dahomey, one of the educationally most advanced of the French colonies, only 10 per cent of school-age children were enrolled in the primary schools. Secondary education figures were lower still. In general, more was done for education in the British and French than in the Belgian and Portuguese colonies. Though Zaire (then known as the Belgian Congo) had probably the largest percentage of primary school enrolment in tropical Africa, it had practically no provision for secondary education, since it was the policy of the Belgian authorities, at least until about 1950, to limit colonial education to the primary school level. When it is remembered that most of the inadequate educational facilities in all colonies were provided by the missionaries and their converts, it will be clear how little the colonial governments did.

The principal objective of colonial governments was to enrich the European countries. For instance, ports, roads, and railways were built mainly to enable the European governments and private companies to tap the resources of the interior of Africa effectively. Whenever European governments or companies invested money in Africa, they did so in areas and on enterprises from which their investments could yield the largest profits most quickly. In short, investments were not meant to improve the economies of the African countries for the well-being of the Africans but to increase the wealth of the European investors. It was, therefore, in minerals and cash-crops (cocoa, rubber, cotton, groundnuts, coffee) which could be exported to Europe to feed the European industries that the colonial administrations and the big European companies were interested. Little was done to develop and improve the production of the food crops on which the lives of the people depended.

As a result, practically every African country came to depend on one or two exportable minerals or cash-crops for most of its income. Zaire depended principally on minerals and rubber, Nigeria on cocoa, groundnuts and palm produce, Ghana on cocoa, Zambia on minerals (copper), and Ivory Coast on coffee and cocoa. Now, any national economy depending principally upon one or two export products is an unstable economy. Whenever the price of any of the crops falls in the world market, the country suffers. This has happened to many African countries since independence. For instance, much of the economic troubles of Ghana and Nigeria after 1960 resulted from the fall in the price of cocoa.

The colonial powers, however, reaped many advantages. They were able to obtain the basic raw materials needed to keep their industries running at home. In addition, the European companies made big profits from organising the purchase and export of the colonial raw materials. No African could compete with the European companies because they always enjoyed official backing and encouragement, and colonial policy generally made it impossible for Africans to acquire the necessary capital and business experience.

Sometimes, the colonial governments established government corporations to buy the colonial cash-crops from the farmers and export them for sale in the world market. Usually, such a corporation was given a monopoly over the buying and marketing of a particular cash-crop, and the power to fix the price to be paid to the African farmers. Perhaps the best examples of such corporations were the Marketing Boards established by the British in their colonies after the Second World War. Under this arrangement, a Marketing Board was set up in each colony for every cash-crop. The reason given was the protection of African farmers against the frequent rise and fall in world prices. As Britain explained it the African farmers of, say, cocoa, would be paid the same steady price from year to year whether the world market price of cocoa rose or fell. In the years when the world price of cocoa rose much higher than the producer price (i.e. the price paid to the farmers), a surplus of money would be accumulated; in years when the world price fell below the producer price, the producer price would still be maintained by withdrawing money from the surpluses that had been accumulated in the good years. In this way, the cocoa farmer would not suffer.

The real reason for the arrangement was, however, that Britain had come out of the Second World War heavily in debt and with her economy shattered, and the Marketing Board system was the British

Government's way of drawing more money than ever before from the colonies. The Marketing Boards usually set the producer prices very much lower than the world prices and the huge surpluses which thus accumulated from year to year were sent to Britain where they were invested in Britain's economic recovery programmes. These moneys were regarded as loans to Britain by the colonies, which were thus being compelled to lend to Britain most of the wealth derived from their products. Moreover, the interest payable on such 'loans' was decided by the British Government and such interest was generally small – 0.5% before 1950, 2% by 1952, 4% after 1952. Between 1950 and 1957 Ghana, from her cocoa alone, lent Britain more than £1,200 million under this arrangement.

Other colonial powers devised similar or different methods for draining the wealth of their colonies. For instance, Belgium drained Zaire heavily during the Second World War, and after the war Zaire was made to write off most of her war-time 'loans' to Belgium.

In short, most of the wealth earned by the cash-crops of the African farmers during the colonial era was spent on the development of European rather than African countries. Moreover, because most of the wealth went to Europe, it was impossible for an indigenous capitalist class to emerge in Africa.

The economic policy planned for the colonies by the colonial powers was that the colonies should serve as both sources of raw materials for European industries and as markets for the manufactured products of European industries. This policy meant that few secondary industries (industries which convert raw materials into manufactured goods) were ever set up in the colonies.

Another important consequence of colonial economic policies was that a few giant European companies came to dominate the economies of African countries. Some of these companies not only controlled the export-import trade but also the mining, the forest resources and a lot of plantation agriculture. The colonial governments did nothing to ensure that these companies returned enough of their huge profits to the colonies for development. For instance, many paid little or no taxes on their exploitation of the mines or on their profits in other enterprises. Some of these companies, like the Unilever group in British West Africa and the Belgian *Société Générale* in Zaire, became so big and powerful that even after independence they and their subsidiaries remained dominant in Africa. Through such companies, European shareholders were able to continue to reap much of the profits from the cash-crop agriculture and the mining industry of African countries after independence.

13

Different colonial governments pursued different land policies. In West Africa, the British did not allow the companies to set up plantations nor did they encourage European settler farmers. However, in the East African highlands (especially in Kenya) and in Rhodesia, white settlers were allowed to take part of the land to establish plantations. The Belgians, French and Portuguese gave colonial lands to the European companies for agricultural plantations. Therefore, while the production of the cash-crops was left in the hands of the Africans in British West Africa, European companies or settlers took part in agricultural production in Kenya, Rhodesia, Ivory Coast, Zaire, Guinea and Togoland. Although the areas taken over by the European companies or settlers were usually a small percentage of the total land area, probably no other issue caused as much annoyance to Africans as the land issue.

Social and cultural effects of colonialism

It is in the field of cultural and social change that the effects of European colonial rule in Africa are most difficult to assess. This is so because it is always difficult to determine all the causes of social and cultural changes in any society. For instance, it could be said that colonial rule caused a lot of contacts between peoples – between Africans of different cultures and different regions, and between Africans and Asiatics and Europeans. But it is difficult to say precisely how much such contacts were due to colonialism and how much to the general improvements in transportation and communication in the world during this century.

The spread of the European type of education has also caused important social and cultural changes. It has produced a new class of African leaders, literate, familiar with the languages and the ways of life of other peoples through their studies and travels, pioneers of a new African society. Literacy has led to the reduction of many African languages into writing, and this has enriched those languages. But colonial rule was responsible for only part of this spread of literacy.

On the other hand millions of Africans living in the remote rural areas experienced little or no direct contact with the colonial machinery. Yet their lives were not wholly unaffected by colonial rule.

European writers have certainly exaggerated the cultural impact of colonialism on Africa. Not only the writings of colonial officials but also those of European scholars and even missionary agents, paint a picture of pre-colonial Africa as a jungle inhabited by barbarians and savages. According to them, the European coloniser brought light and civilisation to this 'Dark Continent'. This picture of Africa provided a justification for colonialism and all its exploitation and oppression. Indeed, it enabled colonialism to be presented as a great and wonderful thing which brought the Africans out of their savagery and made them part of the 'civilised' world. Missionaries painted the picture in lurid colours to convince their congregations, friends and donors back home that their work in Africa was worthy of support.

Every colonial power claimed this duty of civilising the Africans as its mission in Africa. But the French and the Portuguese went further than other European powers in devising a policy aimed at 'civilising' the Africans. This was the policy of 'assimilation'. Since the French and Portuguese convinced themselves that the Africans had no civilisation and that their own civilisations were the best in the world, they decided that the best way to save the Africans from savagery was to turn them into black Frenchmen or black Portuguese speaking the French or Portuguese language, living, behaving and reasoning like Frenchmen or Portuguese. Those Africans who succeeded in attaining this high level of 'civilisation' would then be given French or Portuguese citizenship with all its rights and privileges. They would be separated from the other Africans legally, socially and politically; they would become subject to French or Portuguese laws while the other Africans would be subject to colonial laws; those of them in the French colonies would be entitled to vote and be voted for in elections to the French parliament in Paris; they would qualify to be appointed into high positions in the colonial administration.

However, the view that pre-colonial Africa had no culture and no history is false. The European officials, scholars and missionaries who popularised this image of Africa were ignoring the evidences of rich African cultures – in political, economic and social organisations, in art, music and manners – which were there all over Africa for them to see. Both the French and the Portuguese had in the end to give up 'assimilation' as a policy, the French in about 1920 and the Portuguese in 1961. Though the policy did produce in the French and Portuguese colonies a class of men (called *assimilado* by the Portuguese) who attained a high degree of fluency in the French or Portuguese language and acquired a lot of other French or Portuguese traits, it was a failure in its aim of producing black Frenchmen or black Portuguese. The so-called *assimilado* was the product, first, of a rich African culture from which it was impossible to tear him away completely. Ultimately these men were to join the masses of their countrymen, and indeed provide the leadership, in the struggle to end French or Portuguese colonialism.

In short, through various close contacts with each other in the last hundred years, African and European cultures have learned and borrowed much from each other. African cultures have been strong enough to maintain their indigenous richness though borrowing certain elements from European cultures. It is as people used to say in the French colonies: 'Assimilate but do not be assimilated'; in other words, take from the French culture whatever you regard as desirable in it but do not be taken over by the French culture.

One important change is that in many parts of Africa, colonial administrative and economic activities led to the rise of new towns, in places like ports and mining centres, while the old towns which housed the colonial headquarters grew rapidly in population. This was because paid jobs were available in these places, so that many Africans, literate and non-literate, left their homes and migrated there in search of work under the colonial administration or in the European companies.

The new towns were different from the old African towns in composition and in the type of relationships which grew up in them. They were made up of fragments of families from various regions and various ethnic groups. And these inhabitants were bound together in groups, not so much by their ethnic affinities as by their common economic interests as workers. Soon, these groups were to begin to form themselves into labour unions fighting together for their common good. As will be seen in the next chapter, they also began to form themselves into 'ethnic unions' – each of which was a mutual self-help association for those who had come from the same region. Nevertheless, the new cities served as melting pots in which people of different ethnic origins were thrown together in their daily lives and work. Such close contacts with other people, as well as the demands of life in the new towns, changed the immigrants' way of life. Moreover, it was in such towns that loyalty to the new African countries first developed.

Another facet of these changes was the rise of a working population as a distinct class. Africa had always had its farmers, craftsmen and doctors, but the rise of masses of wage workers congregated in one place because of their employment was a new development.

Traditional family structure was also affected. The indigenous African family was usually a large entity living together in one compound, holding the family land in common, and within which the individual member enjoyed much security and bore considerable responsibility for the welfare of all members. The migrations to the new towns meant tearing away members of the family. Within the new towns a new type of family emerged on the European model of a man and his wife and their children. Moreover, the products of the European type schools could no longer fit easily into the old family system and, in any case, usually had to go far away for jobs. Finally, alien ideas of individual ownership of property slowly crept in and people began to wish to have their own land and their own houses apart. Consequently, in many African communities, more and more small individual family houses appeared side by side with, and sometimes in the place of, the old family compounds.

However, the psychological foundation of the old family system has survived better than its physical structure. Even among the literate and the migrants to the towns, the old obligations for the welfare of all members of the family group has persisted. The average immigrant family of Lagos or Accra or Kinshasa or Nairobi usually houses brothers, sisters, nephews and cousins from the large family at home. And if the city dweller had the means – as a wage or salary earner or a businessman – then he would usually be contributing to the school fees of various young relatives or the maintenance of various old relatives.

On the whole, the cultural effect of colonialism was patchy; stronger in some countries than others, and in every colony stronger in some regions than others. Usually, it was stronger in the urban centres than the rural areas, but its intensity also varied from urban centre to urban centre. Also it was mostly superficial. Indeed, one might liken the cultural effects of colonialism and European influence generally on Africa to acid poured on a wooden carving, eating irregularly into the surface of the carving but leaving its general shape and features essentially unchanged.

2 Liberation movements and the coming of independence

Throughout the colonial era, Africans were continually struggling to regain control of their own affairs. Although they had lost the wars against the European invaders, they never lost the spirit of freedom. The claims of the colonial rulers that Africans were savages, the exploitation of African resources for European benefit, forced labour, the loss of land to European settlers and companies – for all these reasons, Africans increasingly hated European colonial rule.

The way in which the struggle was conducted varied from one African country to another. The African countries differed in their historical experiences and their cultures and, therefore, in the ways in which they expressed their rejection of foreign rule. For instance, in the Maghreb (Morocco, Algeria and Tunisia) the people have a long history of resistance. Centuries before the coming of the French in the nineteenth century, the people of the Maghreb had had to fight a long succession of foreign intruders – the Romans, Vandals, Arabs and Turks. Also, in some of those areas (like the Maghreb and Somalia) where Islam was very strongly established, Islam provided much of the philosophy for the independence struggle, while Islamic brotherhoods formed an important part of the nationalist forces.

Secondly, the policies of the colonial powers themselves differed. For instance, Africans in the British colonies were, on the whole, allowed more freedom of expression and association than those in Portuguese or Belgian colonies. So the liberation movements were mostly peaceful and constitutional in the British colonies, whereas the Portuguese colonies had to fight liberation wars. In countries like Algeria and Kenya where there were many European settler farmers, attempts to recover the land from the settlers was an important theme in the nationalist struggle. The people had to fight not only the colonial power but also the settlers, and the struggle to dislodge the settlers usually led to violence.

However, all the liberation struggles in all of Africa had the ultimate aim of regaining independence. Even when agitations appeared to have narrow immediate reasons – like revolts against taxation, demands for increased employment of Africans in the colonial government service, protests against poor pay for Africans, demands for the return of lands seized by settlers – they nevertheless had as their underlying motive the rejection of foreign domination. All these separate local battles should be seen as parts of the main struggle for independence.

The pace of the progress of the liberation struggle varied from colony to colony depending on conditions there. However, all the liberation struggles tended to develop in three phases.

Phase I: c. 1900–c. 1920

The first phase was marked by rural armed uprisings against colonialism. In the first few years of colonialism, Africans found it difficult to tolerate the new strange things they were being made to do and the strange ways in which their lives were being ordered. For instance, after the Belgian occupation of Zaire, King Leopold's policies were so oppressive that revolts broke out all over the country. The biggest were the uprisings of the Azande (1892–1912), Bayaka (1895–1906), Kasango Nyembo (1907–1917), Bashi (1900–1916), Babua and Budja (1903–1905).

Similar revolts occurred in many other parts of Africa. In some African countries these revolts were carried out jointly by neighbouring peoples who, before the advent of colonial rule, had had little or

18

nothing to do with each other. For example, in East and Central Africa, the Ndebele and Shona of Rhodesia (Zimbabwe), who had once been enemies, revolted together against the British in 1896–7. In 1907, many peoples in south-eastern Tanzania combined together in the Maji Maji revolt against German rule. All these revolts were essentially rural movements occurring at a time when the colonial powers had firmly established their control. They were therefore, in most cases, easily suppressed.

Another type of revolt, not directly political in nature, was also common during these early years. In those parts of Africa where Christianity had made considerable impact people turned to it, usually mixed with indigenous religious symbols and practices, as a means of organising reaction to colonial rule. Usually a separatist Negro Christian Church would arise with a native 'messiah' who would declare that he had been sent to liberate the people. His preachings and activities would then spark off revolts against the colonial regime. There were many such uprisings, but two of the best known are the one led by John Chilembwe in 1915 against the British in Malawi (then Nyasaland), and the one against the Belgians in Zaire during the early twenties led by Simon Kimbangu. Sometimes, as with Kimbanguism in Zaire, the political influences of these messianic movements persisted for many decades.

Phase II: 1920s and 1930s
By the 1920s and 1930s the colonial order had become more developed and African society had witnessed some important changes. European education was producing an increasing number of literate Africans who began to demand increased participation in the administration and government. Many people had moved, and were still moving at an increasing rate, from the rural areas to the main urban centres to seek jobs under colonial governments or in the foreign companies. As a result, the immigrant populations of some leading African towns had grown quite large. Being in closer contact than other Africans with the colonial administrations, they not only knew more about the political, social and economic policies of the colonial governments but also felt more directly the frustrations such policies produced. They had not yet formed themselves into large and powerful workers' unions or trade unions but they were already becoming an important factor in the liberation movement. These were the people who came out in crowds to listen to, and to cheer, the literate leaders when they made speeches about the right of the educated Africans to take part in the government of their country.

Another development in the urban centres in these years was the rise of descendants unions or ethnic unions or progressive unions. As people migrated from their rural homes to come and take up life in the new and often difficult urban environment, they more often received help and friendship from people from their own parts of the country. Ultimately, people who came from the same regions or ethnic groups formed themselves into unions with the aim of enabling members to receive and give mutual assistance. However, these unions usually acquired a political character. In particular, they often became the spokesmen for their areas in demanding social amenities (roads, schools, hospitals), from the colonial government. Moreover, each union usually attracted into its ranks the educated elite from its own part of the country. Many of the men who were later to become great political leaders of Africa acquired their earliest political education by being leaders of these ethnic unions. In Zaire, for instance, Joseph Kasavubu (the future President of Zaire) acquired national prominence as the leader of the ABAKO, the ethnic union of the Bakongo people in the city of Kinshasa. In places like Zaire where the colonial master made the growth of broad-based nationalist politics impossible, the ethnic unions were still the leading political organisations at the time of independence in the 1960s.

During the 1920s the growth of nationalist awareness in Africa received a powerful stimulus from outside – from the black people of the Americas who were themselves seeking political expression. William E. B. DuBois and Marcus Garvey led Afro-Americans to fight against oppression and racial discrimination in the United States, and also showed great interest in the sufferings of Africans under colonialism. Garvey especially taught his fellow Afro-Americans to develop pride in the colour of their skins. He also preached large-scale return of the Afro-Americans to Africa and the freedom of Africa from colonialism, and he prophesied that the redemption of Africa was 'coming like a storm'. He formed the Universal Negro Improvement Association (UNIA) to carry out these battles and he also started a journal entitled *Negro World*.

These ideas and activities stimulated many educated Africans. In many parts of Africa *Negro World* was eagerly read, and branches of UNIA were formed. After Garvey had been imprisoned by the American Government in 1925, DuBois continued the struggle. He tried in particular to bring Black leaders in America, the West Indies and Africa together so that they could co-operate for the liberation of the Black man everywhere. Under his influence, five Pan-African Congresses were held between 1919 and 1945. Also future African leaders, like Nnamdi Azikiwe of Nigeria and Kwame Nkrumah of Ghana, studied in America in the 1920s and 1930s and came under the influence of the Black nationalism of Garvey and DuBois. All these contributed immensely to the growth of the liberation struggle in Africa in the 1920s and 1930s.

Nationalism received further stimulus from the movements which grew up among young Africans studying abroad. The most important was the West African Students' Union (WASU) founded in London in 1925 by Ladipo Solanke, a Nigerian student. The WASU, through its social and political activities, attracted most West African students in Britain. It became an association through which young West Africans abroad acquired much practice in political organisation and political writing. In 1928 Marcus Garvey gave the WASU a hostel in London. In 1929 and 1932 a delegation of the WASU, led by Solanke, visited the main cities of West Africa in order to popularise the WASU, to collect money for it and establish branches of it. The WASU was, therefore, a preparation house for the development of radical nationalism. Many of the future leaders of West Africa acquired their early political education as officers in the WASU.

At that time, the nationalist movement was more advanced in West Africa than in East Africa and there were many differences of attitude between the British and the French colonies. The colonial government of each British colony enjoyed more freedom in managing its affairs than did the French colonial government. In the British system the Governor of each colony advised by his legislative council and executive council, was in charge, with only general guidelines from London. The French system endeavoured rather to evolve a common 'philosophy' of administration for all colonies, and colonial affairs were managed more directly from Paris. As a result, the nationalist leaders of the British West African colonies concentrated their efforts mostly upon influencing the colonial administration on the spot, while those of the French West African colonies had to concentrate more upon influencing Paris directly.

British West Africa

In British West African colonies, the nationalist movement had five main aims: firstly, to influence the administration to employ more educated Africans in top places in the civil service; secondly, to influence the administration to increase the African membership of the legislative council and, thereby, ultimately turn that council into a democratically elected parliament for the country; thirdly, to increase African membership of the executive council and ultimately turn it into a responsible cabinet of the people; fourthly, to reform the local government system and, especially, to persuade the administration to allow, or increase, elected representation on the native authority councils; fifthly, to defend the interests of the African traders against the British and other foreign (especially Syrian and Lebanese) businesses which were gradually pushing Africans out of the trade of West Africa.

In some British colonies, the foundation for these new nationalist activities had been laid before 1920. Lagos in Nigeria, Accra and Cape Coast and the coastal districts in Ghana, Freetown in Sierra Leone and Bathurst in the Gambia – these were known as the 'colonies' proper, the places in which the British had established authority before the scramble for Africa began in the 1880s. The rest of each country was known as the 'protectorate'. Schools had been established in these 'colonies' as far back as the middle of the nineteenth century (earlier in Freetown), and therefore almost all the early literate leaders of British West Africa were in the 'colonies'.

In the 'colonies' protests against British colonial policy had begun long before 1920. The first political association in colonial West Africa was formed in 1897, in Cape Coast in Ghana. It was known as the Aborigines' Rights Protection Society, a branch of an English organisation of the same name. In Lagos as early as 1915, a Lagos man named Herbert Macaulay, grandson of Bishop Samuel Crowther, won popularity for his fearless criticisms of the British colonial administration. And, in almost all the 'colonies', independent newspapers had existed before 1900.

A new phase of the liberation struggle opened in British West Africa in 1920 with the elites of all the British West African colonies trying to form one united nationalist front against the British. In March 1920, the National Congress of British West Africa met in Accra with representatives from Nigeria, Sierra Leone, Ghana and the Gambia. The congress passed resolutions demanding that half of the members of the legislative council in each colony should be elected Africans, that a town council should be set up in every large town, and that four-fifths of the members of each such town council should be elected. Other resolutions demanded reforms in education, medical services and the legal system. The economic actions they wanted taken included the expulsion of the Syrians from the trade of West Africa. Finally, it was decided to form the congress into a permanent organisation and to send delegates to London to campaign for its demands.

However, after the return of its delegation from London, the National Congress of British West Africa was never again able to organise any united action of political importance. Each group of leaders thereafter continued the struggle within their own country.

In 1922, major progress was made when the colonial government granted Nigeria a new constitution setting up a new legislative council which for the first time was to have elected members – three from Lagos and one from Calabar. In addition, fifteen unofficial members were to be nominated by the governor to represent the interests of businessmen as well as the interests of the southern provinces of Nigeria.

Similar constitutions were granted to Sierra Leone in 1924 and Ghana in 1925. The Gambia did not obtain a similar constitution until 1946.

In every case, the unofficial members of the council (elected and nominated) were fewer than the official members. For instance, in Nigeria, there were twenty-six official members to nineteen unofficial members. Moreover, the Governor of each colony was himself the president of each council and he had the power to veto its decisions. Finally, it was only in the few coastal towns (i.e. the 'colonies') that the elections were provided for. Representatives for the 'protectorates' were nominated by the Governor, and they were usually chiefs and not educated commoners. Nigeria's new constitution provided for no representation at all in the new Legislative Council for Northern Nigeria, about half of the whole of Nigeria. The Governor was to continue to make laws separately for Northern Nigeria.

Nevertheless, the new constitutions were widely regarded as a step forward. In Ghana, protests of the elite especially against the numbers of the nominated chiefs from the interior made it impossible for the new legislative council to start meeting for some years. But even there, many of the leaders welcomed the new constitution.

In preparation for the forthcoming elections the elites of the 'colonies' began to form political parties. The most clear-cut example was in Lagos, where in 1923 Herbert Macaulay founded the Nigeria Democratic Party, which won the Lagos elections again and again and remained the strongest political association until the middle of the 1930s. Although its name suggests that it was a Nigerian 'national' party, its activities were limited to Lagos. Nevertheless, its political battles against the British in Lagos marked the real beginning of Nigeria's modern nationalist politics, and that is why Macaulay is today regarded as the father of Nigerian nationalism.

In Sierra Leone and Ghana political associations already formed before the granting of the new constitutions adapted themselves to contest the elections. In Sierra Leone it was the Sierra Leone branch of the National Congress of British West Africa; in Ghana it was the Aborigines' Rights Protection Society.

Being so few in numbers the elected representatives commanded little influence in any of the new legislative councils. Often they found it impossible to work in harmony with the nominated representatives from the interior, who, being chiefs, often took the side of the British administration. So throughout the 1920s and 1930s, the elected representatives demanded that their numbers should be increased, or that the nominated Africans should be literate commoners and not chiefs. But in spite of these agitations, the constitutions of the 1920s remained virtually unchanged until after the Second World War.

French West Africa

In French West Africa, the four coastal areas known as *communes* – Dakar, St Louis, Gorée and Rufisque, all in Senegal – enjoyed conditions similar to the coastal 'colonies' of British West Africa. As in the 'colonies', European type education had been established in the *communes* long before 1900. People born in the *communes*, if they were educated and became Christian, had the status of French citizens, could form political parties, publish newspapers, and be appointed as officials of the colonial civil service. As French citizens they were subject to French laws, whereas the people of the rest of French West Africa were *originaires* (natives) or *sujets* (subjects) and were governed under special laws known as *indigénat*. As far back as 1848 the *communes* had been electing one representative to the French parliament in Paris. It was, therefore, in the *communes* that the foundations of modern nationalist politics in French West Africa were laid.

The year 1914 should be regarded as the beginning of modern African nationalist politics in the *communes*. Until that date it was the Frenchmen living in the *communes* who were elected to the French parliament, although the voters were mostly Africans. In 1914, however, the voters for the first time elected an educated African, Blaise Diagne, to represent them in the French parliament. Blaise Diagne continued to win this election until the end of the 1920s. After his victory of 1914 no European was ever again elected by the *communes*. The small political associations which had been founded in the *communes* by young literate Africans before 1914 rallied round him. By welding all these together he built his own political party – the Republican Socialist Party. In 1919 this party won the elections to the town councils in the *communes*.

Although Diagne was elected only by the *communes*, he was regarded and regarded himself as the representative of all the people of French

West Africa. At first, he proved a very radical fighter for their interests. One of his major political battles was aimed at winning for his countrymen French citizenship while they kept their own culture and their Islamic religion. The French were opposed to this. Their idea of 'assimilation' was that French citizenship would be available only to individuals who were literate, fluent in the French language, and Christian in religion. In 1916, the Senegalese won their case in the French parliament, mostly through the efforts of Blaise Diagne. Since French citizenship carried many benefits, including freedom from forced labour and from arbitrary arrests and degrading punishments by French officials, the other peoples of French West Africa desired to have it also. Until 1946, therefore, the efforts of the nationalist leaders of French West Africa were concentrated on winning French citizenship for their people.

The victory of the Senegalese in 1916 over the question of French citizenship made Diagne more popular in Senegal than ever. As a result, the French administration and the French settlers and companies began to see him as a threat to the whole colonial system. After 1916, therefore, they united to prevent him from winning any more of his radical demands. Finding this opposition too strong for him, Diagne compromised and dropped many of his demands. In fact, he became a strong supporter of the administration over many issues.

From about 1923, therefore, Diagne's popularity in Senegal began to wane. He won the election of 1928 only with difficulty. In the rest of French West Africa, too, the people became disenchanted with Diagne because he was no longer fighting so much for their interests. Indeed, during the First World War, Diagne had accepted the assignment of touring the French territories and persuading the people to enlist in the French army. Between 1931 and 1932, he was appointed Under-Secretary of State for Colonies by the French Government. In this position he had to defend the French policy of forced labour to which the peoples of the French colonies were most bitterly opposed. Diagne lived his last days mostly in France and by the time he died in 1934 he had become more a Frenchman than a Senegalese.

The only other colony in French West Africa with strong nationalist politics was Dahomey. Educated men were very few in the other French colonies, and the French administration maintained a rigid ban on politics. As *originaires* or *sujets* the people had no right to form political associations or publish newspapers. So politics were limited to protests against particular colonial measures and the formation of voluntary associations which were not formally political in their aims. Not until 1937 was any formal political freedom allowed and even this was taken away again during the Second World War, when forced labour was greatly increased.

Although conditions in Dahomey were similar there arose a fearless leader of nationalist agitation, called Louis Hunkarin. Hunkarin had lived in Paris and had come into contact with anti-colonial movements there, including the Black nationalism of Marcus Garvey. Although it was illegal to form political parties in Dahomey, it was not illegal to form a branch of any society which existed in France. On his return to Dahomey, therefore, Hunkarin formed a branch of the 'League for the Rights of Man' and in 1923, under the league's leadership, the people of Dahomey started a movement of passive resistance to force France to reform the colonial system. People refused to pay taxes, workers went on strike, and the markets were boycotted.

Governor Gaston Fourn declared that this was a rebellion against France. He therefore called for troops from neighbouring colonies and declared a state of emergency. The army was used to collect taxes, to destroy villages, and generally to stamp out the movement. A number of leading Dahomeans, including Hunkarin, were sent into exile in Mauritania where all of them, except Hunkarin, died in detention. In this brutal way, the attempt to organise nationalist agitation in Dahomey in the 1920s was crushed.

Nationalist press in West Africa
One important aspect of the nationalist struggle in West Africa in the 1920s and 1930s was the growth of an African newspaper press. African-owned newspapers were to be found in both British and French West Africa, but more commonly in British West Africa. In fact in British West Africa, African newspapers had appeared as early as the late nineteenth century. Most of the newspapers were short-lived. Those which had fairly long spans of life and exerted much influence include the *Lagos Weekly Record*, *The Gold Coast Independent* and the *Sierra Leone Weekly News*. In the French colonies, even in Senegal, most newspapers were owned by Frenchmen. The first African-owned newspaper in the Ivory Coast was *L'Eclaireur de la Côte d'Ivoire* which was started in 1935.

East Africa
With the exception of Kenya, political agitations in East Africa against the colonial administrations were dominated by the European settlers and the Asians. In Tanganyika and Uganda, the legislative councils were given unofficial members in the 1920s, but these comprised only white settlers, representatives of European companies, and Asians.

Not until after the Second World War were Africans allowed.

The reasons for this lack of constitutional progress were that educated Africans were few and that, therefore, nationalist organisations did not appear. The Tanganyika African Association, formed in 1929, was the only nationalist body of any importance to be founded in Tanganyika before the Second World War. But even this had very little popular support; its members being civil servants and teachers whose political activities were closely controlled by the colonial administration.

In Uganda politics developed on separatist rather than broad nationalistic lines. The Baganda, the people of the old kingdom of Buganda who constituted the largest ethnic group in Uganda, were more interested in preserving their separate identity than anything else. In 1900, the British had made a special agreement with the Buganda kingdom giving Buganda a special status within Uganda. Consequently, the Baganda were opposed to any measures for closer union in East Africa, arguing that any attempt to include their kingdom in such closer unions was contrary to the 1900 Agreement. When the Legislative Council was established in 1920, the Baganda, far from demanding African representation on it, bitterly opposed any such representation. Partly because of this, the first Africans did not join the Council until 1945. During the 1920s and 1930s, it was the Europeans and Asians who agitated for increased representation for themselves on the Council.

In Kenya too, the representation on the Legislative Council was limited to the European settlers and Asians until after the Second World War. Also, much of the politics of the country centred on the demands of the Asians for more elected representation. But the 1920s and 1930s witnessed the growth of African nationalist politics, dominated by the Kikuyu, the largest ethnic group in Kenya and the one among whom the European type of education was more advanced than any other Kenyan peoples. Also, the Kikuyu suffered most from the loss of land to European settlers. Although it was the pastoral peoples, such as the Masai, who actually lost the most land, the Kikuyu were growing so rapidly in numbers that any loss of land was bound to cause them greater hardship. Racial discriminations practised by the white settlers made the situation worse.

The first Kikuyu nationalist organisation, the Kikuyu Association (KA) was founded in 1921. Its members were mostly chiefs and it was a moderate organisation concerned mainly with the land issue. The following year, Harry Thuku, a treasury clerk in the colonial civil service, founded the Young Kikuyu Association (YKA) which was a more radical organisation, concerned with the conditions of Kikuyu workers in the urban centres. The older Kikuyu leaders, as represented in the KA, were opposed to the radicalism of the YKA, but neither their opposition nor that of the colonial administration could stop the YKA from growing. The government reacted by sacking Thuku from his job; when he attempted to spread the movement to the rest of the country he was arrested in March 1922. The news of his arrest led to violent protests in Nairobi; the police opened fire and about twenty-five people were killed. Many others were arrested and Thuku himself was banished to a remote northern district.

For some time after this radical Kikuyu nationalism subsided, but it revived when the YKA was re-established as the Kikuyu Central Association (KCA) under a new leadership – Joseph Kangethe as president and Jesse Kariuki as vice-president. On the whole, however, the KCA avoided the more extreme methods of the YKA. In 1928–9, Jomo Kenyatta, then the secretary of the KCA, led a delegation to London to plead the demands of the KCA. In 1931, Kenyatta was back in London to plead the KCA case before the Carter Land Commission set up to look into the Kenya land issue, as well as before the commission which was considering closer union in East Africa.

In 1934 Thuku returned to active politics by forming a new organisation, the Kikuyu Provincial Association (KPA) which was very moderate in its tone and which ultimately replaced the old KA. Its members vowed loyalty to the King of England and promised not to do anything that could cause trouble.

Thus, Kikuyu nationalism was always split between a number of organisations. In 1934, owing to general dissatisfaction with the Carter Land Commission, four of these organisations managed to unite for some time to send a protest to London.

By the late 1930s, Kikuyu nationalism acquired a new character; it began to oppose all things European, such as new agricultural methods and agricultural improvement schemes (like terracing and cattle-culling) and even an electric power project. Also in these years, some nationalist politics began to appear among some of the other peoples of Kenya. For instance, in 1938 a crowd of about 1,500 Akamba marched on Nairobi to protest against some agricultural innovation which touched them. From this time on, the Akamba became friendly with the KCA and from there the KCA extended its influence to another people – the Taita. The KCA was in fact reorganised in these years in order to attract many more members from most parts of the country.

When the Second World War broke out in 1939 the KPA enthusiastically supported the British Government and urged people to enlist for military service. The KCA, on the other hand, was not enthusiastic. In fact, the government soon accused it of having contacts with the enemy – the Italians. For this reason the KCA was banned in May 1940. Some of its leaders were arrested, as were the leaders of the Kamba Members' Association and the Taita Hills Association, both of which were allies of the KCA. These organisations, however, continued to be active underground. The KPA, enjoying government favour, remained the major Kikuyu political organisation operating openly, and was therefore able to increase its membership considerably.

Central and Southern Africa
We shall deal in subsequent chapters with the special cases of South Africa, Rhodesia, Angola and Mozambique. In Zambia, educational progress was very slow, and consequently modern nationalist politics was slow to develop. What little nationalist politics there was in the 1920s was due at first to the influence of people from Malawi where education had made more progress. Indeed, for a long time, most Africans employed by the Zambian colonial civil service were Malawians. In 1923, a Malawi pastor named David Kaunda, father of the future President of Zambia, founded a Welfare Association at Mwezo in Northern Zambia. The constitution of this association stated that its aim was not to subvert the government but to help in 'developing the country'. Even this moderate organisation failed to grow because there were not enough educated people to back it up. In 1928 it was dissolved.

Two years later, other Welfare Associations were founded in places like Livingstone, Broken Hill, Mazabuka and Ndola, all towns along the railway. The association in Livingstone was the strongest and most of its members were government employees and other educated young men, most of them Zambians. The activities of these associations consisted of protests to the government on various aspects of its policies – e.g. the removal of Africans from land along the railway in order to make room for white settlers. But the associations had little or no impact, and it was not until after 1935 that nationalist politics of importance began to develop in the Copperbelt, the centre of Zambia's copper mining industry. Before that date, protest to colonial rule was expressed through religious movements – the Watch Tower Movement or Jehovah's Witnesses. The religious movements continued to be important politically until the 1950s.

By the late 1930s the mining industry in the Copperbelt had become the backbone of the Zambian economy. Large numbers of Africans had come into the mining towns as employees of the mining companies. Soon, popular leaders emerged among them.

The first show of political power by the African miners of the Copperbelt occurred in 1935 when they went on strike, and even rioted, in some of the mining towns. As the African miners became stronger they demanded, among other things, that skilled Africans should begin to take over some of the jobs reserved for Europeans. To defend their interests against the African miners, the European miners formed a union of their own, the Northern Rhodesian Mineworkers' Union (NRMU) which organised a strike in 1940 against rising costs of living. This strike encouraged the African miners to go on strike too, demanding increases in wages. The strike led to some increases in the wages of the African miners, but as yet, they were not sufficiently well organised to form a union or unions of their own.

In Malawi, nationalist politics had developed earlier. Long before 1920 the educated elements formed political organisations, most often the so-called 'native associations'. The first of these, the North Nyasa Native Association was founded in 1912. In 1914 the West Nyasa Native Association was founded and in 1920 the Mombera Native Association.

During the 1920s many more were founded, all moderate in tone, their declared aim being to use legitimate peaceful means to help in developing the country. Their members were government clerks, mission-school teachers, pastors, and educated chiefs. Their political activity was limited to asking the administration to redress wrongs done by government officials and government policies. For instance, they demanded that government officials should stop the practice of arresting women and holding them as hostages because their husbands failed to pay taxes. They also demanded general improvement in education and in the wages and conditions of service of wage workers. In 1929 the West Nyasa Native Association prepared detailed charges alleging that European employers of African labour overworked and underpaid their employees. Other associations asked for more government assistance for the development of cash crops or for the development of livestock farming. But probably most of the associations' energy was devoted to urging the government to increase its assistance to the development of education which by the 1920s and 1930s had greatly slowed down.

In Zaire, owing to the slow development of education up to the 1930s and the rigid government prohibition of politics, anti-colonial protest in the 1920s and 1930s was still dominated by spontaneous rural revolts and messianic religious movements. For instance, in 1919–1921 serious rural uprisings occurred among the Basonge-Meno in Kasai Province and spread to neighbouring provinces. As late as 1931, a similar revolt occurred among the Bapende in Kwango. The colonial government retaliated with a military expedition and not less than 500 people died among the Bapende. Of the messianic religious movements, it will be remembered that Kimbanguism made its appearance in 1921 and in spite of rigorous repression by the colonial government the movement continued to exert strong political influence for decades. Two years after the rise of Kimbanguism, another messianic movement named Kitawala appeared. Kitawala was the Zairean version of the Watch Tower Movement which was very strong in Zambia about the same time. Like Kimbanguism, Kitawala spread far and wide in Zaire and continued for a long time to be politically influential in spite of official repression. No other significant type of anti-colonial movement was able to emerge in Zaire until after the Second World War.

North-west Africa
In the countries of the Maghreb or North-west Africa (Tunisia, Algeria and Morocco) the growth of nationalist politics derived its ideas and methods both from the Islamic religion and European type education. In the struggle against French conquest, Islam had served as a rallying force, particularly in Algeria where French attempts to conquer the country by force met stout resistance from 1830 until 1871. Resistance continued in the desert until 1882 and the conquest of the whole of Algeria was not completed until shortly after 1900, while in the mountainous parts of Morocco, French authority was not established until 1934. For this reason there was hardly any development of modern nationalist politics against colonialism in Morocco until after the Second World War.

In Tunisia, the first African-owned newspaper, the *Al Hadira*, was started as early as 1888. At the beginning of the twentieth century young Tunisians founded an organisation called Young Tunisians, which in 1907 founded its own newspaper, *Le Tunisien*. Its membership was small, drawn mostly from aristocratic young people, so that its aims were not really very nationalistic and it had no popular support. It was not opposed to French colonialism, but concerned mostly with getting the colonial administration to carry out development projects, especially in education.

But the dictatorial nature of the colonial administration and the excesses of the French settlers created widespread discontent and prepared the way for a more radical type of nationalism. Consequently, not long after the founding of the Young Tunisians, a more radical nationalist organisation was formed – the Destour Party. Its aim was to create a new Tunisia based on traditional Tunisian political and legal systems and rejecting most of the French systems represented in the colonial administration. In spite of its radical language the Destour Party never developed a clear plan of action and in 1934 the younger members of the party broke away to establish a new party, the Neo-Destour Party.

It was the Neo-Destour under Habib Bourguiba that was destined to lead Tunisia later into independence. Its method of approach was to work gradually for the development of the country and for the attainment of independence. It began to win strong support among the people and therefore the French administration proscribed it, four years after its foundation, and sent Bourguiba to jail.

In Algeria, the French settlers (called *colons*) were very numerous and enjoyed great political, economic and legal privileges far above the Muslim population of Algeria. This led to the early development of nationalist politics in Algeria. As early as 1912 a group of French-educated Muslim intellectuals formed a party which they called Party of Young Algeria. Their main demands were that the law of *indigénat* should be abolished and that Muslims should be given equal political and legal rights with the Frenchmen. In 1926, a much more radical party was founded – the *Etoile Nord-Africaine* under the leadership of Ali Abd al Qadir. Its ideas were dominated by socialism and by a desire for the unification of the Maghreb. Later, however, under the leadership of Messali Hadj, a self-educated man and a capable organiser, the party turned its attention solely to Algeria. The party, unlike other Algerian organisations of the time, declared itself openly against the continuation of colonialism. Like the Party of Young Algeria, another important party of the time, the *Fédération des Elus Musulman*, founded and led by Ferhat Abbas, favoured assimilation and the granting of equality between Muslims and Frenchmen.

The organisations mentioned above represent the two tendencies in the political awareness of Algerian people in the 1920s and 1930s. Firstly, there were the highly educated Algerians like Ferhat Abbas who welcomed assimilation and wanted equality with the French. Secondly, there were the younger generation of nationalists, most of them not so well educated, who rejected colonialism altogether and wanted an independent Muslim Algeria. It was with the latter group that the future of Algeria lay. Because of their radical views, however, they suffered a lot of official repression. Their organisations were banned one after the other. After the banning of the Etoile Nord-Africaine, the *Parti du Peuple Algérien* (PPA) was founded in 1936. In the 1940s and 1950s these were to be succeeded by the *Mouvement pour le Triomphe des Libertés Démocratiques* (MTLD), and the *Front de Libération Nationale*, or National Liberation Front, which finally led the people of Algeria in their fight for independence between 1956 and 1962.

To sum up
The 1920s and 1930s were still only the start of the liberation struggle all over Africa. Only in a few countries was the liberation movement strong enough to seize important concessions from the colonial powers. Perhaps the best were the British colonies of West Africa where the British began to allow some African participation in decision-making through the legislative councils. But even then, this progress affected almost exclusively the coastal urban centres of British West Africa.

In practically every country in Africa, the early liberation struggle suffered from the very important weakness that it was limited to a few urban centres. Even in a country like Nigeria, where a political party was founded as early as 1923, little or no attempt was made to spread political awareness from the coastal principal town to the rest of the country. The first party in Nigeria to attempt to take nationalist awareness beyond Lagos was not founded until 1934. This was the Nigerian Youth Movement. Even this party started as a Lagos party, called the Lagos Youth Movement; it did not change its name until 1936. Even after that, all it did beyond Lagos was to found branches in a few large towns in the interior; its soul was always based in Lagos. The Neo-Destour Party in Tunisia, also founded in 1934, was similar; it too was the first political organisation in its country which saw the need of taking the nationalist struggle beyond the capital to the rest of the country.

In short, by the middle of the 1930s, nationalist organisations were beginning to emerge which saw the need of spreading political awareness among the masses. The PPA in Algeria, founded in 1936, also deserves mention. But such organisations represented only the beginnings of broad-based nationalist politics.

Egypt as an exception
The only real exception to the general trend, and the only country in which major nationalist progress was made in the 1920s, was Egypt. Egypt enjoyed two advantages. In the first place, British occupation

of Egypt was different in nature from European occupation of the rest of Africa. In 1879, because the Khedive Ismail, ruler of Egypt, had run Egypt into heavy debts to European creditors, Britain and France had established a joint control over Egypt's financial affairs. In 1881, in reaction against the foreign control, the Egyptian army revolted and Britain and France prepared to send forces in. However, the French Government was unable to take part owing to a crisis in France itself, and so Britain alone invaded and occupied Egypt in 1882. The occupation was expected to be short, but the British stayed on, much to France's annoyance. To pacify the French, therefore, Britain had to be frequently announcing that she would soon withdraw from Egypt and this greatly encouraged Egyptian nationalist forces which, thereby, grew very strong.

Secondly, before the British occupation, Egypt had established European type schools and begun to produce a new class of leaders with European type education. By the beginning of the twentieth century she had produced many such leaders and her nationalist movement was therefore very strong. Consequently, Britain was compelled to grant independence of a limited sort to Egypt in 1922.

Phase III: The independence struggle in the 1940s and 1950s

For other African countries, the late 1940s marked the beginning of the third and final stage of the liberation struggle.

In most parts of Africa, the literate elite had grown tremendously in numbers and confidence. In many countries they began to demand full establishment of elected responsible government. Political parties and nationalist newspapers arose to promote these aims. For the first time attempts could be made to rally the whole country in support of the liberation movement. Political activities had extended from the urban centres to the rural areas where considerable numbers of the educated elite were by now to be found.

The greatest impetus to the growth of nationalist forces in these years was given by the Second World War of 1939 to 1945. African countries contributed immensely in men and materials towards the victory of their colonial masters who were allied against Nazi Germany, Italy and Japan. In their efforts to rouse people all over the world against Germany, the allied powers promised in the Atlantic Charter that after the war they would ensure that every nation, large or small, would enjoy the right to choose its own government. Though this promise was meant for European countries only, nationalist leaders all over Africa chose to believe that their countries too would be given the right of self-determination.

Moreover, the war took thousands of Africans outside their own countries, where, in camps and battlefields they saw the true face of the Europeans with whom they worked as soldiers, stewards, cleaners, or cooks. Much of the respect and fear which Africans had accorded to Europeans before 1939 disappeared.

As soon as the Second World War ended, therefore, the final phase of the independence struggle opened. New African nationalist leaders emerged who founded large and powerful political parties and started aggressive newspapers, while African workers founded radical trade unions.

We can only summarise these developments here. In Nigeria in 1944 the National Council of Nigeria and the Cameroons, later known as the National Council of Nigerian Citizens (NCNC) was founded. More than any earlier party, the NCNC made it a point of duty to rally all the people of Nigeria to support the independence struggle. All sorts of ethnic unions, progressive unions and voluntary associations in different parts of the country were encouraged to become branches of the new party. In 1945, Nigerian workers went on a general strike. By supporting the workers the NCNC greatly increased its popularity. In 1946 its top leaders, Herbert Macaulay and Dr Nnamdi Azikiwe, toured Nigeria to raise money to finance sending a delegation to London to protest against a constitution which the Governor was introducing in Nigeria in that year. Although the tour, during which the old Macaulay died, made the party better known in the interior, the delegation's return from London with no important achievement lost the party much popularity. At the same time, friction between the major ethnic groups of Nigeria began to run high. Between 1950 and 1952, therefore, the leaders of Western Nigeria founded a new party, the Action Group, and the leaders of Northern Nigeria founded the Northern People's Congress. Other small parties followed, all agreeing, if on nothing else, on eventual independence for Nigeria.

In Ghana, the United Gold Coast Convention (UGCC) was founded in 1947. Dr Kwame Nkrumah, then studying in Britain, was invited home to be its first secretary. From then on, Ghana became the scene of intense nationalist developments. In 1948 the Ghana workers went on a general strike. Soon afterwards Nkrumah broke away from the conservative men of the UGCC and founded his own party, the Convention People's Party (CPP) which demanded immediate independence and advocated positive action to achieve it. Because of this campaign, Nkrumah and some of his leading supporters were imprisoned.

Unlike the leaders of British West Africa, the leaders of French West

Africa were not yet thinking of independence. They wanted to discard their status of *sujets* and to attain the French citizenship which the four *communes* of Senegal had long enjoyed. In gratitude to her colonies for the great support they had given her in the recent war, France accorded the status of French citizen to all the peoples of the French colonies in 1946. The same year about 800 leaders of French West African colonies met at Bamako and founded a new party, the African Democratic Rally (RDA), under the leadership of Felix Houphouët-Boigny of the Ivory Coast. Other parties were founded in the various colonies, but in almost every colony the RDA or parties allied to it soon became the most powerful. This made Houphouët-Boigny the most powerful political leader in French Tropical Africa.

In its early years the RDA was closely allied with the Communist Party of France because the latter supported the anti-colonial desires of Africans. For this reason the French Government regarded the RDA as a Communist organisation and Houphouët-Boigny as a dangerous Communist.

Kenya's path to independence followed a somewhat different course from that of any other country. There, a major armed revolt, the Mau Mau revolt, started in 1952 with the aim of expelling the white settlers. As a result, the colonial administration declared an emergency, imprisoned Kenyatta and many other leaders and placed a ban on all political organisations until June 1955. But even when this ban was lifted, political organisations were allowed to be formed not on a nation-wide basis but only at district level. Consequently, a large number of local political organisations arose in Kenya, which proved unfortunate because when nation-wide political parties were later allowed, the spirit of intense local loyalty persisted. This made the national parties internally weak and worsened the problems of national unity.

In spite of this unfortunate development, the 1950s saw the steady waning of the dominant role which white settlers and Asians had played in the politics of Kenya. Gradually it became clear that Kenya was to be an African country, not a country dominated by white settlers. The Mau Mau revolt was partly responsible for this. Another characteristic of Kenya nationalism in the 1950s was that it was no longer solely Kikuyu nationalism alone but involved all parts of Kenya.

In 1960 the Kenya African National Union (KANU) was founded mainly by James Gichuru, Dr Njoroge Mungai, Tom Mboya and Oginga Odinga. Kenyatta was still in prison, but at the first general conference of the party, he was elected president and Mboya secretary.

With almost all parts of Kenya represented in KANU, there were great hopes of unity. However, these hopes soon faded. Another group of leaders, some of whom had taken part in founding KANU and some of whom belonged to the old KPA, decided to form another party – the Kenya African Democratic Union (KADU) – in June 1960. An era of intense rivalry between the two parties ensued. In general, though both parties wanted independence, KADU became the champion of the interests of the smaller ethnic groups against KANU which was dominated by the two largest ethnic groups – the Kikuyu and the Luo.

In Uganda and Tanganyika, as in Kenya, developments gradually confirmed that the future belonged to the Africans and not to the European settlers. In Uganda, however, the big question continued as to whether Buganda was to go it alone or become part of Uganda. The Baganda were determined to go it alone and even attain independence separately from the rest of Uganda. Their refusal to change this attitude led, in 1953, to a serious clash with the colonial authorities as a result of which the Kabaka, the King of Buganda, was deported. Ultimately, however, the constitutional arrangements of the 1950s and early 1960s ensured that Uganda, including Buganda, would remain one country. From the developments of the late 1950s Milton Obote emerged as the foremost political leader of Uganda. He was not a Baganda but came from one of the small ethnic groups. In Tanganyika Julius Nyerere became the most prominent leader and his party, the Tanganyika African National Union, founded in 1954, was the party that later led the country into independence.

In East Central Africa, it long remained uncertain which interest would predominate – the interest of the Africans or that of the European settlers. For one thing, European settlers were very many in the countries of East Central Africa – Zambia, Malawi and Rhodesia. For another thing, as early as 1923 the management of the affairs of Rhodesia had passed into the hands of the white settlers, and this situation in Rhodesia was very attractive to the white settlers in Zambia and Malawi.

In 1953 the British Government brought Zambia, Malawi and Rhodesia together as a federation. In all three countries African opposition to the federation led to greatly increased nationalist activities. In the midst of these, the new leaders and the great parties of the future emerged. In 1958 Hastings Banda returned from a prolonged absence in England to take the leadership of the Malawi nationalist movement, the Nyasaland African Congress, founded in 1944. His denunciation of the federation was so virulent that riots erupted. This led to a declaration of emergency in the federation in

1959, the banning of the Nyasaland African Congress and the arrest and imprisonment of its leaders, including Banda. Some Zambian leaders were also imprisoned.

In Zambia, African miners in the copperbelt had begun to form trade unions during the Second World War. In 1949 these combined to form the Northern Rhodesia African Mineworkers' Union (NRAMU). In 1951 the political leaders founded the Northern Rhodesia African National Congress with Harry Nkumbula as president. It was this party that opposed the proposed federation, and when it failed to prevent the formation of the federation it lost much of its popularity. By 1958, when it had again become very popular, a split occurred in the party. The younger men, under Kenneth Kaunda, formed their own party, the Zambia African National Congress (ZANC). When the emergency was declared in 1959 Kaunda was imprisoned and ZANC was banned. ZANC men, however, formed a new party with the name of United National Independence Party (UNIP). When Kaunda was released in 1960 he had become the most popular leader in the country and became leader of UNIP.

Mostly because of unyielding African opposition to the federation, it was dissolved in 1963. The way was thus open for Zambia and Malawi to proceed separately to independence.

In Zaire, the right to form political parties was not granted until 1959, and so there were no nation-wide parties. Nevertheless, throughout the 1950s, various political organisations were formed, mostly ethnic organisations. Some also started as non-political clubs or old boys' associations. Usually, such organisations had to have a government licence before they could exist or hold meetings, but they still managed to discuss politics. The ABAKO was the first organisation, in 1956, to ask for immediate independence.

In Tunisia in North Africa the Neo-Destour Party continued to live precariously – banned at one moment, allowed to exist the next. Of the twenty years between its formation in 1934 and 1954 when the French promised independence to Tunisia, the party leader, Bourguiba, spent about ten in prison.

Break-through to independence
The colonial powers' reactions to the post-war nationalism in Africa varied from place to place. Most of them wished to preserve their freedom of action and to proceed at their own speed. Therefore in places where the nationalist movements were very radical and led to threats of violence, the colonial authorities reacted by banning political activities and imprisoning leaders. Nearly all the future prime minis-

ters and presidents of African countries spent some time in prison in the 1950s.

At first, after the war, the French were grateful enough to their colonies to grant concessions. But this policy was not popular with French settlers and other Frenchmen and by 1948 the official attitude had changed. The colonial administrations received orders to enforce order rigorously. Men like Houphouët-Boigny came under serious pressure. As a result, Houphouët-Boigny compromised and began to co-operate with France. He broke the alliance of the RDA with the French Communist Party and he even became a minister of state in Paris.

These repressive measures, however, could not prevent the march of African countries to independence. From the late 1950s the colonial powers began to withdraw from Africa.

In general, the British were the first of the colonial powers to realise that repression would not do and that some accommodation would have to be reached with African nationalism. Therefore, the British led the way in granting more and more democratic concessions to their colonies and in developing programmes toward eventual independence. Throughout the late 1940s and the 1950s the British took one step after another which gave their African subjects greater and greater control over the affairs of their countries. The climax was reached when in 1957, Ghana celebrated its independence. Things followed quickly after that. By 1965 almost all of British Africa had become independent.

For a long time, the French were inclined to try to find some formula for keeping their empire intact while granting their colonies some measure of internal self-government. In the Maghreb, France was confronted with armed revolts in Tunisia in 1952, Algeria in 1954 and Morocco in 1955. As a result, France granted independence to Morocco and Tunisia in 1956. The problem of Algeria could not, however, be so easily solved as the large number of Frenchmen who had settled and owned land in Algeria were determined that Algeria should always remain part of France. It took seven years of fighting before the French finally bowed to the inevitable. Algeria became independent in 1962.

In the French colonies of tropical Africa, the French continued trying to maintain their control, but though most nationalists were satisfied with the concessions given by France, some began to insist on full independence. Finally, in 1958, the French President, General Charles de Gaulle, proposed to create France and its overseas possessions into a French Community, a sort of French commonwealth of nations but under firm control of France. In September of that year, he presented the proposed constitution of the Community to be voted upon in a referendum to be held in all the French territories. Each colony was offered the choice of voting 'yes' and becoming an internally self-governing republic within the Community, or voting 'no' and becoming independent outside the Community immediately. It was made clear, however, that any colony which chose independence would lose all French aid forthwith. Partly because of this threat, and partly because only a few of the leaders of the French colonies were as yet agreeable to the idea of complete independence, all the French tropical territories, with the exception of small Guinea under Sekou Toure, voted 'yes'. Guinea thus became independent and lost all French assistance, while the other countries went on into the Community.

However, independence was in the air all over Africa. Within a year, some of the West African members of the Community began to agitate for an amendment of its constitution in such a way as to enable them to become fully independent while still preserving links with France in such matters as technical and economic assistance and defence. Between 1959 and 1961 all the French colonies became independent in this way.

As for the Belgians, they continued to assume that they would always keep their Zaire colony, and, therefore, made no attempt to meet the nationalist demands. When Zaire erupted in massive riots in 1959, the Belgians were caught completely unprepared, and were compelled to make a hurried exit from Zaire the following year.

Thus, by the end of 1968, the year in which Equatorial Guinea and Swaziland won their independence, almost all African countries were free of colonial rule. The exceptions were the Portuguese colonies of Angola, Mozambique and Guinea (Bissau), Spanish Sahara, and the two countries of Southern Africa – South Africa and Rhodesia – which were still being ruled by white minority dictatorships. South Africa had been granted independence by the British in 1910, but the independence had been for the white population of the country only. In 1965, the few white settlers of Rhodesia defied Britain and declared Rhodesia independent and thus acquired for themselves the South African type of independence. In both countries, the struggle for the independence of Africans continued.

In the history of the African independence struggle the two most important years were 1957 and 1960. Although five African countries had become independent before 1957, it was the independence of Ghana in that year that affected the whole of Africa most. The year

1960 was the year of greatest achievement when sixteen countries won their independence.

3 Developments in the Portuguese colonies

Portugal was the earliest European colonial power in Africa. During the fifteenth century the Portuguese led the way in exploring the western and eastern coasts of Africa and in starting trade with the coastal African peoples. As a result, they established control over parts of the African coast until the European scramble for Africa in the late nineteenth century, when they claimed the interior territories around these small coastal possessions as colonies.

The Portuguese colonies in Africa were Angola, Mozambique, Guinea (Bissau) and Cape Verde Islands, Sao Tomé and Principe. The three largest are Mozambique (5,000,000 population), Angola (4,000,000) and Guinea (Bissau) which is usually taken to include the Cape Verde Islands and has a population of about half a million. The two small islands of Sao Tomé and Principe lie in the eastern end of the Gulf of Guinea. We shall be concerned here only with developments in Angola, Mozambique and Guinea (Bissau).

Of all the colonies held by European countries in Africa in this century, the Portuguese colonies have suffered the most repression and the crudest exploitation. There are three reasons for this. The first is the Portuguese tradition of colonial rule. From the sixteenth to the nineteenth century the Portuguese used their coastal possessions as sources of slaves for the Atlantic slave trade. During those centuries, too, the Portuguese kings used to reward their families and friends with large colonial estates and sent military expeditions to help conquer such estates, over which the Portuguese owners then exercised almost unlimited power.

When Portugal had built an African empire after the scramble, these former colonial practices were continued in modified forms. For instance, forced labour is no more than a modern version of slavery. Also, just as the Portuguese kings used to grant large colonial lands to individual noblemen, modern Portuguese governments granted large colonial lands to European companies and gave them almost total sovereignty over such lands.

The second factor is the poverty of Portugal herself. With no capital to invest in her colonies to develop their economies, and little or no manufactured goods to import in exchange for their raw materials, Portugal found that the easiest way to derive wealth was to exploit the

41

labour of her colonial subjects, using forced labour which was virtually unpaid for.

The third reason for Portugal's repressive colonial rule was the type of government under which Portugal itself was ruled from the 1930s. Portugal became a republic in 1910, but because the republican government achieved little or no economic progress, the army seized power in 1926. Finally in 1933, Dr Antonio de Oliveira Salazar became dictator. Promising the people of Portugal great economic achievements, Salazar seized all power into his hands, abolished civil liberties and turned Portugal into a ruthless police state, extending the same rule to the Portuguese colonies. It was a major part of Salazar's programme to use the colonies to rebuild Portugal economically and to give the Portuguese a feeling of national greatness. In 1968, when Salazar became too old and too ill to continue to rule, he was replaced by Professor Marcello Caetano, who promised to continue Salazar's colonial policies and did so until 1974.

Race relations and 'native policy'

Although there have been Portuguese settlers in Africa since the sixteenth century, it was not until the time of Salazar that the Portuguese Government began to encourage large numbers of settlers. Salazar not only wanted to make his countrymen interested in the colonies, but also hoped that migration to the colonies might help to solve Portugal's unemployment problems. So the government appealed to Portuguese youths to develop the spirit of adventure and start exciting new lives in the colonies.

As a result of this campaign, the Portuguese populations of the colonies increased between the 1930s and 1960s, from 30,000 in Angola in 1930 to 172,529 in 1960. By 1970, Angola had the second largest European settler population in Africa – 250,000, second to South Africa. By the same date Mozambique had 130,000 European settlers, making her the country with the fourth largest European population in Africa (after South Africa, Angola and Rhodesia). Guinea's Portuguese settlers have always been few. By 1970 their number was 2,000.

The Portuguese have always claimed that, unlike other colonial powers in Africa, they have never practised racial discrimination and cite the thousands of *mestisos*, the mixed-blood products of inter-breeding between Africans and Portuguese, as proof.

However, though the extreme apartheid found in South Africa never existed in the Portuguese colonies, racial discrimination and segregation were always practised there. In the centuries of the slave trade the Portuguese regarded Africans as less than human and raided them mercilessly for slaves. Between the creation of the modern Portuguese empire in the 1890s and the end of the 1950s many laws were passed to define the legal status of the African. According to these laws Africans were designated as *indigenas*, and as such were regarded as 'uncivilised' and subject to many degrading controls. The *indigena* had to carry an identification pass at all times. Failure to produce it to the authorities could result in imprisonment or a term of 'corrective labour'. The *indigena* could not leave his home without permission to look for work, and his children could not attend government schools. In certain areas, a permanent curfew operated for *indigenas*, and no *indigena* could visit any foreign country except South Africa and Rhodesia.

The *indigena* laboured under many economic disabilities. Many of the Portuguese immigrants were illiterate and unskilled, yet they were given first consideration for jobs. Even the menial jobs were withheld from the Africans and given to the Portuguese. In some cases, an *indigena* could not even slaughter, sell or give away his cattle, or withdraw money from his bank account, without permission. In short, Portuguese laws regarded the mass of Africans as savages without civil or human rights.

The laws provided, however, for *indigenas* to graduate into the socially and legally higher class of the *assimilado*. To qualify, an African must be literate, speak Portuguese, earn enough money to support himself and his family, possess the qualities and the social graces deemed necessary for a Portuguese citizen, must not have evaded military service under the Portuguese, nor have deserted from the Portuguese army, and must in general be regarded by the Portuguese officials as a 'civilised' man of good character and acceptable habits. If an *indigena* thought that he satisfied these conditions, he would submit an application to the officials, who would then examine him, asking him and his wife many questions about their private lives. If the officials were satisfied, they would classify him an *assimilado* and issue him an identity card.

On being classified an *assimilado* an African became a Portuguese citizen and enjoyed a lot of freedom. He could move from one place to another in the colony without permission; he was entitled to certain types of job from which the *indigena* was barred; he could not be subjected to forced labour; his children could easily get admission to government schools.

Even so, many Africans who qualified to be *assimilado* never applied for it. Some felt the procedure for obtaining the *assimilado* status too humiliating. Furthermore, becoming an *assimilado* did not give complete equality with the Portuguese. There were still some jobs that the *assimilado* could not be employed to do; and if he did the same job as a Portuguese, he was usually paid less. The *assimilado* usually had to pay heavier taxes than he did as an *indigena*. Finally, the *assimilado* was legally no longer an African and therefore lost his rights to certain things that belonged to him by birth. He could not succeed to a chiefdom, for instance, or take over family land.

For these reasons, and because the number of literate Africans was so small, not more than half of one per cent of the people of the former Portuguese colonies, most of them in Angola, ever acquired *assimilado* status.

Economic conditions

The Portuguese colonies were the poorest in economic and social development in colonial Africa. Yet their natural resources included good fertile soils, mild climates, rich forests, rivers from which hydro-electric power could be developed, and a long list of minerals including diamonds, petroleum, iron, copper, gold, phosphates, manganese and mica.

The chief reason for the poor economic development of the three colonies was the poverty of Portugal. Since Portugal lacked the necessary capital to exploit her colonies' resources, she usually invited other European countries and foreign businesses to provide it. Portugal would then participate as a partner. The companies established under these arrangements were granted lavish and extensive concessions over the land and the mineral resources. Thus, the major development projects in Angola and Mozambique before 1930 – like the building of the ports of Beira and Laurenco Marques in Mozambique and the Benguela Railway in Angola – were carried out with the capital and initiative of other European countries. After 1930 some of the capital for development projects came from the wealth of the colonies themselves. In general, under Salazar, the colonies did better economically. Their budgets were balanced as their products began to earn them considerable wealth in the world market. But the main aim of Salazar was to unify into one single economy the economies of Portugal and her colonies. Politically and economically, Salazar treated the colonies as provinces of Portugal. In that way, Portugal could comfortably live on the wealth produced by the colonies.

The wealth of the former colonies came mostly from their agriculture, forestry and mines. Mozambique's leading export crops were cotton, cashew nuts, cane sugar, tea, copra, sisal, maize, wheat, groundnuts, tobacco and kenaf. Angola depended largely on her coffee exports, but also produced sisal, maize, cotton, cane sugar, oil palm products, manioc, tobacco, beans, wheat, rice, millet and sorghum. Rice was the largest product of Guinea (Bissau), but her two major export products were groundnuts and oil palm products. Millet, maize, sorghum, beans, manioc, sweet potatoes, sugar cane and tropical fruits were also grown. Both Angola and Mozambique raised large numbers of cattle and other livestock. Each of the former Portuguese colonies exported some timber.

The Angola diamond deposits were first discovered in 1912 in the Lunda District. This led to the founding of two diamond mining companies in 1917. Of these, the larger and more important was the Diamond Company of Angola (Diamang), which was established mostly with the capital and initiative of other European countries. Its creators were British, Belgian and American companies and the Portuguese Government. The Portuguese Government granted to this company concessions covering practically the whole of north-eastern Angola, almost one-quarter of the country. Later, after diamonds had been discovered in the coastal areas, the government gave a concession to another company covering most of the Angolan coast.

Petroleum was discovered in Angola early in this century, but it was not until about 1955 that successful mining operations began. The Lobito Fuel Company was established with Belgian capital as a joint enterprise by Belgium and Portugal. In 1957, the Lobito Fuel Company founded a bigger company with most of the capital again coming from Belgium.

Iron has also been mined in Angola, especially at Casinga. As with the diamonds and petroleum, the capital for developing the iron mining came from other countries – Germany, Denmark, Austria and America. The major iron-mining company is the Lobito Mining Company.

Mozambique produces tantalite, iron and coal. The iron-mining was financed with capital provided by a Japanese company called Sumitomo. American companies were granted petroleum concessions.

This system of concessions was also extended to the building of ports, railways and hydro-electric works. In this way the ports of Beira and Laurenco Marques and the Benguela Railway were built. Of such projects, the largest is the Cabora Bassa Dam financed with capital from various European countries and South Africa. The dam, when completed, would be one of the greatest hydro-electric establishments in Africa, providing irrigation water and electricity to Mozambique and parts of South Africa.

45

Large land concessions were also granted for agricultural purposes. Much of the cash crops of colonial Angola and Mozambique were produced on large plantations belonging to foreign companies. Such companies were usually given the fullest authority over everything on their land. They were empowered to enjoy a monopoly of trade, mining and building in their areas, and were also empowered to recruit forced labour from the Africans, to collect taxes from them and to make laws and regulations binding on the Africans. Quite often, they were guilty of abusing their powers and of oppressing the Africans. Quite often, also, the colonial government had no means of learning about these abuses or of redressing them.

From the 1950s, another policy was vigorously pursued in agriculture, especially in Angola and Mozambique. This is the establishment of extensive 'farm colonies' or 'farm settlements' called *colonatos*. Under this policy, which was part of Salazar's campaign to encourage settlement in the colonies, the government provided money for selecting Portuguese families in Portugal, transporting them to the colonies, settling them in the *colonatos*, giving them seeds and livestock to start with, and building roads, hydro-electric and irrigation works to serve the *colonatos*. A few African families were encouraged to settle in some of the *colonatos*. Although the establishment of the *colonatos* increased agricultural production in Angola and Mozambique, it formed part of the policy of taking the land away from the African owners and giving it to foreigners.

The most horrible and most hated of all the Portuguese policies in their colonies was the institution of forced labour, which the Portuguese carried further than any other colonial power. With slavery abolished, Portugal quickly substituted another system which would provide virtual slave-labour. In 1899, she issued the Native Labour Regulations for the colonies. Section 1 of these Regulations stated:

> All natives of Portuguese overseas provinces are subject to the obligation, moral and legal, of attempting to obtain through work the means that they lack to subsist and to better their social condition. They have full liberty to choose the method of fulfilling this obligation, but if they do not fulfil it, public authority may force a fulfilment.

In short, it was the duty of the colonial government to force everybody to work. It was stated that this was part of Portugal's 'civilising' mission. While the African would be 'civilised' by Portuguese education, he would also be developed physically and morally by being taught, through forced labour, to love to work.

Under the system, sometimes called 'corrective labour' and sometimes 'contract labour', any *indigena* could be seized by government officials, or the manager of private companies, and subjected to forced labour, for which he was paid a small wage. As might be expected, the system was open to terrible abuses. Under the 'contract labour' regulations, the former slave owners simply kept their slaves under the new name of 'contract labourers', while the former slave dealers now continued as contractors who went about recruiting 'contract labourers'. These recruitment drives differed little from slave raidings, and treatment of the contract labourers differed little from the former treatment of slaves. The African chiefs were either compelled or bribed into helping to recruit their subjects for contract labour. The law empowered the colonial officials to seize any *indigena* without visible means of livelihood and to force him to accept 'contract labour', which was regarded as 'corrective labour' – i.e. labour to correct his laziness. It was left to the officials to decide who was jobless and who was not, and often they simply decided that any Africans not already working under 'contract labour' were jobless and lazy, and rounded them up for 'corrective labour'. The supervisors of 'contract labourers' often behaved like slave drivers, mercilessly flogging the labourers and subjecting them to all sorts of humiliating and inhuman treatments.

Social developments
Until the 1950s there was very little social progress in the colonies. The money for building roads, hospitals and schools was not available. Also the Portuguese were uncertain of their attitude towards colonial education. They wanted to spread education as a means of bringing the Portuguese language and culture to the people, but many of them also felt that to educate the Africans would endanger continued Portuguese control. Moreover, Portugal was doing little enough to educate its own citizens. Portugal is the most illiterate as well as the poorest country in Europe – the rate of illiteracy in the 1960s being as high as 40%.

Consequently, though Portugal made many high-sounding declarations about the need for education in the colonies, education was given little attention. By 1950–51 in Angola, which was more highly developed in education than the other colonies, there were only 13,586 children in primary schools, 2,277 in secondary schools, and 1,548 in technical schools. Most of this education was provided by church mission schools – especially the Catholic mission – and consisted of a three-year primary course called 'education for adapting' or 'rudimentary education'. Its aim was to introduce the Africans to Portuguese language and culture.

The government schools in the urban centres provided better and longer education. However, the government schools were usually filled mostly by the children of Portuguese settlers; the children of the *assimilado* were accepted if there was room.

Reforms of the 1950s and 1960s

During the 1950s Portuguese colonial policies came under increasing criticism in the world and to silence this the Portuguese began to introduce a few haphazard reforms. They were not ready for a complete change of philosophy and policy, however, and many of the reforms proved impossible to apply.

In 1953 legislative councils were established in the colonies. Each council was to have a majority of elected members. But needless to say, the few literate Africans and some non-literate heads of families were the only Africans that could take part in the elections. To qualify, one had to be a Portuguese citizen born in the particular colony, literate, to have a certain amount of property and pay a certain amount of tax annually. Recognised heads of families, whether literate or not, could also vote. In essence, this was very little gain to the Africans. On the other hand it strengthened the political position of the Portuguese settlers.

In 1960–61, 'contract labour' was declared abolished and all citizens of the colonies were declared Portuguese citizens. The statuses of *indigena* and *assimilado* were abolished and the policy of assimilation was given up. However, in practice, the spirit of assimilation persisted, and so did the old distinctions between the so-called 'civilised' and 'uncivilised'.

One reform which benefited the Africans was the new attention paid to education. Primary school enrolment increased in Angola to 68,759 in 1965 and 267,768 in 1967. The rate of increase was even higher in Mozambique, although more of Mozambique's education was still provided by the Catholic Church. Up to 1965, about 90% of Mozambique's children were still attending Catholic mission schools. The new reforms included an effort to reduce the hold of the church on education, but this was more successful in Angola than in Mozambique. Also, the differences between education in the government schools and education in the mission schools was officially removed. It was laid down that all schools should run the same syllabuses. In 1964 the administration of each colony was authorised to design the school textbooks for its own colony.

African nationalism and the coming of liberation wars

Because Portuguese rule was so harsh, African resistance to it early in this century was very tough indeed. It was a continuation of the frequent wars which the African kingdoms in and around the Portuguese territories had fought against the Portuguese since the sixteenth century. Although the other European powers recognised Portuguese ownership of Angola, Mozambique and Guinea during the 1880s and 1890s, Portugal was unable to take full possession of these countries for many years, because African kingdoms continued to fight in defence of their territories until about 1915 in Angola, until the 1920s in Mozambique and until the 1930s in Guinea.

The repressive nature of Portuguese rule created a tradition of violent uprisings. In Angola, the armed uprisings were unceasing, breaking out in one district one day and another district another day. They continued as late as the years after the Second World War. The story was very much the same in Mozambique and Guinea.

It was not until about the middle of the 1950s that nationalist politics by literate Africans began to appear, due mostly to the fact that the Portuguese authorities rigidly prevented any signs of politics among their colonial subjects. The only African organisations allowed to exist were the associations officially established by the colonial government for the *assimilados*. These were meant to be social and cultural associations and not supposed to discuss political matters at all. The first was the Liga Africana, formed in Lisbon in 1923 for the *assimilados* from all the Portuguese colonies. Similar associations later appeared in each colony. Even these government-sponsored associations were always kept under careful watch. As soon as any one of them showed an interest in politics, the government would remove its elected leaders and impose government-appointed leaders. In these circumstances it was virtually impossible for the literate Africans to organise nationalist political movements. Even after the Second World War, when most African countries began to move towards independence, the Portuguese continued to prevent freedom of association, freedom of expression and of the press in their colonies. Their argument was that the Portuguese colonies were provinces of Portugal, and that therefore the idea of independence did not apply to them.

Consequently, those who wanted to fight for their country's independence were compelled to act in secrecy. They founded organisations pretending to be cultural organisations but which secretly conducted among the people a campaign for national independence.

Needless to say, such activities were very dangerous. The Portuguese checked with extreme violence any challenge to their position. The

Portuguese secret police, which repressed Portugal itself, was introduced into the colonies, and throughout the 1950s reports of African protest and violent Portuguese repression grew. In Angola in February 1956, three Angolan leaders were arrested and deported; in March 1959 hundreds of people suspected of secretly organising nationalism were arrested; in July 150 nationalist suspects were imprisoned in Luanda; more arrests followed in September, and in December came the secret trial and imprisonment of fifty Angolans and seven Europeans suspected of nationalist activities.

In August 1959, fifty striking workers were killed and many more wounded in Bissau, the capital of Guinea. This incident has gone down in the nationalist history of Guinea as the 'Massacre of Pijiguiti'. Later, twenty-one of the workers arrested during the strike were sent to long terms of imprisonment.

In Mozambique, hundreds of Africans were deported or imprisoned in 1948 as a result of a popular uprising in Laurenco Marques. In 1956, also in Laurenco Marques, 49 dockworkers were shot dead during a protest. In April 1960, the police arrested a number of prominent members of the Maconde people of northern Mozambique and took them away to unknown destinations. When the people protested, they were attacked and about 600 of them killed.

Because of these violent repressions, the nationalist leaders of the Portuguese colonies came to the conclusion that violence was the only way of freeing their countries from the Portuguese. Political parties began to spring up which advocated the use of force against the Portuguese. In Angola, the United African Party of Angola (abbreviated as PLUA in Portuguese) issued a manifesto calling upon Angolans to form underground groups which would unite for a war of liberation. In 1956, leaders of the PLUA and other similar organisations met and formed the Popular Movement for the Liberation of Angola (abbreviated MPLA in Portuguese) under the leadership of Agostinho Neto. From 1960, Mozambique nationalists in exile, mostly in Tanzania, began to form nationalist organisations. In June 1962, the largest three of these organisations joined together and formed the Mozambique Liberation Front (FRELIMO) under the leadership of Dr Eduardo Mondlane, a former university professor in the United States. In Guinea, similar movements were founded. Of these the most important was the African Independence Party of Guinea and Cape Verde (PAIGC) founded about 1954 under the leadership of Amilcar Cabral.

From the beginning, there were contacts among the liberation movements in the three colonies. Such contacts enabled them to exchange information and to learn from one another.

The storm burst first in Angola, as neighbouring Zaire attained independence in June 1960. As the peoples of southern Zaire and northern Angola were of the same ethnic stock (Bakongo), Zairean independence caused intense nationalist excitement in Angola. In June 1960, the MPLA sent a petition to the Portuguese Government appealing for a peaceful solution to the problems of Angola. But in reply, the Portuguese authorities arrested leading members of the MPLA, including Agostinho Neto. When a group of people went to the authorities to ask for the release of Neto and others, the police opened fire, killing about thirty and wounding many more. This was followed by military terror in the city of Luanda, the capital of Angola. In September the MPLA appealed to the United Nations Organisation, and in December renewed its appeal to the Portuguese Government and told the whole world that Portugal had turned down all appeals for peaceful solutions to the problems of Angola.

Having thus failed to persuade the Portuguese, the MPLA began to prepare for the use of force. Then in January and February 1961, a strike by cotton workers in the Malange district led to severe Portuguese actions, among them the bombing of many villages and the killing of thousands of people. On February 4–6, MPLA activists carried out attacks on the military barracks, radio station and prison in Luanda. The liberation war had begun.

In March, another liberation movement, the Angola People's Union (UPA) organised a revolt of coffee plantation workers in Primavera in northern Angola. From there, the movement spread to the whole of northern Angola. The Portuguese answered back with maximum force, including napalm bombs which burnt many villages and killed about 20,000 Angolans. In spite of such acts of terror, however, the Portuguese were driven out of most of northern Angola. From about July 1961, the Portuguese began a drive to recapture the north. They succeeded in capturing some important areas, but the UPA guerrilla forces held on to a lot of territory. The UPA was operating in the territory of the Bakongo people of northern Angola, the same people as the Bakongo of the neighbouring independent Republic of Zaire. Because of this ethnic unity, the UPA could easily operate from bases in Zaire. In March 1962 the UPA joined another nationalist movement to form the National Front for the Liberation of Angola (FLNA), under the leadership of Holden Roberto, the leader of UPA. In April, the FLNA announced the formation of a Revolutionary Government of Angola in Exile (GRAE) in Zaire with Roberto as leader, and in August the GRAE began to set up training camps in Zaire. Meanwhile,

Agostinho Neto escaped from detention in 1962 and under his leadership the MPLA united with some small movements and intensified its guerrilla activities.

There were thus two major liberation forces in Angola – the UPA/FLNA under Roberto and the MPLA under Neto. But there were many other small parties and movements. Roberto's party drew its support from the rural populations of northern Angola; Neto's from educated elements all over the country. Another movement – the National Union for the Total Independence of Angola (UNITA) – began guerrilla operations in eastern Angola in 1966 from bases in Zambia. The MPLA soon joined the fighting in this area of Angola also.

In 1963 after years of careful planning, PAIGC started the liberation war in Guinea. Within a short time it controlled substantial portions of the country. One year later, FRELIMO started war in Mozambique. Since its base was in Tanzania in the north-east, its major activities were for years in the sparsely populated north-eastern Niassa and Cabo Delgado provinces of Mozambique.

Portugal reacted to these wars in four ways. Firstly, it sent in more forces and took other military steps to crush the nationalist movements. To deny the guerrilla fighters the support of the rural masses, it began to remove the people from their villages and concentrate them in 'fortified villages'. In addition, any village suspected of helping the guerrilla fighters was simply wiped out and its people massacred. Portugal could not afford the means for fighting these wars, but was supplied with military helicopters by France, bombers and bombs by West Germany and America, and naval boats by America. All these countries, of course, insisted that these military supplies were not meant for fighting in Africa but for the defence of Portugal itself in Europe. Portugal also received increasing help from South Africa and Rhodesia. Indeed, an informal alliance, called ASPRO, developed in Southern Africa between Portugal, South Africa and Rhodesia. More and more, the ASPRO allies exchanged information and co-ordinated their actions against freedom fighters in Southern Africa.

Secondly, Portugal began a campaign aimed at destroying the unity of the various peoples of each colony. For instance, in Angola she recruited the peoples of the south to fight against the peoples of the north in order to create bitterness between them. In Mozambique, because most of the leaders of FRELIMO were from the Maconde ethnic group, the Portuguese tried to convince the other peoples of Mozambique that the movement was exclusively Maconde. The aim was to make it impossible for FRELIMO to recruit followers from among the other peoples.

Thirdly, the Portuguese colonial authorities, from the outbreak of the wars, increased the pace of the reforms begun in the 1950s. Educational development was stepped up, and political changes permitted. In 1968, the property qualifications for the franchise in the legislative council elections were removed so that more Africans could vote. In 1963 economic and social councils were established in Angola and Mozambique to advise the colonial governments.

Fourthly, Portugal granted more and more concessions to big European and American companies so as to involve them in Portugal's ambition to hold on to the colonies. Consequently the nationalist forces became hostile to the economic projects based on the concessions. For instance FRELIMO became very opposed to the construction of the Cabora Bassa Dam, which involved so many European interests.

The liberation movements themselves suffered a lot from lack of unity. Splinter groups were frequently formed, and the rivalry among these various groups was sometimes very intense. Nevertheless, all the colonies, especially Guinea, made considerable progress in the liberation struggle. By 1970, PAIGC forces controlled about two-thirds of Guinea. In Mozambique, FRELIMO forces long controlled the countryside of the north-eastern provinces of Niassa and Cabo Delgado – about one-third of the country. In 1972, FRELIMO forces operating from Zambia in the north-west opened a new front in the Tete province of north-western Mozambique. In Angola, different movements controlled patches of the countryside, forcing the Portuguese to barricade themselves in the main urban centres.

In the liberated areas, the liberation movements carried out development projects, particularly in education. Both PAIGC and FRELIMO did much to provide for education. In 1966 Dr Mondlane said that the most important preoccupation of FRELIMO was the planning, establishment and direction of schools in the liberated and semi-liberated areas. By that date, FRELIMO had established about 100 schools in the liberated areas, with a total enrolment of about 10,000 pupils. It also established in Tanzania the Mozambique Institute to provide secondary and technical education for Mozambique youths. Unfortunately, this Institute had to be closed in 1968. In Angola, the MPLA was at first very much preoccupied with education but later devoted more of its slim resources to fighting rather than building schools. In northern Angola the FLNA continued to do much for education, setting up many schools not only in the liberated areas, but also in Zaire and Zambia.

Between 1969 and 1973 assassination removed two of the ablest leaders of the liberation movements – Eduardo Mondlane, leader of FRELIMO, in 1969, and Amilcar Cabral, leader of PAIGC, early in 1973. These killings however, did not cause their movements to collapse. Under its new leader, Samora Machel, FRELIMO continued to make progress in the war to liberate Mozambique. And in Guinea (Bissau) the remaining leaders of PAIGC were confident enough to declare their country's independence in September 1973 – a step which had been planned before Cabral's assassination. Before the end of the year, Guinea (Bissau)'s independence had been recognised by many countries in Africa and abroad.

In the end, Portugal collapsed under the weight of the colonial wars. By late 1973, its leaders had come to disagree violently, some top military officers insisting that the government should stop the wars and find other solutions to the colonial problem. Early in 1974 these military officers overthrew Caetano's Government and the new government immediately stopped the wars and promised independence to the colonies. Before the end of the year, the whole world had accepted the independence of Guinea (Bissau), and during 1975 both Mozambique and Angola became independent.

4   Developments in African countries under white minority rule – South Africa and Rhodesia

The other African countries where African independence was still to be won by 1975 are South Africa and Rhodesia. Both are former British colonies from which the British withdrew in such a way that the white settlers were left to dominate political and economic life completely and dictate to the millions of Africans. With South Africa is included another country, Namibia or South-West Africa, which will not be directly discussed in this chapter. Namibia was mandated to South Africa by the League of Nations after the First World War, but South Africa has ruled it as a colony ever since and resisted all efforts by African countries and the United Nations Organisation to make it free.

The white minority government of South Africa calls its policy *apartheid*. This means, in theory, that the various races in South Africa -- Africans, Europeans, Asians and Coloureds – shall be kept separate from one another so that each can develop in is own way and at its own pace. In practice, however, apartheid has meant that the few European settlers rule the country, keep all its economic opportunities in their hands, subject the other races, especially the Africans, to the most degrading laws, and turn them into sources of cheap labour for the white minority. Rhodesia has been moving in much the same direction throughout this century, but more slowly, because the white settlers there are far fewer than those of South Africa.

South Africa

The first white settlers in South Africa were of Dutch origin. They came to the Cape of Good Hope in 1652 and founded a settlement which the Dutch authorities wanted as a refreshing station for their ships trading with India. However, the colony's population increased through births and the coming of more European colonists, mostly from Holland, but also from other parts of Europe, especially France and Germany. Gradually there emerged a distinctive white society on the Cape, with a culture and language – Afrikaans – of its own. The new white society called themselves Afrikaners, but are more often referred to as the Boers. Early in the nineteenth century, Britain acquired the colony from Holland, and some Englishmen began to migrate to the colony. These English immigrants, however, never really became absorbed into the Boer society but have remained a distinct group. From the Cape, the boundaries of the colony steadily expanded towards the interior.

From the very first, the white settlers came into frequent clashes with the indigenous African peoples who fought grimly to preserve their land. The first African peoples whom they met, the Koikoi and the San (called Hottentots and Bushmen by Europeans), were too few and not sufficiently well organised to stop the expansion of the white colony. Gradually they lost their grazing land to the white settlers. Some of the Koikoi then moved far away and established new homes in the far interior, but those who remained began to intermarry with the Boers and to accept service under them as servants. From the intermarriages there emerged a group of people of mixed blood now classified as Coloureds.

About the beginning of the eighteenth century, the Boers began to encounter other African peoples. These were the Bantu-speaking peoples, a numerous, intelligent and very virile group who had built well organised kingdoms all over southern Africa. From then on, right into the nineteenth century, the Bantu and the Boers fought a long series of frontier wars in which first the Bantu, then the Boers, had the upper hand. The expansion of the white colony was seriously checked.

Then between 1817 and 1834, the Bantu hinterland experienced a violent revolution – otherwise known as the Mfekane. It started with certain political and military changes among the Zulu which turned them, under the leadership of Shaka, into a very warlike and expansionist state. As the Zulu attacked and destroyed their neighbours, the vanquished fled and attacked other people in their turn. So the destruction and rampage were carried far and wide. This led to the destruction of many states, the emergence of new states, widespread disruption of life and drastic reduction of population in some areas as people fled to other areas for safety. One of the most important consequences was that the near depopulation of certain areas of the Bantu interior let the Boers through. Between 1836 and 1846 they outflanked the Bantu resistance on the frontier and went in thousands into the interior to set up Afrikaner communities there. This march into the interior is known as the Great Trek.

As the Boers came, the Bantu tried to stop them from taking their land. Unfortunately, however, many of the Bantu peoples of the interior had become too weakened by the recent revolution and wars to offer effective resistance. Consequently, the Boers established themselves and began to seize land in all directions, although the Bantu never ceased to resist.

The experiences of the Europeans since the founding of the first white settlement gradually induced a set of terrible attitudes among them. The comparative ease with which they disposed of Koikoi and San resistance made them begin to think of themselves as a race far superior to the Africans. This belief was strengthened by the fact that they were living in the age of the Atlantic Slave Trade and that they themselves began to own African slaves whom they bought from abroad. As their settlement expanded more and more from the Cape so they held their racial beliefs more tenaciously, for, away from the Cape, each Boer family lived on his farm with his family, far removed from other Boers and surrounded by his slaves and Koikoi servants. The Boer farmer found, therefore, that the best way of keeping his slaves and servants submissive, and making them respect his person, was to get them to accept his doctrine that they belonged to an inferior race and he to a superior race. In the end, the Boers built this doctrine into their own brand of the Christian faith, the Dutch Reformed Church, and twisted certain passages in the Bible, especially in the Old Testament, to support it. Finally, in their long conflicts with the Bantu, the Boers found that the racial doctrine served as a means for rallying themselves for the most terrible atrocities against the Bantu.

Meanwhile, at the opening of the nineteenth century, the colony passed from Holland to Britain. And throughout the century, conflicts between the Boers and the British Government were a very important feature of the history of South Africa. One major cause of these conflicts was the Boers' belief that the British Government owed them the duty of expelling the Bantu from the border areas so that they could take over the land. But the British Government, influenced by missionaries and British philanthropists, was often trying to protect the Koikoi servants against inhuman treatment by the Boers, or trying to establish boundaries to put an end to the border clashes. Boer resentment over the British 'failure to do their duty', added to grievances over other issues, was the main reason for the Great Trek into the interior in the 1830s. The Boers were determined to move away from the area under British control.

The Great Trek, however, did not put an end to the Boer-British conflict, but expanded it in scope. On arrival in the interior, the Trekker Boers established three communities – Transvaal, Natal and Orange Free State – and proclaimed that these communities were beyond the border of the British colony and, therefore, not under the control of the British Government. The British maintained that the Trekker Boers were still British subjects and that their new communities in the interior were therefore part of the British colony. From then on, there ensued a conflict between Britain's attempts to maintain its imperial interests over all the white communities of South Africa and the desire of the Boer communities to be free of British control. In these conflicts, British policy was inconsistent, because the British public was opposed to spending money on the colonies. The British Government would annex the Boer republics one day, and give them their freedom the next. After diamonds and gold were discovered in South Africa in the 1860s and 1880s, the British became determined to form all the white communities of South Africa – the Cape, Natal, Transvaal and Orange Free State – into a federation. The Boers, now knowing that their territories were rich especially in gold, resisted the federation plan. This led to a bitter war between the British and the Boers in 1899–1902.

The war ended in the defeat of the Boers and prepared the way for the formation, in 1910, of the federation, called the Union of South Africa. The British handed over control of the former colony to the white settlers and withdrew.

Since 1910 the old rigid Boer ideas of racial separation and white domination have gradually emerged triumphant in South Africa. The story of this triumph falls into two periods: 1910 to 1948, and 1948 to the present. The difference between them is that the goal of white domination has been more ruthlessly pursued since 1948 than before. The dividing line was the election of 1948 in which the most extreme Boer group – the Afrikaner Nationalist Party – campaigned on the promise that it would institute apartheid in all aspects of national life. Its promises of racial separateness and Boer supremacy won the hearts of the Boer peasant population. It therefore won the election and came to power under the leadership of Dr D. F. Malan. This party has ruled South Africa ever since, instituting laws and measures which have wiped out all signs of freedom for the Africans who constitute 70% of the population.

The structure of apartheid
South Africa has a total population of about 21 million. Of this, about 15 million are black, about 3.7 million are white and about 2.6 million are Coloureds and Asians. This means that white settlers represent only about 18% of the population, yet all the political power in the country is in their hands.

Before the Union was formed in 1910, non-whites (including a few literate Africans regarded as 'civilised') could vote in Cape Province. In the other three provinces – Natal, Transvaal and Orange Free State – the right to vote belonged only to white people. In the negotiations leading to the formation of the Union, Cape Province tried in vain to persuade the other provinces to accept non-white voters also. A compromise was ultimately reached whereby each province retained its own electoral rules. After 1910, not only was the Cape system not accepted by the other provinces but the Cape was brought into line with the other provinces. The Africans' vote was the first to be removed, then the vote of the other non-whites. By 1956, only white people could vote or be voted for in elections to the South African parliament. All the other peoples in the Union – Black, Coloured and Asians, about 82% of the population – are denied any voice at all.

In 1959, the white minority government brought forward a measure purporting to give the Africans freedom to rule themselves in their own 'homelands'. This measure – the Promotion of Bantu Self-Government Act – provided for the creation in the African areas of the country of a special homeland for each national group among the Bantu: one for the Zulu, one for the Xhosa, one for the Sotho, and so on. In each so-called 'Bantustan', each African people would elect their own government and rule themselves. The first of the Bantustans, the Transkei, held its first election in 1963.

The example of the Transkei quickly showed what the Boers meant by self-government for the Bantustans. The Transkei Legislative Assembly was far from being a free parliament. It was packed with chiefs appointed by the white minority government of South Africa.

It could make no laws without the approval of the Government of South Africa. All security, even in the Bantustan, was in the hands of white officials and no African had the right to bear arms. Moreover, the government's economic policies make it impossible for any Bantustan to become economically self-supporting.

The Coloureds and the Indians do not even have the chance of having any so-called 'homelands'. All they are allowed are poor suburbs on the edge of the white towns.

These political policies have not arisen by chance. They are the product of a deliberate philosophy which sees South Africa as a white man's country, and indeed the Boer leaders have repeatedly stated that this is their goal. Making the white man the master and owner of South Africa, they have said again and again, is the only way to ensure his survival in South Africa. All non-white peoples in South Africa, the Boers say, must accept their subordination to the whites and their lack of any political rights. J. G. Strijdom, Prime Minister of South Africa in the 1950s, put it this way: 'Our policy is that the Europeans must . . . remain masters in South Africa. If we reject the "master race" idea . . . and if the non-Europeans are given representation and the vote and the non-Europeans are developed on the same basis as the Europeans, how can the European remain master . . .? Our view is that in every sphere the Europeans must retain the right to rule the country and to keep it a White man's country.' His successor, Prime Minister H. F. Verwoerd, said in 1963: 'Reduced to its simplest form the problem is nothing else than this: "We want to keep South Africa White – keeping it White can only mean one thing, namely White domination." ' And in 1970, the Prime Minister, B. J. Vorster added: 'South African nationhood is for the Whites only.'

Economically too, the whites dominate South Africa. More than 70% of the national income goes to the whites; 87% of the land has been designated white areas and only 13% as African 'reserves'. Even then, not all the 13% has been released for the Africans. No African has the right to the freehold title of any piece of land in South Africa. The land that has been allowed to the Africans is grossly insufficient to support the African population. As a result, it is not possible for them to earn enough in the reserves to support themselves and their families. Now and again, whole populations of Africans are removed from their homes on the land designated as white areas and taken to land assigned to them in the African reserves. Such removal has caused serious disruption of life for millions of Africans. Moreover, when a people have been thus removed, they have usually been simply dumped in the open country without any shelter or provisions and left to fend for themselves as best they could. Consequently, life in such new homelands has usually been one of poverty, squalor and disease.

The aim of these economic policies is to turn the black population into a source of ready and cheap migrant labour for the white man's businesses and farms. Since the resources of the reserves are not enough for their economic survival, the Africans are compelled to seek jobs in the white areas – as domestic servants, industrial workers in the mines and factories, or farm workers on the white man's farms. Because the economy of the white areas requires African labour, total separation is impossible; millions of Africans work in areas designated as 'white'. But the apartheid regime has passed a long list of laws to impose racial separateness. Marriage between persons of different races is a crime; mixed racial sports are illegal; public buses, trains, toilets, cinemas, post offices, churches – all are segregated. In the white areas, the Africans have no rights whatsoever. Any African visiting the white areas is regarded as a foreigner and allowed to stay only as long as he is working for a white man or white company. He cannot bring his wife or relations with him unless they too are employed there. His young children born in the white area can live with him there but they must go to the reserve as soon as they attain the age of sixteen. In this way, the African's family life is ruthlessly destroyed.

While living as employees of white people in the white towns, the Africans are crowded together in barrack-like dormitories. Each must carry a passbook giving all the information about him and his employment. Failure to produce this pass when demanded by the police is a serious crime. About 2,000 Africans are arrested and imprisoned every day for pass offences.

Since 1953 when the Bantu Education Act was passed, apartheid has been applied to education. Before this Act, church missions, provincial governments and the Africans themselves had been able to build and run schools for Africans. The Act removed education from the control of these various bodies and handed it to the Ministry of Bantu Affairs. The aim of 'Bantu Education' is to prepare young African minds to accept the Africans' subordinate position in the apartheid state, and to give them only the type of training that will fit them for the subordinate jobs for which the whites need them. Dr Verwoerd, the leading exponent of 'Bantu Education', stated that the free education which the Africans received before 1953 gave them expectations which could not be fulfilled in South Africa, and trained them for professions not open to them. 'If the Native in South Africa today in any kind of school . . . is being taught to expect that he will live his adult life under a policy of equal rights, he is making a big mistake,' said Verwoerd. On another occasion, Verwoerd asked, 'What is the use of teaching the Bantu child mathematics when he cannot use it in practice?' And another Boer leader, J. N. LeRoux, added, 'Who will do the manual labour if you give the Natives an academic education? We should so conduct our schools that the Native who attends those schools will know that to a great extent he must be the labourer in the country.'

Since the Bantu Education Act came into force, therefore, African children have been subjected to a system of education designed to destroy their personalities as human beings. In addition, the schools are starved of money, books and teachers. Schools for African children are run in poor school buildings and overcrowded classrooms. Teachers have sometimes to teach classes as big as fifty because teachers are few; many classes have to be held in the open field because there are no classrooms. Many children have to go without education at all because the schools have no room for them, and a good proportion of those who go to school drop out after a few months. For this education, the African parents have to pay fees. In comparison, education for white children is free, and the government's expenditure on the white child's education is many times its expenditure on the African child's.

To enforce these political, economic and social conditions, the South African white minority regime has made very many coercive laws and developed South Africa into perhaps the most ruthless police state in the world. Mere criticism of the government's actions is a serious offence. For Africans, possession of anything that can be described as a weapon, trespass on the property of a white man – these and similar offences are punishable with death or life imprisonment. The police are given powers to arrest and detain people without trial for up to six months. Stories of terrible tortures of people in police custody are very many. Many detainees are known to have died from torture. The laws protect the police from being held accountable for such brutalities and murders.

African resistance to apartheid
As pointed out earlier, the Africans continued throughout the nineteenth century to fight for their land. The last of these armed risings occurred in 1904. After that, the growing class of literate Africans began to come together to organise nationalist resistance to the ambitions and actions of the Boers. In 1912 they founded the African Native National Congress, later named the African National Congress (ANC), which has provided most of the organisation and leadership for African nationalism ever since.

From the beginning, the ANC decided to use only peaceful and constitutional means to fight for change in South Africa. It did not wish to drive the white people out of the country, but to make South Africa a multi-racial country in which all persons would be equal. Since the white people insisted that uneducated Africans were unfit to govern, the ANC hoped to persuade them to accept literate Africans into positions of responsibility in the country. Through petitions, delegations, appeals to the conscience of the white electorate, the ANC hoped to obtain redress for the wrongs which the Africans suffered, and to achieve the removal of racial discrimination in politics, education, industry, government and social life.

These methods achieved no quick result, however, and therefore African people became impatient. As early as 1913, African workers' strikes occurred. In 1914, African women in Orange Free State demonstrated against passes. In 1919, African sanitary workers of Johannesburg went on strike – one of the first major strikes by African workers. This was followed by a strike by some 40,000 African miners on the Witwatersrand in Transvaal, which was smashed by the police and the army, several miners being killed.

In spite of the government's brutalities, however, the African resistance became more and more radical. African workers employed in industry and commerce began to organise themselves into trade unions. Ultimately, these unions founded a general union, the Industrial and Commercial Workers Union (ICU). Throughout the 1920s and 1930s, the ICU completely seized from the ANC the leadership in organising the resistance of African workers. The ANC itself had internal troubles, and some of its most militant members withdrew.

The years 1935–6 were an important milestone in the history of African resistance. A Boer Prime Minister, Hertzog, pushed through parliament two laws – the Representation of Natives Act which took the vote from the remaining African voters in the Cape Province; and the Native Trust and Land Bill which deprived Africans in Cape Province of their right to buy land outside the African reserves. These bills had the effect of uniting the ANC and the various other African organisations. An All-African Convention was summoned and attended by representatives of most African organisations. An attempt by the radical minority to get the convention to adopt a programme of positive action was however defeated by the moderate majority, and an opportunity for united African action was lost.

The Second World War (1939–45) stimulated African resistance in South Africa just as it stimulated African resistance to colonialism in the rest of Africa. As a result, the ANC was reorganised and strengthened. But perhaps the most important consequence of the stimulus of the Second World War was the founding of the ANC Youth League by university graduates, students, and educated workers. The most prominent leaders of the Youth League were university graduates like Nelson Mandela and Oliver Tambo and educated workers like Walter Sisulu and Anton Lembede. Their motto was 'Africa's cause must triumph'. They criticised the ANC's traditional moderate methods of peaceful protest and advocated direct action.

Under the impact of the Youth League and the workers' movement, the character of the ANC changed. In 1945, it adopted the 'African claims' – one man one vote, equality of all persons before the law, freedom to own land, the abolition of the pass system. When the African Mine Workers' Union organised a great strike in 1946, the ANC came out openly in support of the strike, although the ANC leadership and the striking miners failed to work out an effective programme of joint action.

In 1949 the ANC reacted to the apartheid policies of the new Afrikaner Nationalist Party Government by adopting a programme of action which called for the use of boycotts, strikes, civil disobedience and non-cooperation. Massive demonstrations by Africans, Indians and Coloureds shook the country during 1950. Moreover, all the non-white organisations – Africans, Indians and Coloureds – began to come together. A Joint Planning Council was formed to coordinate their efforts. In 1952 the South African Indian Congress and the ANC cooperated in launching the famous Defiance Campaign of that year. During the campaign, Africans defied a number of apartheid laws, and 8,500 volunteers were arrested and imprisoned for deliberate acts of civil disobedience. Riots broke out in many cities. The government reacted as usual with massive police and military force, and passive resistance to the government was declared illegal.

After this Defiance Campaign, the popularity of the ANC soared among Africans, who were also encouraged by developments in other parts of Africa, where nationalist forces were gradually driving out colonialism. However, under the new wave of repression launched by the government, the ANC under the leadership of Albert Luthuli in 1953–5 returned to a campaign of constitutional, peaceful and moral persuasion, appealing to Africans to exercise restraint and avoid violence. Such appeals were futile. Demonstrations and riots broke out in various parts of the country. When in 1955–6 the government extended the pass laws to women, the women answered with massive riots. To bring the situation under control, the government arrested 156 Africans in December 1956, accused them of plotting to overthrow the government by force, and charged them with high treason. The

63

notorious 'Treason Trials' went on until 1961.

While the 'Treason Trials' were in progress, a split occurred in the ANC. A small group of leading members had become unhappy with Luthuli's insistence on peaceful methods. They also accused the ANC leadership of betraying African nationalism by closely associating with white and Indian opponents of apartheid as well as with communism. In 1958, they founded their own separate party, the Pan-African Congress (PAC). Their first major activity was the organisation of an anti-pass campaign in 1960. On 21 March 1960, an unarmed crowd protesting against the carrying of passes was shot at in Sharpeville. Sixty-nine of the demonstrators were killed and 178 wounded. The ANC denounced the Sharpeville massacre, but the government followed it up with police raids leading to the arrest of many leaders of both the ANC and the PAC. In 1961, some of the ANC leaders were brought to trial under the Suppression of Communism Act; but attempts to prove that they were linked with communism failed and so all were set free. Meanwhile, the government had banned both the ANC and PAC as threats to the peace.

All avenues of open and lawful agitation against apartheid were therefore closed. Rather than disband, both the ANC and the PAC decided to go underground and to begin to use violent means to achieve change in South Africa. A new phase in the African struggle thus began.

Many secret underground organisations have been founded since 1961, the best known being *Umkonto we Sizwe* (Spear of the Nation), founded by the ANC as an armed wing to train guerrillas for the eventual war against the Boers. In the early 1960s, Umkonto conducted a campaign of sabotage which considerably threatened the security of South Africa. The government responded with the arrest, trial and imprisonment of known ANC leaders in 1963, including Nelson Mandela who had become the most prominent man in the ANC. Other leaders of both the ANC and PAC were compelled to flee into exile abroad.

The struggle still continued, however. Both the ANC and PAC continue to be well organised abroad, although attempts to get them to unite against the common enemy have been unsuccessful. Umkonto has also continued to train guerrillas abroad in preparation for the South African war of liberation.

At a meeting in Tanzania in 1967, the ANC adopted a new and far-reaching 'Freedom Charter', which declared the goal of the impending revolution in South Africa to be the creation of a Democratic People's Republic of South Africa, in which government shall be controlled by all the people irrespective of race or colour; all

64

minerals, banks and monopoly industries shall be transferred to the ownership of the state; the land shall be shared among those who work it; equality of all before the law as well as the right of all to work and security shall be guaranteed; education shall be compulsory and free to all.

Rhodesia

Rhodesia used to be known as Southern Rhodesia, one of the three colonies that made up British Central Africa, together with Northern Rhodesia (now Zambia) and Nyasaland (now Malawi). Since the independence and change of names of these two countries, Southern Rhodesia has been referred to simply as Rhodesia. To its African peoples and to the rest of Africa, however, Rhodesia's proper name is Zimbabwe – the name which it will bear officially when its African peoples have won their freedom and taken control of their country.

British rule was established over Rhodesia in the 1890s by a commercial company, the British South Africa Company. Like the Royal Niger Company in Nigeria, the British South Africa Company was given a charter which entitled it not only to control the trade and mineral resources of Rhodesia, but also to establish a government over the country. Again like the Royal Niger Company, the British South Africa Company established its rule by getting the African rulers to enter into treaties whose meanings were not made clear to them, and by making use of military force.

African resistance was very powerful, the last major armed rebellion occurring in 1896–7. After that, company rule gradually became firmly established. The company declared itself to be the owner of the land and began to invite white settlers to come and farm it. Substantial portions of the land were thus taken and given to white settlers, the standard size of each settler's farm being about 3,000 acres.

From the beginning, although Rhodesia was legally a British colony, British control was nominal. Until 1923, Rhodesia was effectively governed by the company. An Order in Council of 1898 provided for the appointment by the British Government of a Resident Commissioner and a Commandant General for Rhodesia, which merely established British imperial presence.

Conditions very similar to those of South Africa soon began to develop in Rhodesia. After defeating the Africans in battle, the company and the settlers seized cattle from them as war reparations. They also seized the best land and pushed the Africans to the poorer land. Africans who remained in the areas claimed by the white people had to begin to pay rents to the white owners. To force the Africans to work for wages on the Europeans' farms, taxes were introduced. Very soon, as the population of the Africans and the number of their cattle increased, the land onto which they had been pushed became too small for them. They began to ask for more land, but the Europeans refused, usually claiming that the Africans were not making good use of the land they already had.

These trends in Rhodesia owed much to influence from South Africa. Most of the earliest white settlers in Rhodesia came from South Africa, bringing their racial prejudices with them.

Political life followed the same trends. From the beginning, the government of Rhodesia was organised and run as if the Africans did not exist. There was no thought that the Africans would ever take any part in the government. The leaders of the company believed that at some future time the company would hand over the government of Rhodesia to the white settlers and thereafter concentrate only on trade; and that Rhodesia would then probably merge with South Africa. When provision was made in 1898 for a legislative council of five elected and four nominated members, the five elected members were elected only by the white settlers. In the years that followed, the elected membership – always of the white settlers – gradually increased.

Most of Rhodesia's early political history, indeed, is a story of the settlers' struggle to wrest control from the company. The company claimed to be the owner of all land not yet assigned, but the settlers claimed that the land belonged to them. The company tried to placate the settlers by granting them more and more participation in the government. The settlers clamoured for more political power all the time and used their growing influence in the legislative council to fight the land issue. In the end, the land issue went before the Privy Council in London, the highest court of appeal in the British Empire. Some missionaries spoke in the interest of the Africans and pointed out that the land did not belong to the company or the settlers but to the Africans. The Privy Council decided that the land belonged to the British Crown and that the company merely held the land in trust. This decision was to the advantage of the settlers, for it enabled the land to be transferred to their government when company government was terminated.

Meanwhile the settlers had intensified their efforts to seize the government of the colony from the company, especially after the First World War. They raised the slogan, 'Rhodesia belongs to the Rhodesians' but by Rhodesians they meant the white settlers only. Finally in 1922, the white settlers were asked to choose in a referendum whether Rhodesia should join the Union of South Africa or become a crown colony with internal self-government and with control over its own police force and army. They chose the latter.

In 1923, therefore, the company's rule was terminated and Rhodesia was declared a crown colony. The 1923 constitution set up a legislative chamber and a cabinet of ministers. There was to be a crown-appointed Governor representing the King of England, but the Governor could only act on the advice of the ministers. The British Government was to be responsible for Rhodesia's foreign relations and to have the power to veto any legislation adversely affecting the Africans. This power of veto however, was never used. In fact the 1923 constitution gave the small white population of Rhodesia freedom to govern Rhodesia as it saw fit, rather as had happened in South Africa in 1910. The relationship between Britain and Rhodesia was more like the relationship between Britain and any of the self-governing dominions in the British Commonwealth. Rhodesia was not a true colony, and the position of the crown-appointed Governor was merely honorary.

Though the white settlers of Rhodesia chose not to join South Africa in 1922, after 1923 they began to build a society based on South Africa's examples. It is important to remember how small the white settler population of Rhodesia has always been in comparison with the African population. In 1930 there were only 48,000 whites and just under two million Africans; in 1960 there were 219,000 whites and about three million Africans; by 1970 there were 250,000 whites to about four million Africans.

The history of Rhodesia since 1923 falls into two periods – 1923 to 1965, and the years after 1965. Until 1965, Rhodesia continued to be nominally a British colony; but in 1965 the white settlers revolted against Britain and declared Rhodesia independent.

Between 1923 and 1965, the white settlers made many laws to entrench themselves as the owners and masters of Rhodesia. Although no laws were made to deprive Africans completely of the right to vote, it was given only to Africans who satisfied certain qualifications. To be able to vote, an African had to command a certain level of income annually, pay a certain amount of tax, reach a certain level of literacy. These qualifications were always so set that only a small proportion of Africans could vote. Whenever the number of qualified Africans increased considerably, the qualifications were raised. In this way, the small minority of white settlers was able to control the Rhodesian legislature set up in 1923.

Before 1923, white areas and African areas of the country had been defined by law. But there was a substantial part of the country not yet assigned to either side. The Africans, for whom the land in the African 'reserves' was proving more and more inadequate, asked for more land from these unassigned areas. Because of the small number of white settlers, a lot of land in the white areas was not being used. Yet the Land Apportionment Act of 1930 not only denied the Africans more land but took away some of the best parts of the land which they already had. The Act gave 48% of all the land of Rhodesia to the Whites (who numbered only 48,000), and 42% to the Africans (who numbered about two million). The remaining 10% was left for game reserves, forest reserves and other uses.

Soon after the passing of this Act, the government began to move Africans from the areas assigned to the whites. This removal of large populations of Africans reached a peak during the 1940s and 1950s. The consequences for the Africans were the same as in South Africa: disruption of life, poverty, squalor and disease.

From the 1920s onwards, the economic conditions of the Africans began to deteriorate very sharply. Before the 1920s, African cattle farmers had produced most of the cattle of Rhodesia. Many of the settlers, unable to compete, had found it more profitable to buy cattle from the Africans to sell rather than produce their own. But from the 1920s, the land available to the Africans was no longer adequate for their needs. Secondly, the white settlers began to use their political power to strengthen themselves against the Africans in the economic field. They also used government resources to provide themselves with experimental farm stations, free expert advice, generous credit facilities, irrigation works, seeds, stocks, and fertilisers at government-subsidised rates. As most of the towns, roads and railways were in the white areas, the African farmers experienced great difficulty in trying to transport their products to the market. Finally, all sorts of measures were taken to make the Africans' maize, a major product of Rhodesia, much more expensive in the market than the white farmers' maize. By the 1940s, the Africans had been more or less ruined economically. Indeed, the African population was by then unable to produce enough to feed itself.

This was just what the white settlers wanted. Increasing numbers of Africans were forced to seek jobs in the white areas – in white businesses in the towns and on white farms in the rural areas. For instance, in the city of Salisbury, the number of Africans in paid jobs rose from 46,000 in 1946 to 75,000 in 1951.

In the towns, the Africans were regarded as outsiders and tenants; they could not take part in town affairs. As in South Africa, Africans had to carry passes and be registered by their employers. Their living conditions were extremely poor. Since the employers and the government regarded the African workers in the towns as temporary residents whose real homes were in the reserves, they provided accommodation for the African worker alone. Such accommodation was provided in compounds built by the employers or in 'locations' built at the edge of the towns by the town authorities. Quite often, the workers brought along their families thus causing unhealthy overcrowding.

Everything was done to make it impossible for the African workers to compete with the white workers. The Industrial Conciliation Act of 1934 and its Amendment of 1937 set up Industrial Councils to settle disputes between employees and employers. Africans were, however, excluded from the term 'employees', which meant that the Africans were denied the benefits of collective bargaining with their employers. Moreover, the Industrial Councils were empowered to regulate the conditions of apprenticeship. This gave the white workers the power of excluding the Africans from the chance of acquiring skills.

Education for African children was provided by the missionary bodies from the first. In 1901, the government granted the missionary bodies £133 towards the education of Africans. Though this grant rose in succeeding years, it always remained very small. By 1910 it had risen to £2,780; by 1930 to £48,000; by 1952 it was £629,590 – a small amount considering the number of African children. In short, African education was left mostly in the hands of the missions.

In contrast, the government began to take over responsibility for providing education for the children of settlers as early as 1900. Ultimately, the government took over many of the mission schools for white children. Not only was education for African and white children separate, the government spent much more on the education of white children than on that of African children.

In 1953, in spite of the opposition of the Africans of Zambia and Malawi especially, Rhodesia, Malawi and Zambia were brought together as a federation. The whites campaigned for the federation with the main argument that it would be economically advantageous to the three countries. The Africans, however, opposed it because it was a way of expanding the Rhodesian system of white domination to the other two countries. African opposition to the federation grew more and more intense until, in 1963, the federation was dissolved.

During the first few years of the federation, a spirit of liberalism and reform showed itself among the leadership of the Rhodesian white settlers. Garfield Todd, who became Prime Minister of Rhodesia in 1953, intended to introduce measures that would considerably conciliate the Africans. Under his leadership, some sections of white opinion began to question the rightness of the attempts which had been made to prevent African competition with whites in economic life. A bill was even introduced to give recognition to African trade unions. Government expenditure on the encouragement of African agriculture was increased. More attention was paid to the provision of education for Africans. Multi-racial university education was started. Some thought was even given to reforming the electoral system in such a way as to give more Africans the vote.

However, this spirit of liberalism was short-lived. In the last years of the federation, the whites became more determined to defend their supremacy. In 1958, Todd's cabinet colleagues forced him out of the government. Todd was succeeded as Prime Minister by Edgar Whitehead, whose government abandoned Todd's reform programmes and immediately started an era of repression.

Two years after the dissolution of the federation, Ian Smith, Edgar Whitehead's successor as Prime Minister, declared that Rhodesia had become independent of Britain. As a result, Britain asked the United Nations Organisation to impose economic sanctions on Rhodesia. The UN asked all countries in the world to stop trading with Rhodesia in certain goods, but South Africa and Portugal continued to do so. In addition, the British Government froze Rhodesian assets in Britain. Though these measures hurt the economy of Rhodesia, it soon became obvious that they were not enough to force Rhodesia to give up its illegal independence. African countries began to demand that Britain should use military force, but Britain preferred to continue to negotiate with the white Rhodesians. Not only did these negotiations fail to change the situation, but the white minority regime grew stronger and stronger. In 1969 a new constitution was introduced which further restricted the rights of the Africans and gave more dictatorial powers to the white minority government. Some writers have called it an 'apartheid constitution'. In 1970, Ian Smith's government declared Rhodesia a republic, thus making the break with Britain complete.

At the end of 1971, however, Britain announced that she had at last worked out a settlement with the white minority regime. The Africans, who formed over 94% of the population of Rhodesia, were not consulted, and the only thing the agreement held out to them was the offer of the vote to those Africans who satisfied certain new property qualifications. It was stated that as more and more Africans satisfied these qualifications, African majority rule would be achieved in Rhodesia. Britain was to grant Rhodesia legal independence as soon as the new arrangement came into force, which it would only do if a majority of African opinion accepted it.

Early in 1972, therefore, a commission under the chairmanship of Lord Pearce was sent from London to find out African attitudes to the settlement. The coming of the commission gave the Africans, whose nationalist leaders were all imprisoned or detained, a chance to voice their opinion and all over the country they overwhelmingly rejected the settlement. Even the chiefs, who have usually been willing tools in the hands of the white regime, rejected it. With this massive African rejection, the status of Rhodesia as an illegally independent country remained.

African resistance

Rhodesia is made up of two major African peoples – the Ndebele of Matabeleland, and the Shona of Mashonaland. Before the coming of the British, the Shona had been subjects of the Ndebele and paid tribute to the Ndebele king.

In the twenty-five years or so following the 1896–7 uprisings, the way African resistance was expressed in Mashonaland and Matabeleland differed. Until 1917, the Shona in Mozambique continued to revolt against the Portuguese. In Rhodesia, the Shona uprisings were not so frequent, but the spirit of rebellion was often apparent. The only serious Shona uprising after 1897 was the Mapondera rising of 1900–3. Mapondera was a great Shona warrior who, during the 1896 uprising, had lived in Mozambique. In 1900 he decided to come into Rhodesia to avenge the defeat of his people and the seizure of their cattle by the British. On entering Rhodesia, he was able to rouse some of the Shona to his support, and until 1903 he continued to constitute a serious trouble to the company's government. His was a losing battle, however. Most of his countrymen did not support him because they were tired of fighting. In 1903 he gave himself up and was sent to prison, where he died shortly afterwards. There was very little further stirring among the Shona until the 1920s.

African resistance in Matabeleland was different. In the first place, among the Ndebele, the hope of reviving their kingship was strengthened by the fact that the sons of Lobengula, the last Ndebele king, had been educated in South Africa and returned with fairly high levels of literacy and were therefore able to argue their case with the British. Secondly the Ndebele were more affected than the Shona by the white land acquisitions. The Ndebele had been deprived of most of their land by 1894 and had failed to recover it in the 1896 uprising. While most of Mashonaland was not yet feeling the seizures of land by the company and the settlers, the Ndebele were already being driven out of their villages or forced to pay rents to white settlers. This land issue kept the Ndebele discontented. To many Ndebele, the revival of the kingship seemed a sure way of recovering Ndebele land.

Lobengula's eldest son, Nyamanda, emerged as the leader of the kingship movement, which gained importance in the last years of the First World War. Nyamanda was supported by Ndebele ex-servicemen who had fought for the British; by most educated Ndebele – teachers and pastors; by the African National Congress of South Africa; by the Aborigines' Rights Protection Society in England; and by most leading men and the broad masses of the Ndebele people. The movement's aim was the restoration of the Ndebele kingship and the creation of Ndebele territory into a separate homeland under the protection of the British Crown. This meant that Matabeleland would be taken away from company rule and be constituted into a protectorate directly under the British Government. The movement set out to achieve this aim by organising the Ndebele into a coherent force and giving them a common voice, and by sending petitions to the King of England. However, the movement failed completely, and in 1923 Rhodesia was handed over to the white settlers.

While Nyamanda's movement was writing petitions to London, another movement had begun to emerge. The leader of this was Abraham Twala, a South African resident in Rhodesia. Twala criticised the methods adopted by Nyamanda's movement and claimed that it had no chance of achieving anything. Experience in South Africa had shown, said Twala, that the salvation of the African lay not with London but with the African people themselves. Twala therefore set out to organise the few African voters in Rhodesia into an association and to use this association to achieve a number of things for the Africans. His movement was, therefore, not a Shona or Ndebele movement but a 'national' movement.

In January 1923, Twala founded the Rhodesian Bantu Voters' Association (RBVA). The RBVA decided to give its support to those white settlers who were demanding the end of company rule and the granting of responsible government to Rhodesia. In exchange the RBVA hoped the responsible government faction among the settlers would promise to achieve certain things for Africans: the right to buy land freely, the removal of some of the restrictions on the African's voting rights, and the provision of higher education for Africans.

The RBVA did not realise, however, that no matter how much support the African gave to the white settler, the white settler could never accept the African as an equal. The RBVA therefore achieved little or nothing after 1923.

Many other associations appeared after 1923 – the Gwelo Native Welfare Association, the Rhodesia Native Association, and others. Because Rhodesia had very few educated Africans, these associations were, like the RBVA, founded and led by Africans from other countries, especially from South Africa and Malawi. These associations had two other characteristics in common. They represented a change from the ethnic nationalism of the pre-1920 period (as seen in Nyamanda's movement) to a true 'national' spirit. Secondly, they were really associations of the small group of educated people and had little contact with the masses of Africans. Partly because they were thus unrepresentative of the African voice, the white government treated them with contempt. The commission set up in 1925 to look into the land issue simply ignored these associations. In 1929, all the associations held a congress and, among other things, voted to oppose the Land Apportionment Bill. In spite of their opposition, the bill became law in 1930. In other matters too, their resistance to the policies and actions of the white minority government achieved nothing.

Towards the end of the 1920s, the African workers in the towns began to organise themselves into trade unions. The founding of trade unions in Rhodesia was influenced by similar developments in South Africa. In 1927 the Industrial and Commercial Workers' Union (ICU) of South Africa sent Robert Sambo to start the ICU in Rhodesia. The ICU of Rhodesia attempted to organise not only the workers in the towns but also African labourers on white farms. These activities alarmed the Rhodesian Government and Sambo, who was from Malawi, was deported. In spite of this, the ICU grew strong among the workers and became the first major mass movement in which both the Shona and Ndebele participated.

The ICU never became strong enough to force important concessions from the white minority government. For instance, its members were not yet prepared for such a radical thing as a strike. Nevertheless, the ICU is important in Rhodesian history as the first mass movement which seriously attempted to overcome ethnic divisions in the Africans' struggle against the settlers. Some of the men who learned politics in the ICU remained prominent in Rhodesian politics until the 1950s.

In the 1930s there were two developments in African politics. The first was the rise and spread, among the Shona, of religious movements similar to Chilembwe's in Malawi and Kimbangu's in Zaire. The Watch Tower movement became very influential among the Shona. Also important was the Church of the White Bird, founded and led by Matthew Zwimba. These movements enabled the Shona to express their rejection of the white government's policies. Their emergence

73

showed that at last the Shona had given up their tradition of armed uprising against the white government and had become receptive to new ideas and methods of resistance. Towards the end of the 1930s, in Mashonaland, there was, in addition to the separatist church movements, a growing tendency towards open criticism and defiance of the white government by Shona chiefs. Perhaps the best known of these chiefs was Chief Nyandoro of Chiota who, because of his bold and frequent criticisms of the government's agricultural policies, was deposed.

The second development in African politics in the 1930s was that more indigenous literate Rhodesians began to play leading roles in the nationalist politics of the associations founded by the educated elite. The number of educated Rhodesians was increasing. In 1934 Aaron Jacha founded the Southern Rhodesian African National Congress, which concentrated on organising the African masses in the towns, but was less successful than the trade unions. After a few years, it faded from the scene, but it was to be revived in the years after the Second World War. The 1920s and 1930s were therefore years of preparation.

The years after the Second World War of 1939–45 were remarkable for the growth of militant nationalism in Rhodesia as elsewhere in Africa. In 1945 the African Railway Workers' Union organised a very successful strike, which not only won the workers increased wages, but also led to the passing of the Railway Act which gave official recognition to their union. During the same year, the ANC was revived, as was the Reformed ICU which began seriously to organise African workers in towns. Another organisation founded at the same time, the African Voice Association, gave its energies to organising and coordinating the discontents among both African town workers and farm labourers. Meanwhile, as part of the general ferment, the Shona became eager for education from about 1946. The fever to send children to school was so great that schools sprang up everywhere and the face of Mashonaland changed rapidly.

All this post-war ferment reached a climax in 1948 with the first general strike in Rhodesia's history. African workers in industry and commerce, joined by domestic servants, went on strike to demand better wages and living conditions. Massive workers' demonstrations occurred. Both the ANC and the African Voice Association supported the strike and helped the workers in their negotiations with the government. The strike led, among other things, to the government's setting up of the Native Labour Boards, thus giving all African workers representation for the first time.

74

Meanwhile, the white settlers' campaign for the unification of Rhodesia, Zambia and Malawi into a federation had intensified. In Zambia and Malawi, opposition to the federation greatly stimulated African nationalism. But African opposition was less strong in Rhodesia. In 1951, the Rhodesian ANC took part in a conference of leaders of Rhodesia, Zambia and Malawi organised by the Zambian leaders. After this congress, some Rhodesian leaders formed an All-African Convention to oppose the federation. But some of the most prominent leaders, like the very powerful Benjamin Burumbo (founder and leader of the African Voice Association) did not join the convention and it soon broke up. In fact, many African leaders were in favour of co-operating with the white settlers in the hope that, after the federation had been created, they would be able to obtain important concessions for the Africans. The federation was created in 1953, and by 1955 most of the African political organisations had become practically inactive. In the place of uncompromising African nationalism, there now arose a spirit of partnership and co-operation with the settlers, and everybody was joining multi-racial organisations. It was at this time that the spirit of liberalism and reform earlier referred to appeared briefly among the leadership of the white settlers. Naturally, this led those African leaders who had advocated co-operation with the whites to believe that they were right.

There was, however, one group of radical young people who refused to take part in this co-operation and partnership with the white settlers. In 1955, this group founded the City Youth League in Salisbury. In 1957, the Youth League joined with the Bulawayo branch of the inactive ANC to found a revived Southern Rhodesia African National Congress under the leadership of Joshua Nkomo. The new ANC, which we shall call Congress to distinguish it from the earlier ANC, immediately became very popular among Africans in the towns, in the reserves and on the white farms. These were the years of the mass parties and rapid advance toward independence in most other parts of Africa (especially West Africa) and the excitement was felt in Rhodesia. Under the leadership of Congress, Africans held mass meetings and demanded 'one man one vote' and majority rule.

But in 1958, as would be remembered, the repressive government of Edgar Whitehead replaced the more liberal government of Garfield Todd. Now those African leaders who had hoped to achieve advancement through co-operation with the whites could see that they had been wrong after all. In 1959, Whitehead's Government declared a state of emergency and banned Congress on the grounds that it was planning to wipe out the white population. Hundreds of Africans were

75

arrested and detained.

Repressive measures generated a new spirit of radicalism among Africans. Parties formed after the banning of Congress were different in many ways from their predecessors. For the first time the African intellectuals, most of whom had abstained from politics, began to take a prominent part in politics. As a result the parties founded after 1959 were truly mass parties of African workers, peasants, farm labourers and intellectuals. Secondly, these parties held public meetings and rallies that drew out immense crowds – crowds bigger than Rhodesia had ever seen before. Thirdly, these parties for the first time began to use physical resistance to white minority rule. Their youth wings organised and trained themselves to use violent attacks on the white regime and all it stood for. Demonstrations, marches, riots, massive damage to property, physical attacks on whites – these became frequent experiences of Rhodesia. For decades, the Africans of Rhodesia had used peaceful methods and made moral appeals to the conscience of their white oppressors. Such methods had failed. Now they were showing that their patience had run out.

The first of the new parties was the National Democratic Party founded in January 1960. On 9 December 1962, it was banned. Ten days later, the Zimbabwe African People's Union (ZAPU) was formed, with Joshua Nkomo as president and the Rev Ndabaningi Sithole as chairman. ZAPU existed for only nine months before it was banned in September 1962 on the grounds that it was using its youth league as a terrorist organisation 'to destroy political liberty and cause deliberate injury to the economy of the country'. Its leaders and hundreds of other Africans were arrested and detained.

With almost all the prominent African leaders in detention or restriction, another party could not emerge until almost a year after the banning of ZAPU. In August 1963 the Zimbabwe African National Union (ZANU) was founded by the Rev Sithole. By then, however, there had developed a rift between his followers and those of Nkomo, who later formed the People's Caretaker Council. For some time, intense rivalry developed between the two factions, but in June-July 1964 both were banned. By 1965 when Ian Smith declared Rhodesia independent, all avenues of African opinion had been destroyed, and all known African leaders, as well as thousands of their followers, had been detained or restricted.

But, in spite of the official repression, African resistance remained very much alive, as was shown early in 1972 when the Pearce Commission came to Rhodesia to assess African attitudes to the proposed settlement between Ian Smith and Britain. With the leading African nationalists behind bars, the duty of organising African opinion fell on the shoulders of Bishop Abel Muzorewa of the Methodist Church of Rhodesia. Under his leadership the African National Council was formed in December 1971, not as a political party, but as a movement seeking to unify all shades of African opinion against the settlement. It was responsible for most of the mass rallies through which the Africans demonstrated to the Pearce Commission that they rejected the settlement. These demonstrations were met with characteristically violent repression by the Ian Smith Government. During the first week of the tour of the Pearce Commission alone, not less than thirty-one Africans, according to Bishop Muzorewa, were killed by the police, 1,000 were arrested and 250 detained. After the departure of the Pearce Commission, the repression and detentions were intensified.

Since the white minority government thus made open political action by Africans impossible some Africans in the 1960s began to believe that only guerrilla warfare could overthrow white dictatorship. The first guerrilla organisation to be formed was the Zimbabwe Liberation Army which came into existence about the time that ZAPU was banned in September 1962. After that, many guerrilla organisations were formed including the youth wings of both the banned ZAPU and ZANU. After the white regime's illegal declaration of independence in 1965, there were increasing reports of guerrilla fighting in Rhodesia. About 1969, an alliance was formed between the freedom fighters of ZAPU and those of the South African ANC, and very bitter fighting was reported in parts of Rhodesia. Perhaps the greatest weakness of these liberation forces was their failure to unite. But even the reports by the white minority government showed that the African liberation forces were gradually becoming better trained, better armed, and better able to win the support of the rural African masses. Thus, though no part of Rhodesia was by the end of 1974 controlled by the freedom fighters, the available evidence showed that *Chimurenga* ('liberation war' in Shona language) was making progress.

Africa since independence – general themes

5   The nature and performance of leadership in independent African states

During the colonial era, western education produced all over Africa an increasing number of the new elite. As earlier pointed out, there were many more educated men in the British and French colonies than in the Belgian and Portuguese colonies. In no country, however, did they amount to more than a very small fraction of the total population.

Products of the high schools and colleges and universities, considerably informed about the outside world beyond their countries and beyond Africa, conversant with the white man's ways, they were the people best qualified to step into the shoes of the colonial rulers at independence. They were not drawn exclusively from any one class of the traditional African society but from all classes. Some, like Sir Ahmadu Bello of Nigeria and Félix Houphouët-Boigny of Ivory Coast, were sons of kings and big chiefs; others, like Sir Abubakir Tafawa Balewa of Nigeria and Julius Nyerere of Tanzania, were sons of peasants. But once they attained their new status, they began to constitute a new class in the new society that was gradually evolving in Africa.

At first, especially in the British colonies, the colonial administrators treated the members of the elite with contempt, and contended that they had become alienated from their own culture by their education and therefore were not qualified to speak on behalf of their peoples. However, in the years before independence, increasing numbers of the elite were employed by the colonial civil service.

The elite were also found in the professions – as lawyers, doctors, journalists, etc. Not a few of these had previously been denied employment in the colonial service. Very few, if any, were yet entering into business. The few industries which existed in colonial Africa belonged to Europeans and employed very few Africans; and commerce was controlled by the European companies and other foreigners like the Syrians and Lebanese in West Africa and Indians in East Africa.

The elite made their greatest impact in politics. It was they who provided the leadership and ideas for the nationalist struggle against colonial rule. And when the colonial masters finally began to allow Africans some participation in the central colonial governments, it was to the elite that they turned, and at independence, it was the elite who took over the administration.

The nature and performance of the leadership which these new leaders have given to independent African countries have been mainly determined by three factors: first, the heritage of colonial rule; second, the way in which independence was won; and third, the problems of the independence era. Colonial government was a government by a small group of people (the white officials) who enjoyed immense privileges over and above the masses of the people. It was a government usually sensitive, and often hostile, to criticism and opposition. Though the elite in every country had denounced the colonial rulers, they had nevertheless imbibed from them many colonial social and political values.

Secondly, independence was usually not a revolution – a change of values – but a change of rulers. The European officials simply left (usually sent off with grand ceremonies) and surrendered the machinery of power to their former auxiliaries in the civil service, the police force and the army and those members of the elite who were in politics. The official mansions which the colonial officials had built for themselves, all the offices and symbols of power and authority were taken over, as they were, by the new rulers.

Thirdly, after independence, the new rulers in every country faced enormous problems. They had to preserve and enhance national unity. They had to prevent the country from being torn apart by ethnic rivalries. They had to show that the new nation was capable of satisfying the economic expectations of its people. They had to find ways of mobilising the people to carry out the programmes of economic and social development.

These enormous problems of nation-building tended to breed, in the new leaders, a certain impatience with all persons and institutions that tended to obstruct or detract from the national effort. So, in practically every African country, political oppositions soon faced trouble. Not only the leaders but most citizens who attached great importance to progress felt that the tasks facing the nation required national solidarity, and that official oppositions were a luxury which African countries could not afford.

In many countries, the opposition did not represent differences of principle but the fears and ambitions of this or that ethnic group. Such opposition parties demanded decentralisation of authority so that the ethnic groups or regions whose interests they represented would be able to manage much of their own affairs. These demands seemed to the governing party to threaten national unity and impede the progress of the national development projects.

Another common experience in African countries after independence was a general waning of the popularity of the government leaders. With the attainment of independence, the excitement of the anti-colonial struggle disappeared. People became more critical of the leaders and of their actions. The inevitably slow pace of economic and social progress was attributed to their failures. In turn the leaders tended to attribute their loss of popularity to the campaigns of the opposition parties.

Therefore, the leaders in power often regarded the opposition parties not only as a luxury but also as a threat. The aim of inter-party rivalry became the destruction, rather than merely the defeat, of one's opponents. And, to achieve this objective, the ruling leaders returned to the practices of the former colonial governments. The colonial laws which had gagged the press were not only preserved but reinforced. To make the judiciary serve its purpose as the colonial judiciary had served the purposes of the colonial regime, the government began to interfere with the freedom of the judiciary. The colonial government's powers of imprisonment, detention, restriction and banishment were revived and reinforced. Just as many of the nationalist leaders in colonial Africa, the 'threats' to the colonial establishment, had gone to prison or restriction or detention, so did many of the opposition leaders in independent Africa, the 'threats' to the new rulers, after independence.

The ruling party bribed as well as repressed the opposition. Promises of money or high positions were held out to the leading members of the opposition party. Government patronage and appointments as well as other social benefits were given only to known members and supporters of the government party. Not infrequently, even things like loans to farmers or scholarships for children were used as rewards to party supporters. All these were designed not only to reward party members, but also to show those in opposition that it paid to belong to the government party.

In some cases, the combination of repression and bribes succeeded in breaking up opposition parties. The ruling party would then announce that it was the demonstrated wish of the people that the country should have only one party. A law would then be put through parliament, making the country a one-party state. But in some cases, the one-party state was passed into law even when many parties still existed in the country. The justification was always the same: to preserve national unity, and to ensure the cooperation of all citizens in the task of nation-building and economic development. Even in countries where the one-party state was not established, it was often suggested as a cure-all. For instance, between 1963 and 1965 in Nigeria, the question was frequently publicly discussed whether Nigeria would not be better off as a one-party state.

Another element with which the leaders of independent African countries had to deal were the traditional institutions – the kings and chiefs. This problem differed from country to country. In most of the former French colonies, the position and prestige of the chiefs had been so weakened during the colonial era that they could not constitute rivals to the new leaders after independence. In most former British colonies, however, the kings and chiefs still commanded considerable respect. They held important positions in the local government set-up and, in countries like Sierra Leone and Uganda, they also enjoyed entrenched positions in the central government.

On the whole, the new leaders showed after independence that they would tolerate no rivalry from the chiefs who were the foci of local patriotisms and so threatened national unity. In the resulting conflicts, the new political leaders, because they controlled the machinery of state, always came out on top. In the kingdom of Lesotho, a conflict between the king and the Prime Minister, Lebua Jonathan, ended in the king's fleeing abroad into exile. In Tunisia, the monarchy was abolished soon after independence. One of the worst conflicts between the new and the traditional leadership occurred in Uganda where the Kabaka of Buganda continued to act as the inspiration to Baganda nationalism and therefore a threat to the unity of the nation. The conflict came to a climax when the army, on the orders of President Milton Obote, attacked the Kabaka's palace and forced him into exile abroad, where he died not long afterwards.

In a few countries, the new political elite, either because they were very few and weak or because the chiefs were still very influential, went into a sort of partnership with the chiefs. Perhaps the best examples are Sierra Leone and Nigeria. In Sierra Leone, because the party in power at independence (the Sierra Leone People's Party under the leadership of Milton Margai) depended largely on the influence of the chiefs for winning elections, it strengthened their influence. A similar pattern was followed in Northern and Western Nigeria. But as the political leaders became more confident, or a more radical group of politicians rose to power, the position of the chiefs became weaker. And the few big traditional rulers (like the Emir of Kano in Northern Nigeria or the Alafin of Oyo in Western Nigeria) who dared to oppose the will of the new leaders found themselves in trouble or in exile.

The new leaders of independent African states also commonly attempted to establish control over independent organisations like students' unions, women's societies and workers' unions, usually justifying themselves by the need to have all citizens working together. In most cases, the battle for control of the independent organisations was long drawn out and indecisive.

In between the political turmoils created by all these conflicts, the leadership of each country concentrated its energies on the task of nation-building and economic and social development. To be able to give undivided leadership in this task was, after all, their justification for their acquisition of all power over the nation. It was also the reason why many citizens were willing to support them. The rate of achievement was determined ultimately by the conditions of each country – the level of its economic development at the time of independence, its natural resources, and the attitude of its people towards hard work and struggle – but it was also influenced by the nature and level of experience of the leaders. In those countries in which independence was preceded by a short period of responsible government during which the new leaders learned to grapple with national tasks, the leadership proved more experienced in conceiving national plans and carrying them out. In other countries, like Zaire, where the colonial authorities had not allowed the emerging leaders any participation in government until the day of independence, the nationalist agitators who suddenly became statesmen made far more mistakes through lack of experience. In some countries, as in Tunisia, the national leadership was so skilful in keeping political conflicts at a minimum that most of its energy could be concentrated on programmes of national progress. In Algeria, on the other hand, the way in which the independence struggle had had to be conducted had so seriously fragmented the national leadership that it could not easily work as a united force.

In no country was the economic and social progress fast enough to satisfy the people. Most people had expected that independence would produce immediate economic miracles as well as a removal of some of the burdens, like taxation, imposed by the colonial regime. In part, such expectations had been created by the promises made by the nationalist leaders themselves during the independence struggle. But after independence, not only did the economic miracles fail to take place, but the burdens of taxation and other social obligations increased. This contributed to the widespread falling off in popularity of the leaders.

Other tendencies exhibited by the leaders further diminished their popularity. After independence, most leaders tended to preserve the privileges characteristic of the colonial regimes. In their long struggle for independence, the elite had fought against the dictatorial colonial rule as well as the inequalities of the colonial society. After independence had put them in power, they still preached the same doctrines of social justice or socialism; some even advocated revolution. Yet, practically every group in power tended to preserve for itself the high privileges enjoyed by the former colonial masters.

For instance, in every country, the colonial salary and wage structure, with all its inequalities, was retained. The colonial officials had earned high salaries, often higher than the economies of the colonies justified, higher in some respects than they could have earned for similar jobs in Europe. With these high salaries had gone a number of fringe benefits – car advance, car basic allowance, furnished subsidised houses, bush allowance, children's allowance, out-of-station allowance – all more or less peculiar to colonial Africa. After independence, these fringe benefits were also preserved almost without change. In many countries, some improvement in wages was introduced with the institution of minimum wages for the lowest paid members of the society. However, the minimum wages were usually not related to the cost of living and salary revisions have usually increased the gap between the super-scale salaries and the low wages.

Many men in high places also began to use their positions to enrich themselves. Official enquiries in many African countries have revealed top-level corruption of all kinds: bribes from persons seeking government jobs, loans or contracts; secret payments by foreign businesses seeking to cheat the country in one way or another; diversion of state money into personal ventures; outright theft of state money or state property or of things belonging to political parties; gifts in cash or kind (e.g. land) from towns or villages desiring amenities provided by the state. It is important to differentiate between these corrupt leaders and the growing number of Africans who, through careful saving and the investment of their energies and talents in business, have acquired wealth. But there are also many businessmen who have done well largely through political connections, through government patronage, government loans and grants, and fraudulent government contracts.

Often, the newly rich elite consumed much of the wealth thus corruptly acquired in maintaining an ostentatious way of life. Big cars, large expensive houses with expensive imported furniture, lavish parties on every conceivable occasion (like weddings or funerals) – these became status symbols over which the elite, especially the politicians and their closest backers, competed. Most of them seem to have believed that flaunting wealth and luxury before the people made them popular with the people.

This wasteful life style was matched by a tendency towards prestige spending in public affairs. Substantial parts of available national resources were spent on big showpieces, such as state palaces, impressive and expensive monuments and stadia, rather than on vital development projects. The palace built by President Houphouët-Boigny is said to have cost about twenty million dollars, about seven million pounds. Even in Dahomey, one of the poorest countries in Africa, the government of President Hubert Maga built, after independence, a palace costing about three million dollars. Biggest of all was Dr Nkrumah's 'Job 600', a complex of buildings completed in 1965 for the meeting of the Organisation of African Unity (OAU) in Accra in that year. It has been widely estimated that 'Job 600' cost between £8,000,000 and £10,000,000. The leaders usually justified these expensive showpieces by saying that they were needed to demonstrate to the world the greatness of the new African nations. The truth, however, is that the new African nations are still far from being great, and prestige spending meant the denial of resources to projects which could improve the standard of living of the people and ultimately make their country great.

For all these reasons, then, disenchantment and cynicism grew among the people towards the leaders. Not infrequently, the attempt to destroy all opposition and dissent appeared, on the surface, to have succeeded. But subsequent happenings usually showed that silencing the voice of dissent did not mean that it had been destroyed. In some countries discontent, denied legitimate expression, burst out ultimately in violent revolts, which seriously threatened national disruption and proved very difficult to control. In some other cases, the leaders continued to appear to be popular with the people – until they were overthrown by the army. Then would follow that strange spectacle which was seen in some African countries in the late 1960s: the crowds which had hailed the leader the day before now turning out to denounce him and pull down his statues and his photographs.

6 Ethnic diversity and the building of national unity

Perhaps the most serious problem that has confronted African countries after independence has been that of internal disunity. It has affected practically every African country, threatening the very existence of some. Its basic source is the ethnic diversity of each country.

The greatest political result of colonialism was the creation of multi-ethnic nation-states all over Africa. Peoples of different cultures, peoples who had always lived politically separate from one another, peoples who had probably fought wars against one another, were made to come together within the same political boundaries, to accept one common citizenship, one national name and one unified administration. Nigeria, for instance, has over 250 ethnic groups, Tanzania over 120, Zambia over 70.

During the struggle for independence, all the ethnic groups suppressed their differences to strive towards the common goal. Since the colonial authorities were looking for pretexts for delaying the granting of independence, clearly independence would not be achieved until the colony showed that all its people were reasonably prepared to work together and present a united leadership.

However, even then there were signs of the future trouble. The changes, pressures and tensions of the colonial experience had gradually forced each ethnic group to discover or rediscover itself. Improved communication within the group resulted in its members coming into closer contact and becoming increasingly aware of themselves as a distinct group with one culture and one language, a group different from its neighbours. Competition between the different groups and regions for the social amenities (roads, schools, hospitals) provided by the colonial government intensified the feeling of unity within each group as well as the feeling of separateness from its neighbours.

Thus, among a people like the Baganda of the Buganda Kingdom in Uganda, the fact that they had been one distinct political entity before the coming of colonialism became vitally important. Since the kingdom remained intact throughout the colonial era, it continued to exist as a rallying focus for the Baganda. Even in places where, like among the Yoruba and Ibo of Nigeria, the ethnic groups had not enjoyed political unity in pre-colonial times, they began to emphasise their cultural oneness and the fact of their difference from other peoples in the colony. Moreover, where there was strong evidence of very close historical contacts between two peoples (as between the Edo and

Yoruba in South-western Nigeria, or the Hausa and Kanuri in Northern Nigeria) some of the educated members of each group now sought to play down or even to disprove such historical contacts. These tensions were generally strongest in British colonies because the French had usually broken up the pre-colonial state systems, accorded the traditional rulers little or no respect, and virtually disregarded the ethnic origins of their colonial subjects. The countries of North Africa experienced few or no inter-ethnic troubles because most of these countries had evolved into distinct nation-states long before the coming of colonialism.

In almost every colony in sub-Saharan Africa, then, nationalism first appeared as a movement of individual ethnic groups or pre-colonial states, not of the whole colony. People of different ethnic origins who migrated into the new towns in search of jobs evolved, no doubt, into a mixed society somewhat different from the rest of the country, but they did not become 'detribalised'. On the contrary, they sought comradeship and mutual support among people of their own cultures and languages and ultimately formed progressive or descendants' unions. In the competition of the various parts of the country for the modern amenities being provided by the colonial administration, these progressive unions became the champions of their own particular areas. They also ultimately established contacts with their homelands and, in this way, assumed political importance. In many countries, these unions constituted the foundations of the earliest political parties.

In a country such as Zaire, which was not allowed to make orderly progress towards independence, political activity was mostly in the hands of the regional and ethnic unions at independence. Practically every locality of Zaire produced its own party or alliance of parties. In no other African country were things as bad as this at independence, but practically every country had its own ethnic divisions.

The general tendency immediately after independence was for these divisions to worsen and grow into crisis proportions. Between 1955 and 1972, a civil war raged in the Sudan between the Arabs of the northern provinces and the black African peoples of the south. In Uganda, Baganda nationalism seriously threatened national unity and once produced a situation of near civil war. Zaire, Chad and Nigeria have experienced civil war caused by attempts of component ethnic groups to secede. In Kenya, there has been a threat of confrontation between the Kikuyu and the smaller ethnic groups. Ghana's unity was seriously threatened immediately after independence by conflicting ethnic loyalties, and in Zambia inter-ethnic rivalries and antagonisms played an important part in national politics.

In trying to explain these post-independence developments, some foreigners have suggested that they are the result of the inability of Africans to run a modern nation-state. Yet problems of national disunity arising from ethnic diversity are not peculiar to Africa. Hardly any country made up of a collection of ethnic groups is entirely free from such troubles. The United Kingdom, Belgium, Czechoslovakia, Yugoslavia and Spain in Europe, India, Pakistan, Malaysia and Indonesia in Asia, Canada and America (to mention only a few) have all experienced tension, violence or even civil war because of the clash of inter-ethnic loyalties. Ethnic loyalties are usually powerful and tend to survive for a long time. For instance, the United Kingdom is very old as a single nation-state, while Belgium was created over 140 years ago. Yet there have been serious signs of strife in our time among the English, Irish, Welsh and Scots of the United Kingdom, as well as between the Walloons and Flemings of Belgium.

In comparison with these countries, the modern nation-states of Africa are very young. Very few of them were created before 1900, and some did not take final shape until the 1920s or 1930s or even later. The two sections of Sierra Leone (the 'colony' and 'protectorate') were not brought together as one country with a common administration until 1924. Though Upper Volta was created as one colony in 1919, it was later (between 1932 and 1947) broken up and divided among neighbouring French colonies, and did not finally emerge as an entity until 1947. In Ghana, the constitutional unification of the coastal areas (the 'colony') with the Ashanti territory did not occur until 1946, and the far northern provinces did not begin to take part in the legislative council until 1950-1. Though the amalgamation of Northern and Southern Nigeria was effected in 1914, the North and South did not become constitutionally and politically one country until 1947-8, when the North was granted representation in the legislative council, which had hitherto been an institution of the South only.

In short, the African countries have not had the benefit of a long period of internal growth and maturity, perhaps the most important factor in achieving national unity. Nor did the colonial powers do much to help them achieve unity; rather, they employed the tactics of divide and rule, which increased inter-ethnic strife.

Finally, after independence competition intensified in each country over the amenities and economic opportunities at the disposal of the new nation-state. This was what independence was mostly about after all: improved conditions of living; new roads, schools, hospitals,

87

industries; improved job opportunities, increased chances of social and economic advancement for the graduates of the schools and colleges as well as for all citizens. Unfortunately, however, national economies could not progress fast enough, and so there were not enough of these amenities to go round.

The competition, therefore, often became bitter and acrimonious among members of the elite for highly paid jobs and business opportunities. Each sought to strengthen his position and promote his interests by associating with men of the same ethnic origin as himself. In the same way, each region used its own literate sons as its champions and spokesmen in the inter-regional competition for modern amenities. For this reason each region wished to see its sons advance in politics, the civil service, business and the professions. Since the regional competition for amenities thus became mixed with the competition among the elite for personal advancements, this enabled the individual members of the elite to claim that their personal successes or failures were the successes or failures of their ethnic groups and regions. They thus transmitted their anxieties and frustrations to the masses of their ethnic groups, so that competition between two leading men for a highly sought job often became competition between their ethnic groups. When it happens, as in Nigeria and Kenya, that some ethnic groups have produced more highly educated men than others, or, because of their larger population, command more political power, then we begin to hear of fears of domination of some ethnic groups by others. This is the origin of that political and social disease commonly called 'tribalism'.

'Tribalism' expressed itself in various ways. Most often, it occurred as confrontation between the national government, usually controlled by one ethnic group or combination of ethnic groups, and a rival ethnic group or combination of ethnic groups, who feared that their interests would be damaged by the policies of the government. The aggrieved ethnic groups then tried to defend their interests by forming or joining opposition parties.

Sometimes, tribalism showed up as conflicts between two neighbouring peoples who might be together in the same political party or not. There was friction for instance between the ethnic groups represented in the Kenya African Democratic Union which was the opposition party in Kenya after independence. In Zambia, too, the ruling United National Independence Party (UNIP) of President Kaunda suffered from such dissensions among its members.

What the ethnic groups and their political parties and movements demanded was simply justice and a fair share of the good things at the disposal of the nation – in Nigeria's political vocabulary, the 'national cake'. Very rarely did an ethnic group reject the nation entirely and try to break away from it. The best known examples of this extreme development occurred in Zaire, Nigeria and Sudan. In some cases where a people was divided by the national boundaries between two countries, the desire of the people to come together has resulted in an attempt to secede from one or other of the two countries. Soon after independence, this happened among the Ewe of Eastern Ghana (who are of the same stock as the Ewe of neighbouring Togoland), and among some of the people of north-eastern Kenya (who are of the same stock as the Somalis of neighbouring Somalia).

All these situations have constituted a great challenge to leadership in African countries after independence and various efforts have been made to grapple with the problem. National propaganda, for instance, has aimed to inspire the spirit of unity, using all sorts of appealing slogans such as, in Nigeria, 'Unity in Diversity', or, in Kenya, 'Harambee' ('Let us all pull together'). The aim was to persuade the peoples that, in spite of linguistic and other differences, they are one and the same people with much in common in their history and their culture, that the observable differences between them are emphemeral, and that inter-ethnic hostilities are no more than a heritage of colonialism. Colonialism, said Dr Nkrumah, 'played upon our tribal instincts. It sowed seeds of dissension in order to promote disunity among us.' Soon after Guinea won her independence, President Sekou Toure declared that with the removal of colonialism, the people of Guinea would quickly rediscover their unity. 'In three or four years,' he wrote, 'no one will remember the tribal, ethnic or religious rivalries which, in the recent past, caused so much damage to our country . . .'

Most African leaders have been inclined to the belief that the best way to reduce or even eradicate inter-ethnic hostilities is to build a strongly centralised national government and channel all political activity into one national party. With a strong government controlling all authority at the centre, and the party in power being the party of all citizens, many have claimed, the ethnic groups would learn to surrender their individuality to the demands of the national good, and all disputes would be settled as they are settled among the members of a family. This is the major argument in favour of the 'unitary' system of government, as opposed to the 'federal' system, in which a country is broken into regions, states or provinces, each with its own government, with a federal government at the centre. It is also the major argument of the advocates of one-party states.

The unitary system of government has been advocated even for large and highly varied countries like the Sudan, Zaire and Nigeria. In some countries, like Kenya and Cameroon, federal constitutions existing at independence were later replaced with unitary constitutions. Similarly, many countries which had two or more parties at independence later evolved into one-party states. The effects of such measures on the problem of national unity cannot yet be estimated. In Tanzania, the one-party state seems to be working smoothly enough, although what that has meant in terms of the advancement of national unity it is too early to tell. In other countries, the one-party system has led to the repression of all dissent, and to serious political problems.

Some other African leaders have taken the view that a federal constitution is the key to national unity. They argue that giving each region (or ethnic group if large enough) power to manage some of its own affairs would reduce tensions and hostile rivalries. Most of these advocates of federation have been the leaders of ethnic groups who found themselves out of the government after independence. Consequently, many well-meaning African leaders of thought have reacted against federalism, fearing that once the regions of a country are given governments of their own, they could easily become pockets of extreme regional or ethnic loyalties and thereby destroy what little national unity there is.

The differences of opinion between the advocates of a unitary system and a federal system have produced more writing and more intellectual activity in Nigeria than in probably any other African country. In the years of preparation for independence, Dr Nnamdi Azikiwe, one of the makers of independent Nigeria, maintained that the decision to make Nigeria a federation in about 1948 was not in the interest of the nation and would have the effect of keeping Nigeria disunited and weak. Many leading Nigerians have continued to express similar opinions. But many other leaders welcomed the idea of federation. Of these, the one who has written most on the subject is Chief Obafemi Awolowo, also one of the architects of Nigeria's independence. In his book, *Thoughts on the Nigerian Constitution*, Chief Awolowo examined the constitutions and political histories of almost all multi-ethnic countries in the world and came to the conclusion that, for any multi-ethnic country, a federation was the most trouble-free constitution.

Nigeria is the country in which federalism has been most consistently tried in Africa. Since independence, perhaps the most important aspect of the constitutional history of Nigeria has been the efforts made to make the federation more satisfactory to the various peoples of Nigeria by creating more states and thereby making it possible for more and more of Nigeria's peoples to manage much of their own affairs directly through their own state governments.

How effective this, or any other constitutional device adopted by African countries will be in solving the problem of national unity, only time can tell. Already, even in the short time since independence, certain developments have taken place which have had the effect of promoting national unity. First, the growth of education has gradually increased the number of people able to rise above 'tribalism'. Secondly, in spite of the economic backwardness of the present, African countries are making some progress in modernising their economies and offering economic opportunities to an increasing number of their peoples. Moreover, even when they quarrel among themselves at home, the citizens of Nigeria or Ghana or Kenya or any other independent African country cannot forget their joint struggles against imperialism. They enjoy a lot of pride also from speaking to the world under the common umbrella of their new nation-state. Furthermore, the facts of living within the same boundaries, sharing the benefits of the same government, operating within the same economy, buying and selling in the same market, going to school together and struggling together against poverty and want – all these have been perceptibly breaking down the emotional walls that separate men of one culture from others.

Although 'tribalism' and sectionalism are still strong forces, the determination to make the new countries work and grow are also growing very strong. The new countries have bred men who have developed material or romantic stakes in their continued existence. Consequently, each secessionist leader has had to fight not only the national forces but also men of his own group who would not accept the dissolution of the country.

As they were leaving Africa just before independence, the colonial officials were saying, 'After we leave, the tribes will be at each other's throats'. It is true that blood has been shed in some places and tension felt in most. But for each instance of bloodshed, there are very many instances in which men of different ethnic origins have taken big strides in learning to live together. For each secessionist movement, there have been hundreds of movements, parties, associations, clubs and societies dedicated to forging national unity.

7   Economic development: problems and progress

A country is said to be making economic progress if its people produce more per head, if more resources are invested into productive enterprises, if job opportunities for the people increase, if cheaper, new and more efficient means of producing things are introduced, if the people are, therefore, provided with more of the necessities of life, and if these improvements are widely available, not to a privileged few but to the people at large.

Judged on these criteria, Africa is the poorest continent in the world. On average, an African earns an income which is about 94% of the income of the average man in Asia, 39% of that in Latin America, 12% of that in Europe, 8% of that in Australia, 5% of that in North America. There are very few African countries in which the annual income per head is much higher than £100 or roughly N200.

For this reason, the greatest battle which African countries have been fighting since independence has been against poverty. Indeed, for probably every African, 'nation building' has meant principally the building of an advanced and virile economy which will make his country strong and himself materially comfortable. In the struggle for independence, independence was seen not merely as an end in itself, but as a means to an end. Independence was to usher in an economic revolution which would improve the material conditions of everybody. This is what Dr Kwame Nkrumah, the man who led Ghana to independence in 1957, meant when he told his countrymen, 'Seek ye first the political kingdom and all things will be added unto it'. Such promises were common to all the writings and speeches of the independence struggles.

After independence, therefore, the citizens of each country have judged the performance of their government mainly on its achievements in the economic field. In turn, every government has regarded economic development as a matter of great urgency, intensified by the realisation that unfulfilled economic promises constitute a threat to political stability. In general, the people's economic expectations have proved greater than any African country has been able to meet quickly. There has, therefore, developed what some scholars now call a 'crisis of expectations', worsened by the fact that in today's world Africans have neighbours (Europeans and Americans) who are economically highly developed and materially well off. Through books, newspapers, magazines, radio, films, television and travellers, most Africans know something of the material comfort of these neighbours, and naturally find their own poverty more difficult to bear as a result. In some countries, the people's disappointment with what they regard as too slow a pace of economic progress has led to actual political troubles.

Difficulties
Many difficulties, however, have confronted the African countries in their attempts to make economic progress. In the first place, the econ-

omic effects of colonialism (see chapter 1) were unwholesome. At independence, the economy of every African country was geared towards exporting cash crops and minerals whose prices were determined, not by the Africans themselves, but by the foreign consumers. Communications and transport facilities were inadequate because the colonial powers had established only those needed for the exploitation of the areas richest in production. The few secondary industries that existed were owned by foreign companies and gave the skilled jobs almost invariably to foreigners. The big commercial establishments were owned by the big European companies; the smaller ones by smaller European traders, as well as by Syrians and Lebanese in West Africa and Indians in East Africa. After decades of huge profits and colonial governmental support, the big European companies were very strongly entrenched and able to destroy any indigenous rival, and very few Africans had the education, capital, experience or technical skills to succeed in business. Every African country was, at independence, importing almost 100% of the manufactured goods used by its people, and also a good proportion of its food.

Secondly, African countries at independence were embarking on their programmes of industrialisation in a very difficult world atmosphere. This is a world in which the highly developed industries of regions like the United States of America, Europe and Japan inevitably tend to compel other countries to serve as markets. The struggle of the beginner against such giants has not been easy.

Finally, in every African country, these problems have been aggravated by bad decisions of the leaders, such as the tendency towards prestige spending, which in turn has meant the denial of resources to investments in vital productive enterprises. Corruption, indiscipline and inefficiency among some leaders have contributed to the lowering of achievement in most countries.

Theories of development

At independence, the general cry was for rapid economic progress, and much debate ensued on how to achieve it. One suggestion was that African countries should adopt the methods of free enterprise or capitalism, in which economic development would be left in the hands of private persons, and the government would devote its energy to providing social services and maintaining the law. This, it was pointed out, was the system which rich countries like the USA, Japan and the Western European nations had employed to achieve their prosperity. Also it would encourage foreigners to invest capital in Africa, an important consideration since lack of capital was one of Africa's major problems. Moreover, it was contended that private persons working for their own profits in their own businesses and freely competing with one another would produce quicker economic development than a government controlling all economic enterprises and serving as the employer of all.

A plan of development based upon the above arguments was advocated in 1953 for Ghana by the famous West Indian scholar, Professor Arthur Lewis. It constituted most of the guide for Ghana's development efforts until about 1961. Similar paths to economic development have been advocated by various African politicians and intellectuals and have been adopted by, for instance, Liberia and the Ivory Coast.

Other African leaders and thinkers, however, advocated that the government should play a prominent part in economic development, especially in industrialisation. They pointed out that the European, American and Japanese type of 'Industrial Revolution' which was achieved through the efforts of private persons, was impossible in Africa because African countries at independence did not have citizens with enough capital and experience to undertake such industrialisation. According to these leaders two alternatives presented themselves: either to let foreign private capitalists come and carry out the 'Industrial Revolution' or to let the government (the only indigenous organisation with the means of raising capital) carry it out. The former alternative was unacceptable because it would constitute an open invitation to foreign economic domination. Therefore, the state must play the leading role in the economy. In other words, African countries should follow a 'socialist' rather than a capitalist path to development.

The socialist approach would, it was said, have the further advantage of enabling the wealth and opportunities of the nation to be distributed equitably among the citizens.

The socialist system was felt by many to agree more with the African way of life. In pre-colonial Africa, land, the chief means of production, was owned not by individuals but by communities or families in common. Within the community or family, every individual enjoyed a great deal of security and bore a lot of responsibility for the security and welfare of all. Economic exploitation of the many by the few, as in capitalism, did not exist. Therefore the socialist system would be more in accord with Africa's own temper and traditions. This particular point has been most clearly developed in the speeches and writings of President Julius Nyerere of Tanzania.

Most African leaders have indeed advocated the socialist approach. Even leaders like Houphouët-Boigny of Ivory Coast who are more inclined towards the 'free-enterprise' or capitalist approach have

94

acknowledged that in the absence of an indigenous capitalist class, the governments of African countries would have to bear the burden of economic development. Also, in economic practice, every African government has adopted a particular device characteristic of socialist economies: the Development Plans. These are guides laid down by the governments to direct the national economies towards goals determined by them, and represent a major participation by governments in economic development.

Among those leaders who have advocated socialism, very few have shown themselves ready to undertake a radical restructuring of the economies of their countries, to nationalise all existing industrial and commercial enterprises, establish state control over all aspects of the economy, and prohibit all private enterprise. Even leaders like Julius Nyerere of Tanzania, Ahmed Ben Bella of Algeria, Modibo Keita of Mali, Nkrumah of Ghana and Sekou Toure of Guinea, who are regarded as the most radically socialist in post-independence Africa, have not attempted to do away with private enterprise altogether. What has been attempted in most places is the establishment of agricultural cooperatives in the rural areas, the building of a state-controlled sector of the growing national industry, and the encouragement of private capital (both foreign and indigenous) to help with industrialisation.

Having rejected the capitalism of the Western World (Western Europe and America), most African socialists advocate 'African Socialism' in order to show that they are not borrowing the ideas of the Eastern World (the Soviet Union, Eastern Europe and China) but that they have invented their own ideas of development. While Eastern World socialism (or communism) holds the view that the socialist society has to be achieved through a successful war of the working classes against the small class of wealthy exploiters in society (i.e. the capitalists and big land owners), African socialism does not believe in class warfare because Africa does not have any classes. African socialism is, therefore, usually described as a development concept springing not from any alien ideas but from the indigenous African society itself. It is something like an African declaration of ideological independence.

Summary of achievements
Although the data available for assessing the rate of economic progress since independence are by no means clear and conclusive, African states have recorded many vital advances.

Since independence, African states have spent much more money on providing education for their citizens. In Africa in general, school enrolment began to increase sharply during the 1950s partly because

95

more and more Africans were participating in government. During the independence decade, the 1960s, enrolment in primary and secondary schools, technical schools, colleges and universities increased more sharply still. In Nigeria, for instance, total enrolment in primary schools increased from 2.8 million in 1961 to 3.1 million in 1968; technical and vocational schools from 6,000 to 12,000; universities from 3,600 in 1962 to over 10,000 in 1971. Free education has been instituted in some places. All this implies rapid improvement in the modernising and productive capacities of African societies.

Since independence, too, the surface of Africa has experienced very intense activity in the building and improvement of transportation networks. Durable roads, telephones and telegraphs have opened up large areas that were formerly almost inaccessible. These improvements have not only helped industrial, agricultural and commercial enterprises, but contributed much to the growth of national unity and to inter-state contacts.

Many African states have invested heavily on the provision of power. The three great dams – the Aswan Dam, the Volta Dam and the Kainji Dam – were all constructed in the 1960s. Mineral oil has been a source of wealth to some African countries, although lack of capital and the requisite know-how has resulted in their giving over to foreign businesses the exploitation of the oil. Consequently much of the profit has gone to enrich foreign nations.

Industry has been perhaps the most dynamic sector of the economies of independent African states. United Nations sources estimate that between 1955 and 1965 the average annual growth of manufacturing output was over 7%, and since 1965 it has grown faster still.

Most of the development in the manufacturing sector has been aimed at producing substitutes for imported manufactured goods. However, manufacturing for export has also increased. Africa's share in world exports of manufactures and semi-manufactures increased considerably in the second half of the 1960s.

As the world recognises more and more the economic potentialities of Africa, foreigners have shown greater eagerness to invest in its development. But Africans themselves, both as governments and as private persons, have been saving more and investing more. A study of a group of 40 countries in various developing regions for the period 1960–65 shows that the contribution of domestic savings to investment was 68% in Africa. However, all the available capital, both indigenous and imported, has been much smaller than the volume of capital needed for a real industrial boom.

The increasing participation of Africans in business has been further encouraged by legislation. In some countries, like Nigeria and Algeria, the governments have made laws to limit and progressively reduce the number of expatriates that the companies can employ. In Ghana, Nigeria and the East African countries, the governments have made various laws aimed at expanding the participation of their citizens in trade and industry.

Agricultural development has not been as fast or as good as industrial development. In comparison with the rest of the world, African agriculture did better before than after 1965, and, in countries like Zambia and Algeria, agricultural production actually declined after independence. Generally speaking, the level of food production as seen against the food needs of the population dropped, because in most countries population has been increasing faster than food production. African cash crops have also generally suffered during the 1960s through bad prices abroad.

For the vast majority of African farmers there has been very little advance in tools and methods. As people get educated, they move away from the land, and although it is a welcome development that people have been going into other enterprises and so diversifying the economy, it also means that new talents, capable of employing new tools and methods, have not been going into agriculture. African leaders are always appealing to the educated youths to go back to the land, but this appeal has fallen on deaf ears because nothing has been done to introduce modern amenities into the rural areas and make them habitable for the new generation of Africans.

However, there have been a few promising developments in agriculture in a few countries. Under government encouragement, farmers in countries like Ghana, Egypt, and Nigeria have been learning to improve their productivity by the use of fertilisers, pesticides and some machinery. Some African governments have also been giving increasing attention to such projects as improved irrigation facilities, supply of farm equipment like tractors, pumps and harvesting machines, supply to farmers of improved strains of seed and provision of technical advice through extension work.

On the whole, by 1975 African economies were still backward and still developing at rates lower than those of other regions of the world. Moreover, most of the labour force was still employed by agriculture, while agriculture still accounted for too large a proportion of all output. Nevertheless, African economies are gradually growing and becoming diversified. And, for the people, the economic progress has meant a steady, though slow, improvement in the conditions of life: better housing, more and improved medical, educational and communication facilities, more money to buy the necessities of life, and the growing availability of greater varieties of consumer goods supplied increasingly by local industries.

8 The development of Pan-Africanism

Pan-Africanism is a product of two closely inter-related factors. The first is the realisation by Africans that they have close cultural affinity, that they have had similar experiences especially in their recent history, that they constitute in the world a downtrodden group, and that they share similar problems and aspirations. The second is the desire of Africans to pull together for mutual support, for their full liberation, and for a more effective voice in the affairs of the world.

Though Pan-Africanism has flowered most since independence, its origins go back to the nineteenth century. It used to be said that the Pan-African idea was entirely a creation of the Black men in the New World – North America and the West Indies – from where it was imported to Africa. But, in reality, Pan-Africanism owed its origin to two separate movements, one in the New World and the other in Africa itself.

From the last years of the nineteenth century, Black nationalism in the New World began to show Pan-African tendencies. The Black nationalists began to speak, not only of their own sufferings in the New World, but also of the sufferings of African peoples under colonialism in Africa. They began to preach that Black men everywhere should unite to liberate themselves. In the early decades of this century, this movement reached its climax under the leadership of such great Black men as Marcus Garvey and W. E. B. DuBois.

While this was happening in the New World, a Pan-African movement had also started in Africa. Its best known champions were Dr Wilmot Blyden and Bishop James Johnson, both of West Africa. Blyden extolled African culture and urged educated Africans to give up European values and return to their own culture. James Johnson championed the 'Ethiopian' movement which advocated the unification of Africa into a single Christian state. He urged the creation of an African Christian Church to be manned entirely by Africans and free of all European cultural attachments. The Christian religion as laid down by this church would then become the religion of the unified African state. The movement envisaged also that the Blacks in the Americas, whom James Johnson regarded as 'Africans in exile', would return home to the unified Africa.

Ultimately, the two movements converged. Between 1900 and 1945, six major conferences were held by intellectuals of African origin from the United States of America, the West Indies and Africa itself. The era of these conferences, better known as Pan-African Congresses between 1919 and 1945, constitutes the first phase of the history of Pan-Africanism.

The first Pan-African conference, convened by Henry Sylvester-Williams, a West Indian lawyer, met in London in July 1900. Its aims were threefold: first, to bring people of African descent in all parts of the world together and thereby serve as a forum through which they could protest against European colonisation in Africa; secondly, to appeal to missionary and philanthropic opinion in Britain to protect Africans against the aggressions of the colonisers; and thirdly, to find ways of establishing more friendly relations between the African and European peoples of the world. These were very moderate aims; they sought friendship, rather than hostility, between African peoples and their European oppressors. Nevertheless, the conference was very important as the first attempt to bring leading persons of African origin together from all parts of the world to deliberate on their common problems. Most of the thirty delegates at the conference came from the United States and the West Indies.

The first of the five Pan-African Congresses was convened by Dr W. E. B. DuBois and it met in Paris in 1919. The second, also convened by DuBois, met in London in 1921; the third in London and Lisbon in 1923; and the fourth in New York in 1927. The Black leaders from the United States and the West Indies were the conveners and chief actors in these four Pan-African Congresses, but some representatives also came from Africa. Blaise Diagne of Senegal was one of the delegates at the first Pan-African Congress of 1919, while a Ghanaian chief was one of the African delegates at the 1927 Congress.

The man behind the Pan-African Congresses was the Afro-American intellectual, Dr W. E. B. DuBois. His idea was to recover for peoples of the Black race all over the world their dignity and self respect, to conduct serious studies into the conditions of Black people everywhere, to disseminate the results of such studies, and to bring the most educated Black people together periodically to discuss, deliberate and formulate action upon the conditions and problems of the Black race. His objective was not to incite the Black people to become hostile to their white oppressors, but to work for peaceful cooperation between the two races in such a way that the white oppressors would be persuaded to consider improvements in the plight of the Black man.

True to these ideas, the first four Pan-African Congresses were moderate in their tone. Generally, they demanded that the colonial masters of Africa should allow Africans some participation in the administration of their countries, and they protested against the degrading treatment of Africans in places like South Africa, Rhodesia and America.

Marcus Garvey, DuBois' great rival in the 1920s, regarded DuBois' ideas as much too moderate. In fact, Garvey, a West Indian who lived in the United States, regarded DuBois as a traitor to the Black race. Unlike DuBois who directed his appeal to the few educated, Garvey appealed to the masses of poor, downtrodden Afro-Americans. He preached racial separateness and appealed to people of the Black race to develop pride in their colour. Unlike DuBois, he was prepared to organise Black people to employ force, if necessary, to drive the European colonisers out of Africa. Also, one of his major concerns was to encourage Black people to form business enterprises in order to challenge the economic domination of the world by Europeans. To this end, he himself founded the shipping company known as 'The Black Star Line'. Finally, Garvey advocated the return of Black peoples in the New World to Africa and the unification of Africa into an empire.

Though DuBois and Garvey were so different in their philosophies, and though they were often very hostile to each other, their ideas worked together to stimulate Pan-Africanism until the 1950s. DuBois had more direct impact on the Pan-African Congresses, but Garvey's ideas exercised considerable influence on the growing elite in Africa. As pointed out in an earlier chapter, his journal, *Negro World*, was eagerly read in many parts of West Africa, and branches of his United Negro Improvement Association were founded in many West African towns.

Among the rising elite of Africa, also, Pan-Africanism was being given expression through a number of organisations which brought together literate Africans from different parts of the continent. One of these was the National Congress of British West Africa which was founded by the leaders of British West Africa in 1919 and which served, for a short time, as the foremost nationalist organisation for the British West African countries. Another was the West African Students' Union (WASU), founded in Britain in 1925, which served, until the 1940s, as the training ground in nationalist politics for African youths studying in Britain. WASU was strongly influenced by the ideas of Marcus Garvey who gave it its first hostel in London in 1928. In 1941, African students in the United States founded an organisation similar to the WASU – the African Students' Association.

Because of this growing Pan-Africanist awareness among the rising African elite, Africans took a more prominent part in the fifth Pan-

African Congress, which met in Manchester in 1945. The planning committee comprised Dr Peter Milliard (from the West Indies) as chairman, George Padmore (from the West Indies) and Kwame Nkrumah (from Ghana) as joint secretaries, T. R. Makonnen (from Ethiopia) as treasurer, Peter Abrahams (from South Africa) as publicity secretary, and Jomo Kenyatta (from Kenya) as assistant secretary. Dr DuBois was invited to preside as 'Father of Pan-Africanism'.

The fifth congress was far more militant than the first four. It demanded an end to colonialism in Africa and called upon the intellectuals, workers and peasants of African countries to unite into mass movements to achieve this. It advised the use of strikes and boycotts and other instruments of 'Positive Action' as means for destroying colonialism. It called for the eventual union of independent Africa. On the whole, this congress was very important to the development of the liberation struggles in Africa after the Second World War. Some of its participants, like Nkrumah and Kenyatta, were soon to become the leaders of the nationalist struggles in their countries.

In the first phase of its history (1900–1945) then, Pan-Africanism brought together intellectuals of African descent from Africa, America and the West Indies. It saw 'Africans' not only as those living on the African continent but as all persons of African origin living in all parts of the world.

The congress of 1945 was followed by twelve years without a significant Pan-African meeting. These were the years when all the politically active members of the African elites were too busy fighting for independence to organise any Pan-African get-together. The spirit of Pan-Africanism was not dead, however. It pervaded the speeches and writings of the nationalist leaders, all of whom claimed to be fighting not for the freedom of their own countries alone but for the freedom and unity of Africa. Pan-Africanism also continued to inspire the thoughts of Black intellectuals outside Africa. For instance, in 1955, George Padmore (the West Indian who had served as joint secretary on the planning committee of the 1945 Pan-African Congress) published his famous book, *Pan-Africanism or Communism*, which clearly analysed the theoretical foundations of Pan-Africanism.

On the whole, Pan-Africanism remained until the late 1950s a movement of the intellectuals and thinkers. In the early days most of these were Afro-Americans and West Indians. From about the 1920s, some Africans (especially those studying abroad) began to take part, and by the time of the 1945 congress, they had become prominent in it. From then on they imported its ideas to Africa and made it play an increasingly important role in the nationalist struggles. But it was not until the independence of Ghana in 1957 that Pan-Africanism became really popular all over Africa. Its champion was now Dr Kwame Nkrumah, the first Prime Minister and later President of independent Ghana.

The year 1957, therefore, marks the beginning of the second phase of the history of Pan-Africanism. One important change was that Pan-Africanism became essentially a movement limited to the African continent. Not only was the role of the Afro-Americans and West Indians greatly reduced in the Pan-African movement, the movement now aimed more at bringing together Africans on the African continent, rather than persons of African origin everywhere.

Secondly, Pan-Africanism since 1957 has been a more practical movement. It has strengthened the spirit of challenge to colonialism and, to some extent, it has given practical support to the movements for the liberation of African countries from colonialism.

Thirdly, Pan-Africanism since 1957 has resulted in the establishment of institutions of a permanent nature (the most notable of which is the Organisation of African Unity) through which all-African or regional cooperation can be expressed. This reflects the fact that Pan-Africanism has increasingly become a movement of a continent of independent nations free to manage their own affairs and to establish institutions of mutual cooperation.

As soon as Ghana became independent, Nkrumah invited George Padmore to become his adviser on African affairs. Accra became a sort of centre from which a steady stream of revolutionary propaganda about African freedom and African unity flowed to the rest of Africa. Dr Nkrumah also made contacts with the leaders of the already independent African countries (like Tunisia). As a result of these contacts, a Conference of Independent African States was held in Accra in April 1958. It resolved to give maximum support to the other Africans still fighting for the independence of their countries. It also decided to plan a bigger conference at which a united strategy would be worked out for the liberation of all of Africa. The outcome was the All-African People's Conference, held in Accra in December 1958.

This conference was one of the most important meetings in the history of Africa. Its delegates were representatives not only of the governments of independent African countries but also of the nationalist movements from almost every African country. Its message to Africa was militant. The delegates returned home with new ideas, new vigour and new tactics for the liberation struggle. The momentum thus gained by the nationalist forces contributed a lot to the achievement of independence by many African countries in the years that followed.

The Second All-African People's Conference was held in Tunis in 1960, and other conferences followed at which the relationship of the African countries with one another and with the rest of the world was spelt out. African states would respect the territorial integrity of one another, would settle all disputes peacefully within the context of Africa, and would observe a policy of 'positive neutrality' or non-alignment in the disputes of the great powers of the world. Finally, in 1963, the Organisation of African Unity (OAU) was created.

The OAU is a league of independent African states. Its supreme ruling body is the Assembly of Heads of State which meets at least once a year. Another organ, the Council of Ministers, which comprises Foreign Ministers of member states, meets more frequently to prepare matters for the final resolutions in the Assembly of Heads of State. The day-to-day administration of the OAU is done by the General Secretariat in Addis Ababa. The chief official of the Secretariat is the General Secretary. From 1963 to 1972, this post was held by a Guinean diplomat, Diallo Telli. In 1972, he was succeeded by a Cameroonian diplomat, Nzo Ekangaki who was succeeded two years later by another Cameroonian, William Eteki M'Boumoua.

The declared aims of the OAU are 'to promote the unity and solidarity of the African states', 'to coordinate and intensify their cooperation and efforts to achieve a better life for the peoples of Africa', and 'to work for the eradication of all forms of colonialism on the African continent'. For these purposes, a number of commissions were set up – to coordinate the solutions provided by African states for social, economic, educational, health and nutritional problems. A Defence Commission was set up and there have been talks about setting up an African High Command. A Committee for Liberation was set up with its headquarters in Tanzania to coordinate assistance to the freedom fighters in Angola, Mozambique, Rhodesia and South Africa.

The record of the OAU to date is one of modest achievements. In a number of major problem areas in Africa, it has intervened with considerable effect. One instance was the Nigerian civil war of 1967–70 which started when the Eastern Region of Nigeria attempted to secede from the country. The intervention by the OAU not only contributed immensely to the ultimate settlement of the crisis, but was partly responsible for restraining the world powers from interfering in such a way as to turn the crisis into an international conflict. Although Africans working together in the OAU have been unable to devise a formula for eliminating the cause of border disputes between African countries, the OAU has nevertheless been responsible for preventing some of these disputes from developing into full-scale wars. The liberation movements in the former Portuguese colonies, Rhodesia and South Africa have received considerable moral and material support from the OAU. On the international scene, the OAU has often enabled African countries to speak with a united voice on world issues. This has, to some extent at least, increased the influence of Africa at the United Nations and in the world generally. Perhaps the most important value of the OAU has consisted in its serving as a forum through which leaders of African countries can meet periodically. Many of these meetings have, it is true, been overshadowed by disputes and disagreements. Nevertheless, they have made it possible for African leaders to be in regular contact and to get to know one another. Many programmes of cooperation have resulted directly or indirectly from these contacts.

The achievements of the OAU have been so modest because the whole Pan-African movement has laboured under various difficulties. For one thing, very few African countries have been willing to surrender any significant part of their newly won sovereignty for the sake of the dream of African unity. Consequently, although all African leaders have proclaimed 'African unity' to be the goal of Pan-Africanism, there has been a sharp disagreement over the meaning of the phrase. Some, like Dr Nkrumah, advocated in the early 1960s that African unity should mean the political unification of Africa into one large state – the United States of Africa. The vast majority of African leaders, however, insisted that Africans must accept the existing African countries as they were, and that African unity should mean only co-operation among these countries. As it was conceived and organised in 1963, the OAU represented a victory for those who advocated the preservation of the sovereignty of the existing nation-states. As such, the OAU has exhibited all the weaknesses that a league of independent nation-states must have.

Differences in national approaches to problems have tended to make the OAU ineffective at various times. This is why, for instance, the OAU has not been as effective as it could be in helping the liberation struggles in Southern Africa. Moreover, the OAU has often been shaken by disputes among its members arising from clashes of national interests – disputes between Kenya and Somalia, between Morocco and Mauritania, between Zaire and the Republic of the Congo, between Ethiopia and Somalia, between Tanzania and Uganda. Not only have such disputes weakened the unity of the OAU, attempts to settle them have consumed much of its energy.

Divisions have also been caused by the differences in the colonial backgrounds of the African countries. The two major groups have been the former British colonies speaking English and the former French colonies speaking French. Both remained closely attached to their former colonial masters – the English-speaking countries as members of the British Commonwealth, and the French-speaking countries as members of the French Community. Moreover, especially during the early 1960s, the language and other differences between the two groups weakened the solidarity of the Pan-African movement. Soon after most of them had won independence, the French-speaking countries met in Brazzaville in December 1960 and formed a separate group known as the Brazzaville Group. At the third meeting of the Brazzaville Group in Yaounde in Cameroon in 1961, they established an organisation for economic co-operation among themselves – the Afro-Malagasy Organisation for Economic Co-operation (OAMCE). They also set up a joint air company known as Air Afrique. In 1961 they formed the Afro-Malagasy Union (UAM) which took the place of the OAMCE and which immediately signed a defence pact with France. Finally, early in 1965 they formed the *Organisation Commune Africaine et Malagache* (OCAM), or Common Organisation of Afro-Malagasy States. Though the members of OCAM claimed that their organisation was within the framework of the OAU, it undoubtedly detracted from the solidarity of the OAU. However, towards the end of the 1960s, the spirit of separateness based upon colonial background appeared to be weakening. From about 1970, OCAM began to break up as some of its members began to resign.

There also developed among the African countries in the early 1960s a major division based upon differences of approach to major issues. Two groups emerged from this division. First, there was a radical group – made up of Ghana, Guinea, Mali, Algeria, Egypt and Morocco – which stood for a militant and aggressive programme to free the rest of Africa from colonial rule. Because this group held its first meeting in Casablanca in Morocco, it became known as the Casablanca Group. Then there was a moderate or conservative group known as the Monrovia Group (also because its first meeting was held in Monrovia in Liberia) and including Nigeria, Liberia, Ivory Coast, Togo and Sudan. The differences of opinion between the two groups concerned not only their attitudes to the liberation struggle but also their attitudes to the rivalry between the two major power blocks in the world – the Eastern Bloc (Russia and her allies), and the Western Bloc (America and Western Europe). Although most African leaders professed non-alignment (i.e. non-attachment to either East or West) which was the declared policy of the Pan-African movement, Africans were nevertheless divided by their attitudes to the Eastern and Western Blocs. On the whole, the Monrovia Group leaned towards friendship with, or even some dependence on, the Western Bloc, while the Casablanca Group was more favourably disposed towards the Eastern Bloc and regarded the Western Bloc as Africa's enemy because the Western Bloc was a friend of Portugal and the apartheid government of South Africa. This division considerably undermined the effectiveness of the OAU and enabled foreign powers to play off African countries against one another. However, this division too became less obvious in the late 1960s and people began to talk less and less of the Monrovia and Casablanca Groups.

Finally, the rapid succession of military overthrows of governments which took place in the second half of the 1960s tended to weaken the OAU. It is not that the military leaders were less interested in the Pan-African movement than the civilians, but that after each coup, each country tended to turn its attention inwards as the new regime had to grapple with the problems of leadership. In this way the Pan-Africanist fervour of the immediate post-independence era waned noticeably, particularly in the declining assistance given during the late 1960s to the liberation forces in Southern Africa.

Many movements of local co-operation have arisen in different parts of Africa, inspired partly by the Pan-Africanist spirit and partly by local needs for co-operation. Some of these have taken the form of attempts at political union – like the Mali Federation (made up of Mali and Senegal), the Ghana–Guinea Union, the movement for the union of Egypt and Sudan, the movement for a union of the Maghreb. However, none of these so-called unions ever got off the ground, for the simple reason that, though there might be compelling economic reasons for such unions, no country has really been willing to lose its independence and become a province in a bigger country.

Other movements of local co-operation have placed emphasis on economic co-operation. The greatest of these up to 1975 was the East African Community. The East African countries have a longer history of co-operation than countries in any other region of Africa probably because they all belonged to one colonial power, Britain, and developed many areas of joint services. After independence, these joint services became areas of co-operation. The East African Community, created in 1967, provided for an East African common market, common services and a Development Bank. This purely economic arrangement has been shaken on a number of occasions by political disputes – for instance, the dispute between Uganda and Tanzania following the military coup in Uganda in 1970. Nevertheless, it has been the most significant project of regional economic co-operation in post-independence Africa. In 1975, the countries of West Africa agreed to found the Economic Council of West African States (ECOWAS), a sort of West African common market.

Finally, since independence, Africa has witnessed considerable improvement in inter-state transportation and communication, an improvement achieved through the co-operation among the various countries. Of the lines of communication resulting from such co-operation, perhaps the longest is the projected Lagos-Mombasa road to link West Africa with East Africa.

9   Independent Africa in the world comity of nations

The emergence of African nations is one of the most revolutionary developments in the recent history of the world. Until the 1950s the history of international relations concerned only the nation-states of Europe, North America and the Eastern bloc. But during the 1960s, this situation was radically changed, and perhaps the greatest of the changes was the appearance, in rapid succession, of so many African nation-states. In fact, one might speak of the 1960s in world history as Africa's decade. By 1970, African votes at the United Nations numbered more than forty, which in itself made Africa an important factor in world affairs.

There are important differences in the nature of the foreign demands on the attention of the African states. For one thing, different regions of Africa face different areas of the world and are therefore subject to different types of pull. For instance, as North Africa faces Europe and the Middle East the North African states are affected more directly by developments in Southern Europe and the Middle East than are other African states. On the other hand, East Africa is a part of the world of the Indian Ocean, and therefore is directly affected by developments in Asia.

More differences arise from different colonial heritages. For instance some African states speak to the world in English, others in French, Portuguese or Italian. Cultural and linguistic affinity, as well as economic ties which go back to colonial times, tend to pull English-speaking African states towards Britain and the English-speaking world, and the French-speaking African states towards France and the French-speaking world. Moreover, the diplomatic practices of the former British colonies are moulded considerably by British tradition while those of former French colonies are moulded by French tradition.

Nevertheless, African countries, as members of the world comity of nations, have many common characteristics, are confronted by very similar basic problems, and therefore their foreign policies show the same fundamental outlines.

The first of these characteristics is that as sovereign states, the African states are very young. The older a state is, the longer the history of its foreign policy, the clearer its basic national ideology, and the less likely is its foreign policy to be affected by the whims and personalities of its leaders. The states of Europe have existed for so long that they have developed corporate personalities, traditions, reflexes and directions of their own. The African states, on the contrary, have not yet developed any such corporate personalities, and their foreign policies are frequently distorted by their leaders' personal attitudes. A change of leadership, therefore, has often occasioned changes of foreign policy. For instance, under Nkrumah, Ghana was the champion of aggressive African nationalism; but under Busia, Ghana tended to shrink into its shell, found it possible to expel the nationals of other African states, and became one of the few African states supporting the idea of dialogue with the apartheid regime of South Africa. Yet another dramatic change of policy occurred after the removal of Busia from power by the army. His successor, Colonel Acheampong, immediately denounced the idea of dialogue with apartheid.

Another common characteristic is that no African state yet has much influence in the world. Power is the great regulator of the relations among sovereign states. As used here power means not only military power but economic prosperity, sheer size, political stability at home and credibility abroad, etc. Judged against these criteria, no sovereign African state as yet has any significant power. At the United Nations, for instance, all the African voices put together are small in comparison with the single voice of the United States or the Soviet Union or Britain. But for the universal revulsion against apartheid, South Africa would easily command more weight in the world than all the sovereign African states put together. Though South Africa has only 6% of the continent's population, she controls about 75% of the income and output of Africa south of the Sahara. In the words of the leader of the Nigerian delegation to the OAU Conference in Kinshasa in 1967, Africa is today hardly more than a continent of competing beggar-nations.

Finally, African states are engaged in foreign policy for basically the same objectives: to ensure worldwide respect for their independence, integrity and unity, to promote their economic prosperity through actions aimed at ensuring favourable balances of trade and the attraction of aid and investments, to ensure peace and co-operation among African states, to eradicate all forms of foreign domination on the African continent, to ensure respect for the black man in the world, and to contribute to the achievement and maintenance of peace and justice in the world.

Non-alignment

As African countries became independent, most of them proclaimed that their interests in the world would best be served by a policy of 'non-alignment', in other words not becoming attached to either of the two rival power blocs (Eastern and Western) in the world, and not taking sides in their disputes. It was a doctrine of newly independent nations seeking to assert their freedom and identity on the international scene.

The concept of non-alignment had first developed among the Asian nations as they became independent after the Second World War, during the late 1940s and early 1950s. Then in 1955, the Asian countries and the few independent African countries came together as a bloc of non-aligned nations at the Afro-Asian Conference held in Bandung in Indonesia in 1955. The independent African countries which sent delegates to the Bandung Conference were Egypt, Liberia, Ethiopia and Libya. Sudan and Ghana, which were nearing independence, also sent representatives. The Bandung Conference was followed by similar conferences in the years that followed, and as African countries became independent, the number of African delegates at these conferences increased. At the Belgrade Conference in 1961 ten African countries were represented, and at the Cairo Conference in 1964, twenty-eight. From these conferences emerged the Afro-Asian Bloc or Afro-Asian Solidarity Group, which made its influence felt particularly in the United Nations Organisation, and was ultimately extended to include the Latin American countries. This group (made up of African, Asian and Latin American countries) is referred to in international politics as the 'third world' – the Western and Eastern Blocs being the first and second worlds.

From the first All-African People's Conference in 1958, the stand of the Pan-African movement in the world was declared to be one of non-alignment. This principle was reasserted by every subsequent conference, and was finally inserted into the charter of the Organisation of African Unity in 1963.

As it ultimately developed, non-alignment was a political as well as an economic doctrine. Its major objective was the avoidance of involvement in the disputes of the big powers. Since the African countries were new on the world scene and were economically and militarily weak, they felt that the best way to preserve their freedom was to stay out of the cold war between the powerful nations, and to unite and co-operate with one another. Such co-operation would enable them to exert a united influence on world affairs and thereby save the world from being destroyed by the rivalries of the great powers. Non-alignment therefore condemned nuclear weapons, big power interference in the affairs of weak nations, the making of military pacts by weak nations with powerful nations, and the granting of military bases to any of the big powers by any of the third world nations. These were the main political aspects of non-alignment.

Economically, non-alignment came to mean, first and foremost, the avoidance of economic dependence on any big power. Since every African country entered upon independent nationhood with its economy closely tied to that of its former colonial overlord, it became part of the aim of economic independence to reduce such ties by seeking trade and economic relationship with other nations – especially with comparative strangers like the United States, the Soviet Union, the Eastern European countries, Japan and China. Finally, it became one of the major principles of economic non-alignment that economic aid from the rich nations to the African nations should not have 'strings' attached to it. Indeed, some African leaders ultimately advocated that African countries should prefer 'multilateral' aid (aid through such joint bodies as the World Bank and the International Monetary Fund) to 'unilateral' aid (aid made directly by one country to another). It was argued that this was the only sure way of obtaining aid without strings.

Non-alignment in practice
After independence, each African country established diplomatic relations with many countries abroad, including countries of the Eastern Bloc. This was an important way of asserting national freedom on the international stage. Moreover, in many issues affecting the world, African countries very quickly showed that they would not be bound by the opinions of others. Thus, most African countries showed that they were critical of United States intervention in the affairs of Vietnam and of the Soviet Union's armed intervention in Czechoslovakia. In spite of the United States' opposition, many African countries accorded recognition to the People's Republic of China as the legitimate Government of China. And, at the United Nations General Assembly, most African states spoke from year to year in favour of the admission of the People's Republic of China to the United Nations. In 1961, when the Soviet Union proposed the establishment of a three-man body (a 'troika') to take the place of the Secretary-General of the

United Nations, the African states, like the Western powers, opposed it on the grounds that it would weaken the United Nations Organisation. But when the Soviet Union proposed an immediate suspension of all nuclear tests (without any international inspection) pending the conclusion of a general arms control agreement, African countries supported the Soviet Union against the Western powers. On the total elimination of colonialism and white minority dictatorships from the African continent, the Eastern Bloc has usually supported the African stand. In short, African states at the United Nations have freely supported whatever proposals appear to them to serve the purpose of ending colonialism, of safeguarding the sovereignty of weak nations against the interferences of big powers, or of ensuring the peace and survival of the world itself.

Economically, most African countries after independence developed commercial relationships with new partners all over the world, again including countries of the Eastern Bloc. Direct African trade with countries like the Soviet Union, the United States, China, Japan and the Eastern European countries, which was small or non-existent during the colonial era, showed rapid increases during the 1960s, while the percentage of African trade with the former colonial powers declined.

Most African countries also felt free to seek economic, technical and military assistance as well as investment capital from all available sources. It has, however, been the universal concern of all African countries to prevent foreign aid, from whatever source, from leading to the establishment of foreign political influences. African suspicion of foreign influence has produced many dramatic changes in their relationships with foreign powers. An unsuccessful attempt by the Western powers to use economic aid to rope Egypt into a Western-sponsored military alliance in the Mediterranean led to sharp disagreements between Egypt and the Western powers in 1956. After that, Egypt began to receive much economic and military assistance from the Soviet Union, but Egyptians always ensured that this should not lead to the growth of Soviet influence over their country. In 1972, popular suspicions of growing Soviet influence led to a sudden expulsion of Soviet technical and military advisers from Egypt. During 1964 the governments of Zambia, Malawi and Niger reacted sharply against Chinese attempts to influence the internal politics of their countries.

The experiences of the African countries have shown, however, that for weak and poor nations there is a limit to non-alignment. The commercial ties with the former colonial overlords could be loosened only gradually. Many were so strong that there was little that could be done about them in the years immediately following independence. Even after a decade of formal independence, the former metropolitan companies still dominated the economies of many African countries. Moreover, for its development, every African country required financial and technical assistance as well as foreign capital, and the need for such assistance tended to make many countries somewhat subservient to their former colonial rulers, no matter how much noise was made about aid without strings. Some countries like the Gambia and Dahomey were so poor that, for many years after independence, they could not even pay the day-to-day expenses of government without financial grants from their former colonial masters.

The way in which economic weakness can frustrate non-alignment is perhaps best illustrated by the attitudes of the African countries to the European Common Market or European Economic Community (EEC), an economic organisation of a number of Western European countries including most of the former colonial powers. Before the independence of most of the French colonies in 1960, France had applied for them to become associate members of the EEC. After 1960, the negotiation was continued. Associate membership of the EEC was made to look very attractive to the newly independent African countries. It would provide something like a guaranteed market, and even special prices in some cases, for their products. Moreover, the EEC set up a Development Fund from which money would be drawn to give aid to the associate members.

Many African leaders, however, warned African states against joining the EEC on the grounds that they would be tied to the economy of Europe and compelled to remain as sources of raw materials for the industries of Europe. Membership would also make it difficult for the African countries to speak with free voices in the affairs of the world, and even attach African states to the Western Bloc in the cold war. The EEC, said Dr Nkrumah, was aimed at harnessing the African countries to satisfy the 'profit-lust' of the imperialist powers and to prevent African states from following an independent non-aligned policy in the world. 'If we do not resist this threat,' he said, 'and if we throw in our lot with the Common Market, we shall doom the economy of Africa to a state of perpetual subjection to the economy of Europe. This will, of course, hinder the industrialisation of our young African states. It is impossible to think of economic development and national independence without possessing an unfettered capacity for maintaining a strong industrial power. The activities of the Common Market are therefore fraught with dangerous political and economic consesequences for independent African states.'

Such warnings, however, could not detract from the apparent economic attractions offered by associate membership of the EEC, and in 1963 eighteen of the French-speaking African countries joined the EEC as associate members. They included even such a radically orientated country as Mali. Moreover, from 1965 other African states – Nigeria, Kenya, Uganda, Tanzania – began to apply for associate membership.

Because they lack power and influence in the world, too, African states have failed to remain as politically non-aligned as they would wish. They have continued to belong to such organisations as the British Commonwealth and the French Community – two organisations whose real objectives are to sustain British and French influence. Not infrequently, African leaders whose countries belong to these organisations have made romantic statements about the international brotherhood which such organisations foster. But the truth seems to be that they have remained members only because they expect such membership somehow to enhance their influence in the world, and to increase their chances of obtaining economic, technical and military assistance from the former colonial rulers. Through such organisations as the Afro-Malagasy Union (UAM) and the Common Organisation of Afro-Malagasy States (OCAM) which replaced it, French influence continued to be very firmly maintained in African affairs.

Many of the French-speaking countries entered into military pacts with France at independence. For many years after independence the Government of Senegal continued to harbour French military forces in Senegalese towns. When Chad Republic was faced with internal insurrection, it called in the French army. Similarly, when Kenya, Uganda and Tanzania were faced, at different times in 1964, with mutinies among their armed forces, who were revolting especially against the retention of British commanders, they summoned the British army to their rescue.

African economic and military dependence on Western European countries not only made nonsense of non-alignment, but also made it impossible for African states to defend African interests against Western European powers. Thus, when France began to test atomic bombs in the Sahara Desert in the early sixties, the African states could not take any effective action. The countries of the Brazzaville Group backed France. A few countries, notably Nigeria, broke off diplomatic relations with France, but France received too much support from other African countries for such a step to be other than a diplomatic disaster. Similarly, when the white minority regime of Rhodesia unilaterally declared Rhodesia independent in 1965, African states, acting under the umbrella of the OAU, demanded that Britain should use force to end the illegal independence. At a meeting of the Foreign Ministers of the OAU member-states held in Addis Ababa in December 1965, it was unanimously agreed to break off diplomatic relations with Britain, but only nine countries (Ghana, Mali, Guinea, Tanzania, Congo, Mauritania, Sudan, Morocco and Egypt) did so. Indeed, most of the African members of the British Commonwealth behaved as if they were anxious to shield Britain from any joint pressure by African countries. Uganda and Nigeria were particularly responsible for getting two Commonwealth conferences called on the Rhodesian issue – as if to tell the rest of Africa that the Rhodesian issue was a Commonwealth and not an African affair. As a result, the countries which had broken off diplomatic relations found themselves in a diplomatic mess, and each had to find a way of tamely re-establishing relations with Britain.

Another major consequence of the weakness of African states has been their tendency to rely unduly on the United Nations to solve their problems for them. Much of the African offensive on white minority dictatorships in Rhodesia and South Africa and on Portuguese colonialism in Africa was shifted to the floor of the United Nations General Assembly. In co-operation with other countries of the third world, African states succeeded in getting the United Nations to set up a Committee on Colonialism as well as an international body charged with the duty of administering Namibia. However, attempts to get the United Nations to fix dates for the ending of colonialism in Africa have failed; and the apartheid government of South Africa has refused to hand over Namibia to the United Nations body. On the whole, the over-reliance on the United Nations has been a confession of impotence, bringing little or no positive advantage. Not a few prominent Africans have expressed the view that only force can change the situation in Southern Africa, but most Africans know that Africa does not command the economic and military strength for such a venture.

Finally, the attitude of many African governments to the Soviet Union, China and other Eastern Bloc countries immediately after independence was moulded largely by Western propaganda. Such propaganda portrayed the Soviet Union as the source of all political insurrections and a threat to all orderly government in the world. As a result, many countries passed laws banning Soviet or communist literature, and excluding the Soviet Union and other communist countries from the list of foreign countries to which their passports could be used to gain entry. Almost everywhere, citizens who had studied or travelled in the Soviet Union were held in great suspicion by the authorities. As the years passed and the African leaders came to see more of international affairs, these fears wore off considerably, but in the early sixties they were very strong indeed, especially among the Monrovia Group.

Indeed, as we have seen, differences of attitude to the Western and Eastern Blocs were an important factor in the division of Africa into a Monrovia Group and a Casablanca Group. The division of Africa enabled foreign powers to play off African leaders against one another. For instance, the Western press painted leaders like William Tubman of Liberia, Félix Houphouët-Boigny of Ivory Coast and Sir Abubakir Tafawa Balewa of Nigeria in glowing colours and contrasted them unfavourably with Nkrumah and Sekou Toure. Inevitably, this introduced a note of personal animosity among leaders into African affairs and, thereby, weakened African solidarity.

The experiences of African states on the international scene then, have been those of young, weak states finding it difficult to maintain their freedom of choice and of action in a world dominated by the rivalries among a few giant powers. Quite often, Africans critical of their countries' performances in international politics attribute such performances to failings in the leaders, but far more important is the immaturity, poverty and weakness of the African states themselves.

10 Military interventions in politics in Africa

In the years before independence in Africa, the army played no noticeable part in politics. The colonial armies were small and were led by expatriate officers. They were a creation of colonialism, and employed only to satisfy some purpose of the colonial rulers – like internal 'pacification' or border defence. Consequently, in the politics of liberation the armies did not, because by their nature they could not, participate. There were occasional scattered mutinies against officers or in protest against poor service conditions, but none of these mutinies aimed at taking over the government. The Portuguese colonies and Algeria were the only countries to win independence through military action. The politics of the liberation movements in other countries was essentially an affair of the mass parties, trade unions and nationalist leaders.

Consequently, at independence nobody reckoned that the army would play much part in the politics of any African state. In fact, some African leaders even regarded the army as unnecessary. Yet, within a short time of independence, Africa became the scene of a whole rash of military *coups d'état*. In country after country, the occupants of the presidential palaces were removed, sometimes executed, and into their positions moved the men from the military barracks.

The first of these coups occurred in Egypt in 1952 when a group of Egyptian officers toppled the monarchy. It was followed six years later in November 1958 in the Sudan when officers led by General Ibrahim Abboud seized control. On 19 June 1965 a military junta seized power in Algeria, and there followed, in quick succession, similar events in Zaire (25 November 1965), Dahomey (22 December 1965), Central African Republic (1 January 1966), Upper Volta (3 January 1966), Nigeria (15 January 1966), Ghana (24 February 1966), Nigeria again (29 July 1966), Burundi (28 November 1966), Togo (13 January 1967), Sierra Leone (22 March 1967), Sierra Leone again (April 1968), Congo-Brazzaville (4 August 1968), Mali (19 November 1968), Sudan (25 May 1969). After Sudan, it seemed for over a year as though the wave of coups might have ended. But in January 1971 another one occurred in Uganda, and in January 1972 yet another in Ghana.

The second half of the independence decade (the 1960s) might therefore be called the era of military *coups d'état* in Africa. Nigeria, Ghana, Sierra Leone, and Sudan have had more than one each, but Dahomey holds the record with more than five.

The reasons for military overthrows of governments vary from country to country; nevertheless certain common trends are discernible. First, there was a tendency for the ruling parties and leaders to lose some of their appeal and popularity after independence was won and the mass excitement of the anti-colonial struggle extinguished. Economic promises could not be fulfilled quickly enough; and the lot of the masses improved little while most of the leaders could be seen to be corruptly enriching themselves. In some countries, the people's disappointment led to so much social commotion that the army was compelled to step in to prevent total collapse. For instance in Dahomey, not only was the government after independence unable to increase the wages of the urban workers, it couldn't even pay them any wages at all for some time. This led to riots during which some of the workers openly appealed to the army to seize power and save the nation from chaos. The rapid succession of military take-overs in Dahomey has resulted mostly from the economic failures of its governments.

In most countries, however, it was not so much the disappointment of the people over the poor economic performance of the government as their poor handling of the political situation that led to military intervention. Faced with the growing scepticism and even hostility among the people, the leaders often set out to recapture the enthusiasm and unity of the pre-independence period. Their methods, conditioned by those characteristic of the former colonial regimes, were forceful, ultimately violent. Criminal proceedings against political opponents, legal restrictions on their political activities, rigging of elections, rewards to opposition parliamentarians to 'cross the carpet', intimidation of the supporters of political opponents and, ultimately, the use of force and of terrorist tactics against opponents – these were the measures adopted in an attempt to enforce unanimity.

This increasing use of force tended to increase the importance and confidence of those institutions in the society best equipped to handle force: the police and the army. Moreover, when opposition political groups and parties and associations were denied the opportunity for lawful political action, they often began to resort to force to press their rights and demands. Now, the more the opposition employed force to press their demands, the more the ruling parties had to rely openly on the police and army to maintain order, and the more the police and army gained in importance and confidence. In the end, the police and army found that they were the only organisations with the discipline and power to maintain order, prevent the country from disintegrating, purge the country of corruption and restore the confidence of the common people in the government. In both Nigeria and Ghana, for example, the growth of political violence made it necessary to bring out the army to maintain order. In the end, the army took over.

In short then, the major causes of military *coups d'état* were popular disaffection and the failure of the civilian leadership. However, sometimes even the armies themselves suffered internal tensions, which led to their intervention in politics. Such tensions were sometimes caused by ethnic loyalties penetrating into the army. Rivalries among ethnic groups in the country reached the men in the army, and not infrequently, personal rivalries among the military officers tended to be fought out with the weapon of 'tribalism'. Also, when a certain ethnic group was heavily represented in the army but the government was in the hands of another and hostile ethnic group, divisions based on regions or ethnic groups quickly developed in the army. For instance, resentment of Milton Obote's treatment of the Kabaka of Buganda and the Buganda kingdom seems to have been important among the grievances leading to the Uganda coup of 1971.

Another type of tension within the army was caused by rivalries among the older and newer indigenous officers. In most African armies, the topmost African officers at independence had been recruited by the expatriate officers at the lowest level and had gradually risen through the ranks over the years. In the years shortly before and after independence, however, more Africans were recruited into the officer corps. Inevitably, since the level of education had generally risen in those years, the newly recruited officers were men of higher education than their superiors; sometimes even university graduates. This circumstance usually generated tensions, and not a few of the coups in Africa were aimed at the military leaders as much as the politicians.

The military in power
No matter for what reason they seized power, the average military officers were characterised, on their assuming office, by a puritanism and a distaste for wasteful and ostentatious living, which made them sharply different from the politicians whom they had displaced. Everywhere, the leaders of the coups promised incorruptible leadership, justice to all, release of political prisoners, national reconciliation, confiscation of the wealth corruptly acquired by politicians, more purposeful economic direction, quick return to civilian rule after fair elections. In return, they asked the people to show confidence in the new government, to stop taking the law into their own hands, and to co-operate in the task of purging the nation of corruption.

In practically every country where a coup occurred, its immediate effect was to create general relief and revive enthusiasm and hope among the people. The promises of the soldiers carried ready conviction because the soldiers appeared so different from the politicians. Warring factions laid down their arms and the country quickly returned to peace and order.

One of the commonest promises made by the armies on seizing power was that their regimes would be merely 'corrective' and that they would soon give way to new civilian rulers. In only a few cases has this promise been quickly fulfilled. In Sierra Leone, the junior officers who organised the second coup (April 1968) handed over almost immediately to civilians. The first military regime in Ghana also fairly quickly returned the country to civilian rulers after supervising the drawing up of a new constitution to guarantee future stability.

In most other countries, the army has tended to stay in power indefinitely. The military regime under General Abboud in the Sudan stayed in power and became corrupt and inept, until it was thrown out by a civilian uprising. In Egypt, the military rulers evolved into a political movement not long after seizing power and banned all other political parties. Their political movement has ruled Egypt ever since. The military regime which came to power in Zaire in 1965 has followed the pattern of Egypt.

The case of Nigeria is somewhat different. The military regime which took over in January 1966 had hardly settled down before it was overthrown by another group of officers in July. The new rulers soon began to make arrangements for the creation of a new constitution as a prelude to return to civilian rule. But the outbreak of violence in parts of the country and the coming of a civil war put a stop to such arrangements. As soon as the civil war was over, the military rulers promised that, after their programme of post-war reconstitution had been carried out, they would hand over to a civilian government in 1976. On 1 October 1974, however, that promise was withdrawn.

In no African country did the army come into power as a political group with definite political programmes and ideologies. The leaders of the African coups were mostly men hurried into political intervention by the threat of national chaos and collapse. Their military take-overs were different from military take-overs in places like Cuba under Castro. There is no doubt that they were sincere in their promises to eradicate corruption, destroy the roots of ethnic and regional rivalries and antagonisms, promote economic prosperity, cure social inequalities, all very quickly. But all these ventures are in themselves very difficult ventures even for experienced statesmen or seasoned revolutionaries. Not only did social reforms move more slowly than was promised, but exposure to politics sometimes affected the high moral discipline of the army and led many military rulers to begin to behave like their civilian predecessors.

Such behaviour naturally disappointed the people. In Ghana, the people became disenchanted with the army not long after the 1966 coup and this encouraged some young officers in the army to attempt to topple their leaders from power. Similar disenchantment led to students' riots in the Sudan and also a coup attempt by some young army officers against the Abboud Government before it was finally overthrown by popular revolt. In Nigeria, the corruption and lavish ostentation of the second military regime led to a third coup in July 1975.

Case histories of selected independent states

11 Ghana

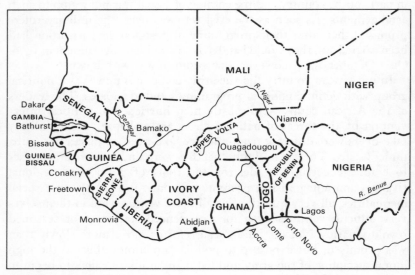

Independent West African states

In 1951 Ghanaian nationalist forces won a major victory when the colonial government agreed to grant limited internal self-government, or responsible government, to Ghana. From then until 1957 a popularly elected government managed the country's affairs, supervised by the colonial authorities. Then on 6 March 1957, Ghana became completely independent.

The architect of Ghana's independence was Dr Kwame Nkrumah, leader of the Convention People's Party (CPP). He dominated Ghanaian politics for fifteen years until, in 1966, his government was overthrown by a military *coup d'état*. Since then, the army has ruled Ghana – except for a short time when Ghana had a civilian government under the leadership of Dr K. A. Busia. Dr Busia himself was overthrown by another military coup in January 1972.

Preceding chapters have dealt with Ghana's foreign policy under Nkrumah. This chapter is concerned only with internal developments.

Economic developments

Ghana's economic development under Dr Nkrumah falls into two periods – 1951–61, and 1962–6. Before responsible government was granted to Ghana in 1951, the colonial Governor had drawn up a Ten-Year Development Plan, and soon after the West Indian scholar, Professor Arthur Lewis, was invited to advise the government. Professor Lewis' *Report on Industrialisation and the Gold Coast* was submitted to the government in 1953, and together with the Governor's Ten-Year Development Plan, provided economic strategy until 1961. Moreover, until 1957, Dr Nkrumah and his colleagues, although controlling much authority, were still under the supervision of the colonial government, and the Minister of Finance was a British official. During 1951–61, therefore, Ghana's economic development was still dominated by British ideas; the colonial structure remained virtually unchanged.

The guidelines laid down in Professor Lewis' report suggested that great emphasis should be placed on agriculture. A healthy and growing agriculture would provide 'both the market for industry and industry's labour supply'. Without these, quick industrialisation was impossible. Also, a growing agriculture would supply the food needed by the growing population and the growing industrial working population.

Next to agriculture, the second greatest priority should be given to the provision of public services – education, transportation, communication. These were regarded as more urgent than the building of industries because only the government could provide public services whereas many different agencies including private persons could build industries.

As far as building industry was concerned, the duty of the government was to make Ghana attractive to foreign investors with both the capital and the expertise. The government should clearly set down the rules under which foreign investment would be allowed to operate: in what industries foreign capital was allowed or not allowed; in what industries foreign capital was allowed only in partnership with indigenous capital; what rules would govern employment, etc. Ghana should concentrate on building those industries for which the raw materials were locally produced – processing vegetables, vegetable oils and fruits, brewing beer and soft drinks, manufacturing of cement, building materials, wood products and chemicals.

These were the lines which the government of Ghana tried to follow, more or less, until 1961. When Dr Nkrumah came to power under the responsible government arrangement in 1951, he accepted the Governor's Ten-Year Development Plan, although he shortened the period of its fulfilment to five years and increased the total amount of money that was to be spent. In 1957, it was announced that the plan had been fully implemented. Then in 1959 a Five-Year Development Plan was issued for the years 1959–64, with the main objectives of providing more educational facilities, and better social services generally. It aimed to create at least 600 industries, some by the state and some by private enterprise.

On the whole, there were considerable economic and social achievements in the years 1951–61. One of the most important was the eradication of the swollen-shoot disease which had threatened to destroy Ghana's cocoa farms. The only effective remedy was to cut the diseased plants. To win the farmers' support the government provided for compensation for the trees cut. The farmers were also taught the use of insecticides to control other cocoa diseases. Ghana's cocoa production doubled between 1951 and 1961, and by 1961 Ghana produced 40% of all the cocoa sold in the world market. At the same time, encouragement was given to the expansion of other crops like coffee, bananas and rubber in the tropical forest areas, and cattle, corn and other grains in the grassland areas, as well as the production of timber and the mining of gold. By 1960, the three leading exports were cocoa, timber and gold. There was also considerable investment in industries, although the ambitious targets of the Development Plans were not reached.

The mileage of hard-surfaced all-season roads almost doubled during the decade, and feeder roads were built for the benefit of the farming population. The railway network was extended. The port of Takoradi was expanded, and a beginning was made with the building of Tema harbour, the largest artificial harbour in Africa. Pipe-borne water was supplied to most towns and sizeable villages. The production and supply of electricity increased sharply. Communications were improved through the establishment of postal, telegraph and telephone facilities. Under Nkrumah's educational programme in 1951–61, enrolment in primary and middle schools quadrupled. In 1952, Ghana made elementary education free for all – the first country to do so in Africa – and in 1961 it was made compulsory. A very ambitious programme of providing health facilities was embarked upon – including regional and district hospitals, health centres and clinics.

On the whole, then, Ghana made good progress between 1951 and 1961. Between 1951 and 1960, the economy grew at a regular rate of 8%, a very high rate for any country. The picture was, however, marred by certain very important weaknesses. In accordance with Professor Lewis' guidelines, the Ghana Government offered all sorts of attractions to foreign investors, such as tax exemptions or low rates of taxation on profits, low duties or even no duties on imported raw materials, laws guaranteeing the safety of foreign capital, tariff laws to protect goods produced and promises of loans to help foreign businesses, etc. But in spite of all these, the influx of foreign capital was far short of what was expected, not more than 15% of the total investment. Almost all the improvements, therefore, had to be financed from internal sources, something the government had not bargained for. These sources were seriously threatened from about 1960, when the world price of cocoa, Ghana's chief source of income, began to fall.

Also the importation of machinery to build industries, the provision of public facilities, and the increase in private consumption all called for a rapid increase in imports. Between 1952 and 1961, imports rose by 115% while exports increased by only 34%. This was a very serious balance of payments problem, and it was worsened by certain practices of the foreign companies and foreign banks, both old and new. Since the government's policy allowed great freedom to the foreign companies, many of them were able to repatriate so much of their profits as to injure the economy of Ghana.

Obviously, much more wealth was flowing out of Ghana than was coming in or being produced. The capacity of Ghana to pay for her imports was falling.

As a result, Ghana began to draw heavily from her reserves abroad. These reserves came from Ghana's own cocoa-produced wealth, which the colonial authorities had sent to Britain and invested in the British economy. Between 1959 and 1961 especially, the reserves fell very rapidly. By 1961, the situation looked very grim indeed.

Dr Nkrumah took the view that the attempt to develop the country through a capitalist approach had failed. The achievements were not good enough; the troubles which resulted were too serious. Always a believer in socialism, Nkrumah now turned to socialist methods. Through its government, Ghana would control its own economic destiny. It would now wipe out the neo-colonialist control of its economic life and make it fully free. Moreover, a socialist approach meant that Ghana's economic progress would benefit all its citizens.

Rather than become a country in which the few would be very rich while the masses wallowed in poverty, Ghana would grow into a country in which all citizens would have equal opportunities to develop to the best of their abilities and earn respectable standards of living. A visit by Dr Nkrumah in 1961 to the Soviet Union, where he saw socialist planning at work and was promised considerable Soviet assistance, strengthened his faith further in the new approach. But he was not going merely to imitate the Soviet Union; instead he would draw the principles of his own socialist planning from the peculiar African conditions of Ghana. In 1961, therefore, Ghana was asked to get ready for the second revolution in its history – a revolution based on the principles of African socialism.

The Five-Year Development Plan (1959–64) was abandoned. In July 1962, the CPP adopted Dr Nkrumah's proposal of a new party programme – a 'Plan for Work and Happiness' – which declared socialism to be the objective of all future economic development in Ghana. Then in March 1963, the new official socialist plan, the Seven-Year Development Plan 1963–70, was adopted by the Ghana parliament.

The ultimate aim was to achieve a full socialist state in Ghana in twenty years. State control would be gradually established over the economy, but not by nationalising existing private enterprises. Rather, the government would greatly increase the rate of its investments in industries and other enterprises so as gradually to surpass all private investments, foreign and indigenous put together. For the time being, the government would continue to welcome private investments in certain areas of the economy; foreign investors would be required to re-invest a good part of their profits. But certain industries would be reserved only for state investment. These would be so well run that they would make good profits which would be used to establish other state industries.

The plan thus envisaged a huge increase in the government's investment in productive enterprises – some £190 million a year. This should have meant that expenditure on building public facilities and providing social services would be reduced because, in a poor country like Ghana, not much money would be left. However, Dr Nkrumah was determined not to reduce such expenditure but considerably to increase it. So the plan also provided for vastly increased expenditure on the building and maintaining of roads, schools, hospitals, and communications services.

How was Ghana to find the money? The plan envisaged that much of it would come from direct and indirect taxes, from the profits made by its industries and other enterprises, and from the profits of the Cocoa Marketing Board. The people would be encouraged to live frugally and save more of their personal incomes. But much money would also come from external aid. Ghana expected to get substantial aids from the East, but she also hoped to continue to receive aid from the West, mostly in the form of loans.

Having thus laid his plan, Nkrumah went to work. To introduce more new crops and modernise agricultural methods, tools and practices, state farms were set up which would show the farmers how to change their methods and tools. In 1963, a State Farms Corporation was established, which by 1966 had 135 state farms employing about 21,000 farm labourers. At the same time there were 34 Workers' Brigade farms to spread improved agricultural methods. The government decided to buy other crops from the farmers in the same way that the Marketing Board had been buying cocoa since colonial times. The Cocoa Marketing Board was therefore given power to buy, not only cocoa, but also groundnuts, bananas, palm oil. Finally, an attempt was made to form the farmers into co-operative movements. Each co-operative was required to become a member of the United Ghana Farmers' Council.

Meanwhile, the government had pursued its policy of building industries. The giant Volta Dam was completed to supply cheap electricity to the whole of Ghana. Completed also were the port of Tema and Tema Township with facilities for the greatest industrial area in West Africa. In Accra and other centres, industries of all types sprang up. By 1966, there were 64 state industries, and many private industries. A State Enterprises Secretariat was set up to co-ordinate the management of the state industries.

The state also went into commerce. The large import and retail company of Leventis was bought and made the foundation of a National Trading Corporation. The volume and variety of goods manufactured inside Ghana grew very rapidly. To reduce the commercial dependence on Britain, trade with Eastern countries was greatly increased. Regulations controlled the sale of some goods and fixed the prices of others. An import licence system enabled the government to control imports and foreign exchange.

Social welfare developments were also continued. More clinics and hospitals were built. In 1963, school books were made free for all children. By 1965 Ghana had three universities.

Unfortunately, however, the system did not work out as successfully as was hoped. The state made reasonable profits on its commercial ventures, but not in agriculture and industries. The state farms were managed very inefficiently, and by the end of 1965 were running at a total loss of £17 million. Of the industries, more made losses than made profits. The heaviest losses were recorded by the Mining Corporation and the Ghana Airways.

There were many causes for this unhappy state of affairs. One was lack of faith in the new programme by most of the top civil servants and other leading citizens. Another was lack of experience. For instance, most of the persons employed in the state farms were not experienced agriculturists, managers and farm hands. Most were persons employed simply because they had basic education, or were enthusiastic about the farm projects, or were loyal to the party, or had no other jobs. Very often politicians forced the managers to employ their friends or relations. Ultimately because of lack of knowledge and experience, morale fell. Thus it was common for the crops of the state farms to waste away unharvested, or to be stolen. Many of the industries invested far more capital or employed more workers than were really needed. The co-ordination done by the State Enterprises Secretariat was very poor, and there was therefore duplication and waste, especially in purchasing. Finally, the private enterprises contributed immensely to the failure of the state enterprises. The big colonial companies especially were so well established and so powerful that they found no difficulty in sabotaging the state enterprises that now tried to compete with them. They bribed the managers of the state enterprises, evaded the import control and foreign exchange control regulations, and thereby continued to make big profits while the state enterprises made big losses.

The failure of the state enterprises was particularly serious because the money for establishing them was largely borrowed from abroad. The hope that more money would be realised from the export of cocoa was extinguished by the continued fall in the price of cocoa in the world market. Revenue from indirect taxes was increased by greatly raising the customs duties on imports like cloths, vegetables, fish, coffee, tea and tobacco. In 1961, the government's decision to deduct 5% as compulsory savings from the salaries of all persons earning £150 and above, led to a general strike when the deductions started in September. Ghana received some foreign aid towards the implementation of her new policy, but most of the money from external sources came as loans. From 1961 to 1966, the nation's foreign debts rose from $16.3 million to $395 million.

Inevitably, all these developments began to affect the masses of the people. Ghana's small traders and importers, the market women, saw their small business gradually wiped out by the new regulations. The market women, who had always supported Nkrumah, gradually turned against him. Also, the inefficiency of the new food purchasing and distribution system discouraged farmers, thereby depressing food production, and disrupting the supply of the available food to the towns. By 1965, Ghana was faced with drastic shortage of food. Food became very expensive in the towns, making life difficult for the urban population. Moreover, the supply of imported consumer goods – milk, shoes, sugar etc. – became inadequate.

While the hardships of the people grew worse, many of the national leaders made themselves very rich through all sorts of corrupt practices, and showed off their ill-gotten wealth before the people. Moreover, the government made the situation worse by indulging in fantastic expenditures on prestige projects like 'Job 600'.

Political developments

Ghana attained independence under a unitary constitution. The various opposition parties had attempted without success in the last three years before independence to make the country a federation. The main opposition parties were the National Liberation Movement (NLM), the Northern Peoples' Party (NPP) and the Togoland Congress (TC), all founded about 1954 to defend the interests of particular ethnic groups.

The NLM represented the Asante of central Ghana, the largest single ethnic group in Ghana and the chief producers of Ghana's leading export crop, cocoa. The party advocated federation to enable the Asante to manage much of their own affairs. It was also committed to defending the interests of the Asante cocoa farmers. In fact, the immediate reason for the founding of the party in 1954 was the decision of the Nkrumah Government not to increase further the price paid to cocoa farmers, although cocoa prices were at that time increasing in the world market. The government planned to use the surplus to finance national development, but the NLM argued that this was tantamount to making the Asante people the beasts of burden for national development. A federation, the NLM hoped, would remove the central government's control over cocoa.

The NPP also supported federation so that the people of the northern territories, whom it represented, would be able to have local autonomy. But the intention of the TC was different. It represented the Ewe people of the far eastern provinces of Ghana, who were ethnically the same as most of the people of neighbouring French Togoland. The Ewe of Ghana, who were great cocoa farmers, saw that the Togolese farmers earned much higher prices for their cocoa than they did, because Togolese cocoa was subsidised by France. The aim of the TC, therefore, was to break the Ewe territory completely from Ghana and merge it with Togoland.

At independence, the political atmosphere of Ghana was seriously poisoned by all this sectionalism and tribalism. The CPP stood out as the defender of national unity, using propaganda which appealed to nationalist sentiment and ridiculed members of the opposition as backward-looking tribalists. Even before independence, political violence had become common. In the pre-independence elections, the chiefs in the opposition areas, who overwhelmingly supported the opposition parties, used their power to prevent the CPP supporters, usually the young educated elements, from holding meetings and rallies. In Asante, the NLM organised armed bands to intimidate villages supporting the CPP, and the CPP sent in its own bands of armed men, called Action Troopers. At independence, riots broke out in many towns in the Ewe area, riots so serious that the army had to be sent in.

Once in complete control after independence, the CPP began to use its power against its opponents. Official pressure was brought to bear on the chiefs to weaken their support for the opposition. Some of the most unfriendly chiefs were deposed or arrested. Government jobs and government influence were used to promote CPP members and supporters. The Asante province was weakened by being split into two. Inducements were offered to the opposition members of parliament to 'cross the carpet', and the strength of the opposition in parliament was thereby gradually reduced.

Ultimately, the government began to pass laws to increase its powers to deal with the opposition. A law of November 1957 made local and ethnic parties illegal and made tribalism a criminal offence. This law forced all the opposition parties to dissolve, but their leaders immediately came together and founded a single national opposition party – the United Party – under the leadership of Dr Busia, until then the leader of the NLM. In the same year, a Deportation Act was passed, giving the government power to deport undesirable aliens. Then in 1958 came the Preventive Detention Act giving the government power to detain a person for five years without any trial and without even being accused of any specific offence. Other laws made the penalties for treason and sedition more stringent, and made it a serious offence for any Ghanaian to make false statements capable of injuring the reputation of the nation.

These laws steadily demolished the opposition. Many opposition politicians were clamped into detention. Dr Busia fled into exile abroad and ultimately lost his parliamentary seat. By 1960, the opposition was hardly a force to be reckoned with. Between 1957 and 1960, the number of opposition parliamentarians fell from 27 to eight. On July 1, 1960, Ghana was made a republic with Dr Nkrumah as President; and in January 1964 Ghana was made officially a one-party state, with the CPP as the only party.

By this time, however, cracks had occurred in the CPP itself. Until 1961, the CPP had stood strong and united against all its opponents. But the change in economic policy in 1961–2 caused serious differences in the party. Some of Nkrumah's top colleagues, like Komla Gbedemah, Minister of Finance since independence, were not enthusiastic about, or were even opposed to, the new economic philosophy. Then, in accordance with the new socialist philosophy, Dr Nkrumah put a limit on how much property the party and government leaders were allowed to have, and each leader was called upon to surrender everything above that limit. The more radical elements became the most powerful elements within the party, pushing out the former front-line leaders, who were now regarded as 'conservative' or 'reactionary'. In October 1961, six ministers, including Gbedemah, were asked to resign, and six others were publicly asked to give up their excess belongings. The powers of repression which the government had built up in the years since 1957 were now being turned against its own leaders. Gbedemah fled into exile abroad.

Then, in August and September 1962, two attempts were made on the life of Dr Nkrumah. Suspicion immediately fell on three ministers – Ako Adjei, Kofi Crabbe and Tawai Adamafio. These three, with two other suspects were brought to trial, but the three ministers were acquitted for lack of evidence. Party loyalists raised an outcry against the verdict and Nkrumah nullified the decision of the court, had the ministers re-arrested and retried by a judge appointed by himself. They were found guilty and sentenced to death, although Nkrumah later commuted their sentences to long prison terms. Meanwhile, more attempts were made on Nkrumah's life.

From then on, Dr Nkrumah withdrew from the public and surrounded himself more and more with yes-men and flatterers who deceived him about the conditions of the country and the mood of the people. And, as a result of the economic hardship which the people suffered and the growing political instability in the country, the people became more and more alienated from him and his government. In February 1966, while Dr Nkrumah was on a visit to Asia, the army and police moved in and seized power, to the great rejoicing of the people.

From Asia, Dr Nkrumah flew to Guinea where he was royally welcomed by President Sekou Toure and proclaimed co-President of Guinea. In April 1972 Dr Nkrumah died in an Eastern European hospital, widely mourned in Africa as a great champion of African freedom and African unity.

Ghana after Nkrumah

The military government which took over in February 1966 inherited many serious problems. Most important, it had to re-establish the people's confidence in the government, and to try to revive the economy. Various commissions of enquiry were set up to investigate the widespread suspicions of corruption against the former ministers and government functionaries. The most serious economic problem was the national debt: the loans which the Nkrumah Government had borrowed abroad. Since the economy was very weak and imports continued to be greater than exports, the military regime could find no solution. Cocoa, too, was still doing poorly in the world market. Some of the state industries which were performing poorly were sold to private businessmen, but this hardly touched the economic problem. Indeed, the foreign debt increased.

In one area, however, the military regime performed creditably. Within as short a time as possible, it supervised the drawing up of a new constitution. In 1969, it supervised parliamentary elections under the new constitution and then handed over to a popularly elected civilian government. Dr K. A. Busia, who had returned from exile after the overthrow of Dr Nkrumah, became Prime Minister. He came to power with a lot of popular support and good will. His Progress Party (PP) won 105 seats in the 140-seat assembly. But his regime was short-lived.

After he was overthrown in January 1972, many explanations were given for his removal – including allegations that his government had been corrupt, and that his policies and actions had intensified 'tribalism' in the country. Available evidence suggests that there was considerable truth in these allegations. Almost as soon as Busia came to power, the public began to hear about innumerable corrupt practices by the PP ministers. The fact that the ministers soon began to compete with one another in buying expensive new cars, building expensive houses and establishing businesses made the public believe the stories, and a growing number of Ghanaians soon began to say that the new civilian rulers were no less corrupt than Nkrumah's ministers. At the same time, the feeling grew that Dr Busia, as an Asante, was using his power to favour the Asante unduly in the civil service, the army and other branches of government, while discriminating against the smaller ethnic groups, especially the Ewe.

The major cause of Busia's fall, however, was his inept performance as a leader. It was soon obvious to all that he had little or no control over some of his ministers. His lack of ability to take firm decisions was clearly demonstrated by his actions on the question of apartheid in South Africa. He started by supporting the idea that independent African countries should begin to have dialogue with the South African Government, but his view on the question was publicly changed (for and against) not less than five times after this by his spokesmen.

In Africa at large, his regime progressively became unpopular. He offended African nationalist feelings everywhere by his views on apartheid. And he made his reputation much worse still by expelling the citizens of other African countries from Ghana.

At home, he took many clumsy steps that offended the army leaders; for instance, his government publicly vilified two leading army officers and had another publicly tried on a charge of stealing. Then the government's decision to cut down the budgets of the armed forces spread disenchantment to the rank and file of the army.

No doubt the economic problems Busia inherited were immense. Internally, the economy was still badly dislocated; abroad the foreign debt was a nightmare; and among the masses of the people, expectations were very high. But Busia proved incapable of deciding upon, and pursuing, any clear course of action that could inspire public confidence. About the national debt he never had any clear policy, and the nation watched in confusion, nervousness and disgust as the Prime Minister and his top men went about holding endless unproductive meetings with Ghana's creditors. Among the cocoa farmers, disappointment about the falling prices of cocoa was turned into outright hostility to the government by changes in the operation of the Cocoa Marketing Board. The practice had always been that the Board supplied money to the cocoa-buying agents at the beginning of each cocoa season so that the agents could pay the farmers when the farmers delivered their cocoa at the stores. But under the new system the Board would no longer supply the buying agents with money in advance. This meant that the agents could not pay the farmers until they had actually sold the graded cocoa to the Board. Naturally, the delay created a lot of hardship for the farmers and turned them against the government.

Meanwhile, between the government and the trade unions, an outright confrontation developed. The main cause of this was Busia's attempt to control the Trade Union Congress (TUC) by forcing it to accept officers selected by the PP. When the TUC refused to accept the PP-selected officers and elected its own independent officers, Busia declared war on the TUC, accused it of being an agent of Nkrumah's CPP, and proposed a law to disband it. The workers went on strike, but hundreds of them were arrested or dismissed from their jobs, and the TUC was disbanded. The hostility of the farmers was a little thing compared with the hostility that now grew among urban workers.

By 1971, Ghanaians had become so disillusioned with the Busia Government that many began openly to express their desire to have Dr Nkrumah back in power. By mid-1971, the threat of Nkrumah's new popularity had grown so much that Busia had to adopt stern measures to stop talks about Nkrumah and the sale of Nkrumah's photographs.

The final blow to the reputation of the Busia Government was its decision in December 1971 to devalue the cedi, the national currency, by 44%. No doubt, some devaluation was necessary; and a devaluation of between 20% and 25% was urged by the experts as well as by Ghana's foreign creditors. The drastic 44% devaluation dampened the spirits of the nation and caused widespread consternation and fall of morale. A month later, the army, under Colonel I. K. Acheampong, took over.

12 Nigeria

Nigeria went through a decade of responsible government before independence. From 1951, popularly elected governments managed the affairs of the nation, under supervision of the colonial officials. Gradually this supervision lessened as a result of nationalist pressure. Finally, on 1 October 1960, Nigeria became independent.

By 1951, thanks to the constitutional measures taken in the late 1940s, Nigeria was already a federation, with three members, called regions – the Northern Region, the Eastern Region and the Western Region. In 1963 the Midwest Region was carved out of the Western Region. Then in a major restructuring of the federation in 1967 twelve states were created to replace the four regions.

Economic developments
Economically, Nigeria has made immense progress since 1951. It was then a typically underdeveloped country, depending heavily upon a few cash crops – cocoa, palm oil, palm kernels and groundnuts – and a few minerals, notably tin. Cocoa was the great foreign exchange

earner. Practically all the import trade, and most of the export trade, was controlled by a few giant European companies. The three great companies – United Africa Company (UAC, a member of the Unilever Group of companies), Compagnie Française de l'Afrique Occidentale (CFAO), and Société Commerciale de l'Ouest Africain (SCOA) – controlled most of Nigeria's commerce. Most of the rest was in the hands of the Syrians and Lebanese. There were hardly any manufacturing industries. Foreign businesses also controlled all banking and insurance, as well as a substantial part of the transportation trade. Very few, if any, Nigerians were employed by the foreign businesses in any responsible position and therefore hadn't had any experience in the running of big business. Beyond the main centres of British administration – Lagos, Ibadan, Kaduna and Enugu – very few towns had electricity or pipe-borne water. Schools were few, much fewer in the Northern Region than the other two regions. Tarred roads were rare, and large areas of the country were without roads altogether.

However, Nigeria had great potentialities. The most thickly populated country in Africa with territory spanning forest and grassland latitudes, Nigeria had the potential ability to produce a great variety of agricultural crops. Its abundant mineral and forest resources were mostly still untapped. Its people were reputed to be industrious and ambitious.

From 1951 on, with Nigerians managing more and more of their own affairs, these potentialities began to be transformed into actual development. In comparison with Ghana, Nigeria has experienced little discussion of, and less experimentation with, ideologies of development. In the years immediately after independence, two of the largest political parties, the Action Group (AG) and the National Council of Nigerian Citizens (NCNC) began to advocate different brands of socialism. The AG advocated Democratic Socialism and the NCNC Pragmatic Socialism. But both appeared to want the rapid increase of indigenous participation in the economy so as to free the economy from foreign control. Both were therefore anxious to encourage not only state enterprise but also indigenous private enterprise. To weaken foreign control quickly, the AG also wanted the nationalisation of certain important industries – e.g. banking and insurance – over which foreign control was very strong. But most of the leaders of the nation opposed the idea, saying that talk of nationalisation would only scare away the foreign investors whom the country needed to attract. When a group of young NCNC leaders issued a statement demanding the nationalisation of a wide range of enterprises, most of the top national leaders repudiated the statement and assured the foreign businesses that nationalisation would never take place in Nigeria.

This does not mean, however, that the governments of Nigeria left economic development wholly to private enterprise. To do so, since very few Nigerians had any capital or business experience, would have been to hand Nigeria over entirely to foreign capitalists. The governments of Nigeria have invested substantial amounts in productive ventures. In the first place, they inherited certain businesses from the colonial government: the Railway Corporation, the Coal Corporation, the Electricity Corporation, the Produce Marketing Boards. Nigeria's share in the old British West Africa Airways was constituted into a federal government corporation – the Nigeria Airways. All these were developed into huge state monopolies representing an enormous volume of investment.

In the second place, soon after 1951 the governments began to invest money into new enterprises. Each of the regions created a Development Corporation charged with channelling the government's investment into viable industrial and agricultural projects. State-owned industries and agricultural establishments sprang up all over the country. Some of the ventures were owned entirely by the state; but others, especially the processing industries, were established in partnership with foreign private capitalists. The volume of state investment steadily increased over the years, creating housing estate companies, banking and insurance companies, a national shipping line, inland transportation companies, hotels, commercial television and radio broadcasting companies, agricultural estates, and a wide range of processing industries. Of the state enterprises one of the biggest is the Kainji Dam and hydro-electric establishment on the River Niger put up at a cost of over £90 million to supply electricity to the whole country. An iron and steel industry is planned too.

A certain amount of co-operative enterprise has also been fostered by the governments. For instance, in the Western Region a farm settlement project was started in the 1950s in the hope that the educated young men attracted to these settlements would become the pioneers of a new generation of co-operative farmers, using modern agricultural tools and techniques and marketing their crops co-operatively. Small consumer co-operatives were also started in different parts of the country, as well as produce marketing co-operatives for the producers of cash crops such as cocoa.

There has been considerable investment by private businesses, mostly from other countries. By adopting tax policies and other measures favourable to foreign investors, the Nigerian governments have attracted a lot of foreign capital. Because of its great economic potentialities, Nigeria has been, to foreign investors, one of the most attractive countries in West Africa. Even so, the influx of foreign capital has never been as large as the governments have hoped. For instance, in the first Development Plan drawn up after independence, most of the planned investment capital was expected to come from external sources, but only a small part was received.

Nevertheless, foreign capital has played a very important part in the industrialisation of Nigeria. Some of this was invested in partnership with the governments and some independently. The old colonial companies have shifted part of their capital away from commerce to processing. Probably most of the incoming foreign capital has gone into the petroleum industry, perhaps the most spectacular development in Nigeria's recent economic history. Started in the 1950s, petroleum mining grew rapidly in the 1960s and by 1970, Nigeria was one of the ten greatest producers of crude petroleum in the world. This petroleum boom came at a time when the nation's greatest foreign exchange earner, cocoa, was rapidly collapsing in the world market, and so saved Nigeria from Ghana's experience of large and persistent foreign trade deficits. Because Nigeria lacks the capital and technical know-how, the oil industry has been developed entirely by foreign capital and foreign expertise. However, about 1971, some indigenous participation in the oil industry began.

Private indigenous participation in the industrialisation of Nigeria has steadily increased over the years. Ever since Nigerians began to manage much of their own affairs in 1951, the governments of Nigeria have encouraged indigenous private enterprise through government contracts and loans, favourable laws and regulations limiting the number of expatriate staff the foreign companies can employ. An industrial Development Bank has also been created to foster industrialisation, the government making sure that an increasing percentage of its loans for starting businesses go to Nigerians.

At first, almost all the growing indigenous investment went into businesses like commerce, transportation and the building trade. But increasingly, Nigerians have been going into processing too. The shortage of consumer goods during the Nigerian civil war (1967–70) prompted many Nigerians to go into big export-import businesses as well as small-scale processing industries. The trend has continued after the war, producing by 1972–3 what might truly be called an indigenous business boom. In 1972, this development encouraged the Nigerian Federal Government to pass a law defining the areas of the economy where foreign investment would be allowed or not allowed.

Roughly, the law classified the whole economy into three categories: businesses in which only indigenous investment would be allowed; businesses in which foreign investment would be allowed only in partnership with indigenous investment; and businesses in which foreign investment could operate without restriction. This law came into full force in 1974. By 1973, it was already influencing many of the big foreign companies to sell their shares to Nigerians for the first time, or even to sell their businesses outright.

The Nigerian economy, therefore, is 'mixed'; state enterprise exists side by side with co-operative enterprise, with foreign private enterprise, and with indigenous private enterprise. The combination of all these enterprises has led to considerably rapid economic growth for Nigeria – one of the most rapid in Africa. Since 1951, the economy has been growing at rates ranging between 7% and 9%, producing a rapidly growing volume and variety of made-in-Nigeria goods: textiles, shoes, tyres, cement, aluminium goods, building materials, beers, soft drinks, canned fruits, vegetables and meat, vegetable oils, soaps, cocoa products, electronic equipments, furniture and carpets.

Many of the state ventures have not done too well, for basically the same reasons as in Ghana: inexperience of the officers and interference by politicians, resulting in the investment of too much capital, the employment of too many people (a lot of whom are unsuitable), poor co-ordination, and waste. The businesses established jointly by state and private capital have generally done much better. A recent survey of the agricultural and industrial projects of the Western Nigeria Development Corporation showed that many of them, far from making profits, were a constant drain on the funds raised by the Western State Government from other sources.

Another weakness of the Nigerian economy is that comparatively too little attention has been paid to agriculture. Most of the attention given to agriculture – such as research and the encouragement of improved techniques and tools – has been given to the few cash crops (cocoa, palm produce, groundnuts) which are important to the governments because they earn foreign exchange. For instance, though the price of cocoa has continued to suffer seriously in the world market, by 1974 much effort was still devoted to encouraging farmers to expand cocoa acreage. Only a few new food crops have been deliberately encouraged, for instance, rice in southern Nigeria and cane sugar on the Niger valley. In parts of the north, too, some of the state governments have dammed rivers to provide farmers with water to irrigate their farms. But on the whole, the tools and methods of farming have remained unchanged. One major consequence of the poor conditions of rural life is that the educated youths of the rural areas have been migrating to the urban centres at a rate far beyond the capacity of the urban centres to provide them with jobs. Urban unemployment has therefore risen to alarming proportions.

In the provision of public amenities, Nigeria has made much progress since 1951. Education has taken more than 25% of the annual budget of every government. Primary and secondary schools have sprung up in most parts of the country. In 1956, primary education was made free in the Western Region. Because the Northern Region started from a weaker foundation than the Eastern and Western Regions in 1951, educational development has been less advanced in the north; at independence in 1960, the north, with about half the population of the country, had only 41 of the nation's 883 secondary schools. However, progress has been much faster since independence, and particularly since the creation of more states in the north in 1967. Nigeria has greatly expanded post-secondary education. Between 1960 and 1972, the number of universities increased from one to six. Between 1951 and 1972, the total mileage of tarred roads was multiplied many times; so were the numbers of hospitals and clinics, and the number of communities supplied with clean pipe-borne water.

Political developments
All this economic and social progress took place against a political background which was far from happy. The major trouble was the growth of regional and ethnic rivalries and antagonisms. As a result of British policy, by 1951 the North and the South had had very little political contact with each other. Naturally, lack of knowledge of each other bred fears. Because the Northern Region had received far less education than the two Southern Regions it had produced far fewer educated leaders. This increased northern suspicions and fears of the South. On the other hand, as the population of the Northern Region was bigger than the two Southern Regions (East and West) put together, the North had an advantage over the South in the struggle for control of the central government, since the rule was 'one man one vote'. Not only was the South hostile to the North, but the East and West were also rivals, each believing itself to be the most advanced in the country and suspecting the other of manoeuvring to take an unfairly large share of the 'national cake'.

The formation of political parties reinforced these antagonisms. In the last years of the Second World War, it had seemed as if a single party, uniting all Nigerians, might emerge. But by the time the first elections were held in 1951–2 to the Federal and Regional legislatures, three main parties had emerged – the National Council of Nigeria and Cameroons, later changed to National Council of Nigerian Citizens (NCNC), the Action Group (AG) and the Northern People's Congress (NPC). The three parties were based in the three Regions. The NPC was exclusively a party of the North; the NCNC was a party of the East, although it had a considerable following in the West and North; the AG was a party of the West, although it later had considerable following in the North and East.

None of the Regions, however, was a homogeneous entity. Each was made up of one large ethnic group and a number of small ethnic groups, and between the major group and the small groups, there was intense rivalry and hostility. In the North, the major ethnic group was the Hausa-Fulani, sharing the Region with the Kanuri of the Lake Chad area, and the large collection of small ethnic groups in the Niger-Benue valley called commonly the Middle Belt peoples. In the West, the Yoruba were the major ethnic group; to their south-east were the many ethnic groups collectively called the Mid-west peoples. In the East, the Ibo were the major ethnic group; to their south were many other peoples often referred to in politics as COR peoples (Calabar, Ogoja and Rivers peoples).

Politics within each region was usually a very tense affair. The majority ethnic group dominated the ruling party – the Yoruba the AG, the Hausa-Fulani the NPC, and the Ibo the NCNC. Among the small or minority ethnic groups there was usually a lot of bitterness, caused by the complaint that the powers of the regional government were being used to give an unfairly large share of the new developments – schools, hospitals, roads, state appointments – to the majority ethnic group. Ultimately, the minority peoples began to demand a separate region of their own. So intense did their complaints become that a Minorities Commission was set up in 1957 to investigate their fears. Though the Commission admitted that the fears expressed by the minorities were well founded, it did not recommend the creation of new regions. And so Nigeria went into independence with three regions. But the complaints of the minorities never really diminished. In the Middle Belt area of the Northern Region, it produced violent revolts against the regional government.

Meanwhile, politics at the national level had established its own pattern. Each of the three big parties was ambitious to win the elections to the federal parliament and control the federal government. To achieve this, the NPC tried to win all the seats in the North – but never succeeded in doing so. The NCNC and AG each tried to win seats outside its base region, usually by exploiting the grievances of the minorities in other people's regions. In this way, the NCNC became very strong in the Mid-west area of the Western Region, and the AG became strong in the Middle Belt area of the Northern Region and, to a lesser extent, in the COR area of the Eastern Region. The exploitation of the minorities' grievances in each other's regions, however, only increased the hostilities between the big parties.

The NPC always won the largest number of seats in the federal elections. But since no party ever won an absolute majority, some sort of alliance had to be entered into in order to form the federal government. In the consequent political manoeuvrings each party endeavoured to put members of its own ethnic group in such important national positions as would enable the group to get a good share of the 'national cake'. Principles hardly came into it. In such circumstances, a rivalry between two prominent men for an important national job usually became a major dispute between their two ethnic groups, a dispute which would echo loudly through the political parties.

Finally, corruption and nepotism were very common. People in important positions used such positions to enrich themselves and advance their relatives. Leaders in power all over the country were very intolerant of opposition and criticism and did everything to stamp out opposition – everything from bribes to false arrests, imprisonment and other forms of legal harassment. The common experience of parliamentary oppositions after independence was for their numbers to dwindle as their members 'crossed the carpet' to the government benches. Violence became part of the national political tradition.

Such conditions were bound sooner or later to lead to a major crisis, and from 1962 on they did. At that date, the NPC and NCNC were in control of the federal government, having formed an alliance after the pre-independence election of late 1959. The AG was in opposition in the federal parliament. Dr Nnamdi Azikiwe, until 1960 leader of the NCNC, was national President; Sir Abubakar Tafawa Balewa, deputy leader of the NPC, was Prime Minister; and Chief Obafemi Awolowo, leader of the AG, was the Leader of the Opposition. In the Regions, the AG was in power in the West, under Chief S. L. Akintola, deputy leader of the AG, as Premier. Chief Akintola's government was confronted by a fairly strong NCNC opposition. In the North, the NPC was in power, with Sir Ahmadu Bello, leader of the NPC, as Premier. And in the East, the NCNC was in power with Dr Michael Okpara, Dr Azikiwe's successor as leader of the NCNC, as Premier.

The crisis started as an internal rift in the AG, splitting the party into two factions, one supporting Chief Awolowo, and the other supporting Chief Akintola. In May 1962, the rift led to physical violence among parliamentarians on the floor of the Western House of Assembly, the regional legislature. Thereupon, the federal government announced that law and order had broken down in the West, declared a state of emergency over the region, suspended its government and legislature, and appointed an administrator to manage its affairs. Leading Western politicians, including Chief Awolowo and Chief Akintola, were restricted. Chief Akintola ultimately formed his supporters into a separate party, the United People's Party (UPP).

When the emergency expired, Chief Akintola was returned to his position as Premier in January 1963. Meanwhile, the NCNC-NPC allies in the federal government had begun to use the Western crisis as a means of destroying the AG opposition to their government. The NCNC parliamentary opposition in the West was asked to support Chief Akintola, and a UPP-NCNC alliance was thus formed to rule the West. Chief Awolowo and some of his leading supporters were arrested, brought to trial on charges of plotting to use force to overthrow the federal government, and sentenced to varying terms of imprisonment.

Meanwhile, a major constitutional development took place. The Mid-west part of the Western Region was carved off and made into the Mid-West Region.

Soon the NPC-NCNC alliance began to break down. When it was formed in 1959 most people had expected that the NCNC, having more educated and more experienced politicians than the NPC, would be the dominant partner, in spite of the numerical superiority of the NPC. Things did not work out that way. Though less formally educated, the NPC men proved extremely able politicians. By 1963, there was no doubt that the NPC was master of the alliance. The NCNC men were becoming disillusioned and dissatisfied. Moreover, it was becoming obvious that it was the NPC, and not the NCNC, that was really benefiting from the developments in the West. Chief Akintola leaned more towards the NPC, and it gradually became obvious that his UPP was becoming a means of establishing NPC influence in the South. The NCNC was becoming alarmed.

This was the mood of the alliance when the national census was conducted late in 1963. Most southerners had expected that the results would show that the North in reality had a smaller population than the South, and thereby terminate the North's numerical superiority in the federal parliament. But the results confirmed that the North had a bigger population. This led to an uproar in the South, with many prominent people, among them leaders of the NCNC, charging that the census figures were rigged. The NPC-NCNC alliance cracked right open.

In 1964, the final break came. In the first half of that year, Chief Akintola succeeded in persuading most of the NCNC leaders in the West to join forces with him to form a brand new party – the Nigeria National Democratic Party (NNDP) – to control the West. With the announcement of the formation of the NNDP, the NCNC lost most of its Western leaders and a good proportion of its Western rank-and-file support. A dramatic political realignment now took place, with the NPC and NNDP pulling together, and the NCNC and the AG (which had remained remarkably popular among the ordinary people in the West) pulling together. As the federal election of December 1964 approached, two hostile national alliances of parties confronted each other – the Nigeria National Alliance (NNA) formed by the NPC and NNDP, and the United Progressive Grand Alliance (UPGA) formed by the NCNC and AG.

The election campaign of that year was a rough and violent affair. Candidates were kidnapped and spirited away, and their opponents were then declared returned unopposed. Violence erupted everywhere. The UPGA charged that the NNA was rigging the election. The President, Dr Azikiwe, asked that in view of the terrible happenings, the election be postponed, but the NNA insisted it must go on. The UPGA then decided to boycott it. But in the North where the NPC was in power, the election went on, and the NPC carried off practically all seats. In the West, where the NNDP was in power, the election also creaked through, in spite of determined and violent opposition by the UPGA. With the UPGA people not voting, the NNDP won the majority of Western seats. In the Mid-West, the Premier, though an NCNC man, changed his mind at mid-day and ordered the election to go on. It was therefore only in the East that no voting took place. The NNA won an overall majority.

But that was not the end of the crisis. The President announced that he could not, on the basis of such an election, call anybody to form the government. And so, for a few days, the nation swayed on the brink of total ruin. However, a compromise was ultimately reached by which the NNA agreed to include some NCNC men in the government after the elections were held in the East. This compromise could not last. There was no love lost between the NNA and the NCNC.

Meanwhile, a much bigger crisis was approaching. 1965 was the year in which the life of the legislature of the Western Region would expire. Chief Akintola had to dissolve the legislature and call for a new election. The campaign that ensued was the worst in Nigeria's history. From all indications, it seemed that the UPGA (or even the AG alone) had enough popular support to win the election. But it was also obvious that the NNDP was not going to give up so easily. Some NNDP leaders publicly stated that their party would win, with or without the people's support. As the election day (October 11) approached, strange and terrible things began to happen. Some electoral officers issued nomination papers to some candidates and then vanished, to avoid issuing papers to other candidates. Candidates and electoral officers were kidnapped. In this way, some NNDP candidates were declared returned unopposed, but the UPGA still hoped that popular support would carry them through to victory.

Probably nobody will ever be able to penetrate the strange happenings of October 11–12 to arrive at the true results of the election. Both sides claimed victory, but since the NNDP claim was backed by the official channels, the NNDP went on to form the government. Unprecedented violence then erupted almost all over the region against the persons and property of NNDP members and supporters, as well as against the institutions of government. Hundreds of people were killed. The police and army were massively drafted to the West to no avail. By January 1966 probably most parts of the Western Region were beyond the control of the Regional Government.

In the early hours of 15 January 1966, the army took action. The Prime Minister, Sir Abubakar Tafewa Balewa, the Premier of the West, Chief Akintola, and the Premier of the North, Sir Ahmadu Bello, were killed. So were a number of leading military officers. The planners of the *coup d'état* were young officers, many of them university graduates. Although they failed to seize power completely, they caused enough disruption to make the continuation of the civilian government impossible. The remaining federal ministers therefore handed over to the loyal section of the army, under the leadership of Major-General Aguiyi Ironsi, commanding officer of the Nigerian army.

Ironsi became Head of the Federal Military Government, and military governors were appointed to head the regional governments. Most Nigerians, North and South, welcomed the overthrow of the politicians. But Nigeria's troubles were not as yet at an end. There were many factors contributing to a new growth of inter-ethnic tension, chiefly General Ironsi's attempt to replace the federal government with a more strongly centralised one. The name 'Regions' was scrapped, and each region became simply a 'group of provinces'. Then a law was made to unify the top levels of all the civil services of the country. People who shared the view that a unitary set-up would be the best for Nigeria hailed these changes. But events soon showed that the regional system and regional interests were too strong to be thus abolished. In particular, since the North still had far fewer highly educated people than the South, the attempt to unify the top levels of the civil services appeared to be an attempt to flood the Northern civil service with Southerners – especially with Ibos, General Ironsi himself being an Ibo. Increasingly commonly, the January coup came to be described as an Ibo coup.

At the end of May, following the law unifying the civil services, violence broke out in some Northern towns against Ibo people living there. Then in July, another group of military leaders, mostly of Northern origin, toppled General Ironsi. The second coup brought Lieutenant-Colonel (later General) Yakubu Gowon to power as Head of the Federal Military Government.

By then, however, the nation had travelled very far along the road to division. In an attempt to revive the spirit of unity, the new government released political prisoners and called representatives of all regions together to discuss a new constitution. But late in September, while the constitutional talks were in progress in Lagos, the national capital, another and more terrible round of violence erupted against Ibos in parts of the North. As a result, the Ibos began to flee from all parts of Nigeria into their own region of origin. The constitutional talks broke off.

The military governor of the East, Colonel Odumegwu Ojukwu, who had neither reconciled himself to the events of the July coup nor recognised General Gowon as Head of the Federal Military Government, now called upon all Ibos to return to the East as Ibos were not wanted in Nigeria. He also asked non-easterners living in the East to leave. The country was obviously disintegrating. All attempts to reverse the situation through talks and conferences failed. Finally, in May 1967, Colonel Ojukwu declared the East to be no longer part of Nigeria but a separate country with the name Biafra.

The Federal Military Government immediately mobilised the army to stamp out the secession. The Nigerian civil war had started. It was destined to go on for thirty long months during which thousands of Nigerians were killed by Nigerians on the battlefield, towns and villages and farms were destroyed, and hundreds of millions of pounds were expended on the work of destruction. However, the nation was preserved as one.

When the war came to an end in January 1970, the military rulers announced a programme of reconstruction, at the completion of which, in 1976, they would hand over the government to civilians. The country had been carved out into twelve new states in the turbulent months of 1967 just before the civil war started. The reconstruction programme now included the drawing up of a new constitution to establish a final shape for the federation. It also included the rebuilding of war damages and the holding of a new national census.

The Federal Military Government was widely commended for the generous and sensible way in which it treated the former secessionists once hostilities came to an end. Largely because of this, the task of national reconciliation advanced much faster after the war than most people would have dared to hope. Before 1970 was out, most of the persons displaced from their jobs in various parts of the country by the crisis had returned to their pre-war positions. By the time the war came to an end, also, the division of the country into twelve states had completely changed the national political atmosphere. The old North and South, and the old fears of Northern or Southern domination were out of date. So were the old confrontations between the minority and majority ethnic groups in the old Regions. Moreover, the new states were twelve new centres of development, progress and challenge, twelve new channels through which people could seek personal advancement.

The years following the end of the civil war witnessed immense economic and social progress in the country, especially in the states. Nigeria's mineral oil production expanded rapidly, until Nigeria became one of the seven largest producers of crude oil in the world. This meant enormous financial resources, enabling the country to embark on ambitious programmes. The Third National Development Plan announced in 1973 is one of the most ambitious yet in the history of Africa. In 1974 the government announced its decision to start free primary education for the whole country.

However, the military regime also became progressively unpopular in these years. One major cause of this was the world-wide inflation which made life difficult for the common man. But perhaps most of the trouble arose from General Gowon's failings as a leader. A kind and generous man, General Gowon seemed increasingly to lose the ability to tackle difficult problems. For instance, when the results of a general census conducted in 1973 led to nation-wide disputes, General Gowon set up a review committee and promised a final statement – which never came. To growing demands for the creation of more states in the country, he frequently answered with promises of action – which were never fulfilled. In response to popular wish, he announced in 1974 that the state governors would be replaced, but every day seemed to see him further away from action on the matter. The nation became burdened with a growing accumulation of unresolved problems.

To make matters worse, official corruption became more apparent than ever before. And, as the revelations of corruption shook the country, the government appeared more determined to protect the corrupt leaders than to do its duty to the nation.

Finally, when General Gowon announced on 1 October 1974, that he no longer intended to surrender power to an elected civilian government in 1976 as earlier promised, his remaining popularity rapidly disappeared. On 29 July 1975, he was overthrown in a bloodless *coup* organised by the lower military officers. A new regime came to power under Brigadier Murtala Mohammed.

13 Sierra Leone

Sierra Leone had a longer experience of British imperialism than any other British colony in West Africa. British political interest in the area began in 1787 when some prominent British men helped some liberated African slaves in Britain to come and settle on the coastal parts of modern Sierra Leone. At first the colony was expected to be self-governing, but in 1808 it became a crown colony. The other parts of what is now Sierra Leone were not acquired by the British until 1896, when the British proclaimed a Protectorate over the territories adjoining the Colony, thus creating the Colony and Protectorate of Sierra Leone. It was not until 1924 that the Colony and Protectorate were given the same government. The constitution of that year created a single Legislative Council in which the people of the Colony (called the Creoles) and the indigenous peoples of the Protectorate (called 'up-country' people) were represented.

Like Ghana and Nigeria, Sierra Leone enjoyed a short period of internal self-government before attaining independence in 1961. In 1951, the Governor granted some Sierra Leoneans ministerial portfolios, although all policy-making was still under British control until 1953. Then some African ministers were given policy-making power, and the leading African minister, Dr (later Sir) Milton Margai, became Chief Minister. The most important ministeries – Finance, Foreign Affairs, Defence – remained, however, under the Governor's control.

A small country with very limited human and natural resources, Sierra Leone had a population, in 1960, the year before independence, of just over two million. Sierra Leone was also a very poor country, with the overwhelming majority of its people subsisting on peasant farming. Of cash crops, Sierra Leone produced some palm oil and kernels, coffee, cocoa and groundnuts. In 1950, these represented more than half of her total exports. By 1960, less than 50,000 Sierra Leoneans were employed in jobs earning salaries and wages, and far less than half of these were employed in commerce and industries. The rest were employed by the government in administration and public works.

Although Sierra Leone experienced western education much earlier than other parts of West Africa, her first mission schools having been built in 1787 and Fourah Bay College having been established in Freetown in 1827, it was still backward educationally in 1950. Especially among the up-country peoples of the Protectorate, only a small percentage of the children were attending school. Education did not really come to the Protectorate until the beginning of this century. Until the 1920s, all the Sierra Leonean students in Fourah Bay College were Creoles from the Colony.

Sierra Leone also had problems of disunity at independence. There were long-standing antagonisms between the Creoles and the up-country peoples. Because of their British culture, their British way of dressing and living, and their higher standard of education, the Creoles had long developed the tradition of looking down on the up-country peoples as primitive and illiterate. On the other hand, the up-country peoples despised the Creoles as strangers in the country. The Creoles had opposed the 1924 constitution merging the Colony with the Protectorate, because they resented being given the same administration as the 'primitive' peoples of the Protectorate. And, when a constitution was proposed in 1947 giving the Protectorate a larger representation in the Legislative Assembly, the Creoles vigorously protested – although the Creoles were less than 7% of the peoples of the Protectorate. The arguments over this constitution produced about three years of bitter and abusive attacks and counter-attacks between the Creoles and the up-country peoples which greatly worsened the relationship between the two.

There were also rivalries and suspicions among the up-country peoples, originating in the colonial era. When education at last began to come to the Protectorate, educational opportunities were very unevenly distributed. The Mende area in the south received far greater educational facilities than the northern territories. As a result, when Sierra Leoneans began to take part in the government of their country in 1951, most of the prominent up-country political leaders were Mendes. This caused resentment among the northerners – the Temnes, Limbas and others – and by the time of independence, they had become quite hostile to what they regarded as a 'Mende domination'.

Above all, at independence, the Sierra Leonean leadership was extremely conservative, probably the most conservative group of leaders that ever led any African country into independence. This leadership consisted of the more educated and richer Creoles in the Colony (renamed Western Area after independence) and the chiefs and more educated persons in the up-country provinces. In the Western Area the Creoles continued to cling to their British ways and British manners and to refer to Britain as 'home'. Indeed, many Creoles found it difficult to be enthusiastic about independence because independence involved weakening age-old ties with 'the mother country'.

In the provinces, the influence and authority of the chiefs had always been upheld by the British. As a result, at independence the chiefs still exercised considerable authority over their people. The Paramount Chiefs were the powerful heads of the local administrations, and through their courts they wielded immense powers. They were responsible for the maintenance of law and order in their chiefdoms, with power to permit or prevent public meetings. Using all these powers, they could fairly easily crush whatever political party dared to oppose their interests or their influence. Even for years after independence, the chiefs were still able to make their people do forced labour for them and to pay all sorts of taxes, such as palm wine tax. At the national level, the independence constitution strongly entrenched the chiefs' influence in the national legislature by reserving for them a substantial number of seats. In practically all other African countries, the independence legislature was made up of two chambers – a lower chamber called House of Assembly or House of Representatives, and an upper chamber called the Senate. The lower chamber, the real seat of power, was made up of elected commoners, while the upper chamber was made up of chiefs. In Sierra Leone, the independence constitution created a one-chamber legislature in which the chiefs were given a guaranteed number of seats. This made the chiefs very powerful in the national political system, since they had so many effective votes.

Moreover, most of the highly educated men who emerged as prominent political leaders from the up-country were sons of chiefs or were at least closely related to chiefs. This was because the sons of chiefs had benefited from colonial education more than the children of commoners, partly as a result of deliberate British policy to train members of the traditional ruling class as leaders of the new society, and partly because the chiefs had more money than the commoners to educate their children. There was therefore a very close association between the new political leaders and the chiefs. The ruling party at independence – the Sierra Leone Peoples Party (SLPP) relied mostly on the power and influence of the chiefs to win elections. The common people, therefore, could hardly obtain protection from the SLPP Government against oppression by the chiefs. Moreover, since it could count on the support of the chiefs at elections, the SLPP never really needed to build a proper party machinery to canvass for the support of the common people.

For these reasons, nationalist politics in Sierra Leone before independence was an affair only of the leaders. No attempt was made to inform or involve the people or arouse their enthusiasm; the only issue was the rivalry of the leaders for power. Each group of leaders sought the favour of the British colonial overlord, and so Sierra Leone's nationalist leaders were more often defenders, rather than critics, of British colonialism. The leader of a British parliamentary delegation which visited Sierra Leone just before independence reported on the people's ignorance regarding independence: 'Many times we were asked, "Why are you leaving us? You have been our friends and have helped us. Why do you want to go?"' In many parts of the country, influential persons secretly told the delegation that their people were opposed to immediate independence. Most common people felt that independence was something which would serve the interests of the politicians only. So great was the popular ignorance that a few months before independence, the SLPP Government announced its plans to launch a campaign to 'explain to the people what independence means'.

This intense conservatism of Sierra Leonean leadership and nationalism was mostly a product of the slow pace of social change in the country during the colonial era. Not only was the growth of education much slower than in Nigeria or Ghana, so was the rate of urbanisation. By the 1950s, Sierra Leone did not have the large numbers of educated youths and large urban wage-earning population which were contributing to the growth of radical nationalism in Nigeria or Ghana. As a result, the traditional institutions, reinforced by British backing, retained their power and influence and occupied a position from which they could direct national affairs.

So in 1961 Sierra Leone was very poorly prepared for self rule, and the task of economic and social progress was slow and accompanied by serious political troubles after independence.

Economically, perhaps the most important development has been the expansion of Sierra Leone's mining industry. By 1970, the mining of diamonds, both industrial and gem diamonds, had become Sierra Leone's most important industry. The value of diamond exports in 1970 amounted to 61 million American dollars, nearly all of it to Britain. By 1970 also, Sierra Leone was exporting about three million tons of iron ore. Bauxite mining also increased, and 552,000 tons of bauxite was exported in 1971. Another mineral of some importance in Sierra Leone's economy is rutile or titanium oxide. Sierra Leone's deposits of rutile are believed to be perhaps the richest in the world. Rutile mining, however, is yet only on a small scale. By 1970 about 44,000 tons was exported; in 1971 this fell to about 28,000 tons. The diamond mining rights were owned entirely before independence by British interests, but in the years after independence the Sierra Leonean Government acquired 51% shares in the diamond business. Most of the capital for the rutile mining has come from the United States. By early 1972, American businesses controlled all shares in the rutile mining industry. Bauxite mining was also controlled by American and Swiss interests by that date.

Although the expansion of mining has considerably increased Sierra Leone's total exports, the total volume is still very small. In 1971, total exports amounted to about 103 million American dollars, and total imports to about 115 million. Large-scale illegal diamond mining and smuggling have deprived the country of much of the revenue and foreign exchange that could have been derived from diamond exports.

More than 80% of the population of Sierra Leone was still engaged in agriculture by 1974. The main agricultural export crops – palm produce, cocoa, coffee and groundnuts – showed little or no expansion after independence. Also, Sierra Leone had to increase her imports of food, even of rice, the chief food crop produced by the country. In 1970 alone, six million American dollars' worth of rice were imported.

Social development has also been slow. Education expanded more rapidly after independence than during the colonial era. Fourah Bay College was converted into a full-fledged university not long after independence, and a university college was opened at Njala in the north. But even by 1963 not more than 24% of school-age children were attending school, and by 1970 the total illiteracy figure was still over 70%. The expansion of health services was also slow.

The major criticism usually levied against the SLPP Government of the first seven years of independence (1961–7) is that it never produced any plan of economic and social development. All it did was to live from day to day, yielding to local pressures, building a school here, a health centre there, a bridge somewhere else, all with no definite plan.

Not surprisingly the country soon ran into political trouble. Under the first Prime Minister, Sir Milton Margai, the country remained fairly stable, largely due to Sir Milton's personality. Cautious and conciliatory by nature, Sir Milton was a leader under whom political hostilities could hardly get out of hand. No situation, no matter how bad, could make him lose his coolness or hurry him into precipitate action. His opponents often criticised him and accused his government of being unprogressive both in its domestic and foreign policies, but they could not easily lose their personal respect for him.

However, Sir Milton died in April 1964 and was succeeded by his brother Mr (later Sir) Albert Margai. Ambitious, aggressive, and with an exaggerated opinion of his own popularity in the country, Sir Albert was a completely different man from Sir Milton. Very soon it became obvious that Sir Milton's cautious type of leadership was more suitable for maintaining the political stability of Sierra Leone.

At this date the ruling party, the SLPP, had members in all parts of the country (up-country people as well as some Creoles). But its leadership was predominantly Mende, and in the up-country areas its strength depended mostly on the chiefs. Because the total number of Creoles in the country was small, the Creoles had ceased to be a strong political force by independence. Those who were interested in politics had had to join the parties founded by the up-country people. The leading opposition party was the All Peoples Congress (APC), founded in 1960, the year before independence. The APC had grown out of the resentment of the northern elite (Temnes, Limbas, etc.) against 'Mende domination', though on the whole it never irresponsibly appealed to tribalist sentiments. Its leader was Siaka Stevens, a Limba.

But the difference between the APC and the SLPP was not merely ethnic. In the northern territories open opposition by the common people to the chiefs' oppressive rule was stronger than in the rest of the up-country areas. In 1955–6, the people of the northern territories had revolted violently against their chiefs, and the spirit of open defiance of chiefs remained strong there. The APC leaders were the educated northerners who supported the common people against their chiefs. They were not as highly educated or as rich as the SLPP leaders; very few of them were related to chiefs, and since they could not count on the support of the chiefs, they had to build a powerful party machinery for reaching and convincing the people.

The APC was, therefore, a better organised and more radical party than the SLPP. It sought, not that chieftaincy should be abolished, but rather that it should be made more democratic and less oppressive and cease being a political instrument of the ruling party. In other respects, too, it spoke a more radical language than the SLPP. For instance, it was critical of the SLPP's 'open-door' policy towards foreign businesses. Again, it did not seek to discourage foreign businesses from helping to develop the resources of the country, but rather that they should be more strongly controlled by the government and that the government should encourage the growth of indigenous enterprises too.

By 1964 the APC had won some supporters outside its northern base. It had some Creole members. It also had allies among some minority ethnic groups outside the north (such as the Kono) who were also opposed to 'Mende domination' and to the oppressive rule of their chiefs. In the 1962 election, the first national election in which the APC participated, it had found it impossible to get people to stand as its candidates in many constituencies, and the chiefs had used their power to prevent its members from campaigning. After the election, the pressure by the chiefs had continued, coupled with promises of high appointments or even money to attract the few APC parliamentarians away to the SLPP. But the APC managed to keep almost all its men, and even expanded its influence.

This was the situation when Albert Margai took over as Prime Minister. On the whole, Albert proved a more progressive leader than Milton. Although he did not change Milton's approach to economic matters, he did attempt to reduce the growing unemployment by sponsoring agricultural projects and small industries in which the government had shares. Abroad, he expanded his country's contacts beyond Britain, and developed diplomatic and trading relations with new partners, including the Soviet Union. Unlike Sir Milton, he led Sierra Leone into very active participation in the politics of Africa. For a time he became one of the most outspoken African leaders in the cause of African liberation in Rhodesia, and quite a close friendship developed between him and Dr Nkrumah, the high priest of African freedom and African unity.

But in the political arena at home, he was increasingly involving himself in trouble. This was not entirely his fault, however. The political situation did not allow for much manoeuvre. He believed that his party, the SLPP, should be organised more like a party. But when he tried to undertake such organisation, he ran into stiff resistance within the party itself. For a party so closely linked with the chiefs, there was no way of reorganising to win the support of the masses, without antagonising the chiefs and their supporters. With Milton as Prime Minister, the chiefs could always count on the support of the government whenever any troubles arose between them and their subjects. To their annoyance, the chiefs found that Albert could not be counted upon to give them such unfailing support. As time went on, although the chiefs' support for the SLPP remained unshaken, their support for Albert wavered.

Moreover, there were powerful elements within the party who had not forgotten or forgiven the fact that in 1958 Albert had led a revolt against the SLPP leadership. In 1958 a group of young men (mostly

Mende like the leaders of the SLPP) had left the SLPP and founded another party, the Peoples National Party (PNP). Albert had been their leader. Although the PNP men had later returned to the SLPP fold, Albert's attempts now to reorganise the SLPP looked like a bid for unlimited power for himself by putting his former PNP colleagues in important positions, and Albert's own behaviour increased such suspicions.

Among non-Mendes in the SLPP, the appointment of Albert to succeed his brother was seen as a demonstration of Mende domination. Some were never reconciled to the appointment. The Creoles, who had found it fairly easy to accept Milton as national leader, could not forget the aggressive part which Albert had played in the 1940s and 1950s in the confrontations between the Creoles and up-country peoples. Partly because of this and partly because of the excessive ambition which Albert began to exhibit once he became Prime Minister, many Creoles found him intolerable.

As soon as he became Prime Minister, Albert launched a massive propaganda campaign to project himself not only as a great national hero but also as a prominent leader of Africa – 'Albert Margai of Africa'. Where Milton had gone quietly about his business, Albert never passed through the streets without police outriders, noisy sirens, and clumsy attempts by government officials to assemble a cheering crowd. At the same time, every attempt was made to suppress news of the opposition, and the persecution of opposition elements was increased. In October 1964 Albert impetuously dissolved the Freetown city council, mistakenly believing that his popularity was so great that it would carry the SLPP into victory in the ensuing election. But the APC won that election. Albert reacted by taking more repressive measures against the opposition. Finally in 1965, he decided to eliminate all opposition. A motion for a one-party state was actually put through parliament and a commission set up to draw up the guidelines for a new constitution. But the idea was fiercely contested, not only by the opposition but also by SLPP men who saw it as an attempt by Albert to give himself autocratic power. In the face of this growing opposition, the one-party state idea was given up.

Meanwhile, the government was becoming notorious for corruption. Reports of shady deeds by very high persons in the government were often circulating in the country, and opposition spokesmen were frequently accusing the government and leading SLPP politicians of improper or corrupt practices ranging from bribery to nepotism to smuggling. Ministers on official tours of parts of the country were known to receive lavish gifts from the towns and villages which they visited and then to use government money to transport such gifts to their homes. Usually, the government had no satisfactory answer to the accusations and rumours of corruption. Indeed, on many occasions leading members of the government and ruling party made statements which created the impression that their sense of public morality was extremely low and that they believed their high public positions entitled them to perform with impunity acts that would normally be regarded as immoral or even criminal. These things contributed much to the growing unpopularity of Albert's government.

Albert's collapse finally came in 1967. Parliament was dissolved in February and the elections fixed for March, first the election of ordinary members on March 17, then that of the chiefs on March 21. During the campaign, violence erupted in many places. However, in spite of the use of the powers of government and the chiefs, the APC won a majority of the ordinary members. Sir Albert still expected, nevertheless, that after the election of the chiefs he would win an over-all majority. But that was never to be. On the morning of March 22, before the results of the chiefs' election were in, the Governor-General called Siaka Stevens, the leader of the APC, and swore him in as the new Prime Minister.

This action of the Governor-General has been the subject of arguments since. Some people have insisted that he ought to have waited for the result of the chiefs' election before naming a Prime Minister. Other people, however, have argued that the election of ordinary members was the real decisive issue, since the practice had always been that the elected chiefs joined whichever party already had a majority of ordinary members. The Governor-General took this view.

The appointment of Siaka Stevens was not allowed to go through. While he was being sworn in, the head of the army, Brigadier David Lansana, who was widely known to be a supporter of Albert Margai, ordered his troops to surround the State House, thereby holding both Stevens and the Governor-General captive. Apparently, Lansana was not trying to seize power but to hold the stage until the elections were completed and a Prime Minister was appointed on the final results. But other leading officers refused to support him. On March 23 they arrested Lansana, suspended the constitution, and established a military government.

The country was shocked. In spite of all the efforts of the military government to make itself popular with the people, most of the people remained hostile to it. Then one year later, junior military officers revolted against their superiors and seized power. But the makers of this second coup kept their promise of quickly returning the country to civilian rule. On 26 April 1968 Siaka Stevens was installed as Prime Minister on the basis of his electoral victory of March 1967.

Siaka Stevens came to power in 1968 with a lot of popular support and enthusiasm. Even among the Mende, many were willing to accept his leadership. In March 1969 he dissolved parliament and ordered new elections, and his party came back with a larger parliamentary majority. His government has proved, on the whole, more far-sighted and better able to make plans than his predecessors'. It was under him that state control was established over a substantial part of the diamond mining industry. While keeping the channels of aid and investment from the West open, he also succeeded in attracting aid from the Soviet Union.

But the political stability which followed his return to power in 1968 was short-lived. Some Mendes had never reconciled themselves to the Mende loss of power and therefore remained hostile to Stevens. Even within Stevens' own party, disagreements arose, leading to angry resignations of some of his ministers. Both within the army and among civilians, many people suspected Stevens of having communist tendencies. In 1970, the opposition crystallised into a new opposition party, the United Democratic Party (UDP). The UDP leaders accused the leaders of the government of corruption and diamond smuggling. Violence flared up, with both parties attacking each other with political thugs. In September, the Prime Minister declared a state of emergency and arrested the leaders of the UDP and a number of soldiers on charges of plotting to overthrow the government. Treason trials followed. Early in 1971, two attempts were made on the life of the Prime Minister, and another attempted army coup ended in failure. On 23 March 1971, at the request of the Prime Minister, the neighbouring Republic of Guinea sent forces to Sierra Leone to support the government.

Siaka Stevens managed to survive the storm. On 19 April 1971, the tenth anniversary of the independence of Sierra Leone, the country was declared a republic. Siaka Stevens became executive President, elected for a five-year term.

14 Liberia

Two African countries – Ethiopia and Liberia – preserved their independence when the rest of Africa became European colonies and protectorates in the late nineteenth century. Liberia is much younger than Ethiopia, dating its existence from 1822, when some freed slaves were transported from America across the Atlantic and landed at Monrovia to start a new life in Africa. The organisation responsible for bringing them there was the American Colonisation Society.

Until about the middle of this century when colonialism came under pressure all over Africa, Liberia was frequently threatened with being taken over by one European power or another. The first of these threats came in the 1840s, when the Government of Liberia, which was still controlled by the American Colonisation Society, decided to raise money by levying customs duties on goods imported into the country. The British Government, which owned the neighbouring colony of Sierra Leone, refused to recognise the right of the Liberian Government to levy customs duties. Consequently many British traders refused to pay the duties. In 1845 Liberian authorities seized a British ship for refusing to pay; the British came in with a warship, seized a Liberian trading ship and began to threaten Liberia. Liberia asked the American Government for help, but this was refused. As a result, the people of Liberia decided to take their destiny into their own hands. In 1847 they issued a Declaration of Independence, and Liberia thus became an independent country in the world.

But Liberia's freedom was not yet out of danger. The United States of America refused to recognise the independence of Liberia for about 15 years. Moreover, as the century drew to a close, Britain and France, having shared out the rest of West Africa as colonies between them, regarded Liberia's independence as a threat to their hold on their colonies. They feared that Liberia's example would encourage the other countries of West Africa to agitate for freedom.

Unfortunately, Liberia itself was very frequently in financial difficulties and obliged to borrow money from her enemies – especially from British companies. And when Liberia could not pay the debts, the British seized the opportunity to try to limit its sovereignty. For instance, between 1909 and 1912, because Liberia could not repay loans to the Liberian Rubber Corporation, a British company, the company urged the British Government to take over Liberia. The British Government, with the support of France, then proposed an arrangement under which the finances and army of Liberia would be placed under the supervision of European experts. To preserve her sovereignty Liberia appealed to the United States of America for help. Some American banks agreed to lend Liberia the money to pay off the British loan, on condition that Liberia agreed to place the administration of her customs under an American controller. Liberia had to agree, and so an American was appointed to administer the customs and finances of Liberia. Liberia thus became a semi-colony of America, and when in 1917 America went into the First World War, a European war which had nothing to do with Liberia, Liberia had to follow.

Liberia's semi-colonial ties with America did not prevent continued British intrigues. British businesses in Liberia, especially the Bank of West Africa, tried throughout the war to bring about Liberia's financial collapse so that the British Government might take over. When in 1915 the Liberian Government was confronted with a serious revolt among some of the indigenous peoples, the British alleged that the Liberians were unable to maintain order and therefore tried to take over part of the country. Again in 1930, the British got the League of Nations to investigate allegations that slavery was still being practised in Liberia. As a result of this inquiry, the European powers tried to place Liberia under an international control. Although Liberia managed to avoid losing her sovereignty completely, she was compelled to lose a substantial part of her territory to the British during the 1880s, and a yet larger portion to the French in 1892. As a result, Liberia is now no more than one quarter of her original size.

Let us turn now to Liberia's economic history. The leaders of the early settlers tried to encourage their people to take to agriculture, but without success. Most of the leading settlers preferred to become traders, or teachers, or priests in the church, or seek government employment. The settlers, or Americo-Liberians, gradually took over trade on the coast from the indigenous African traders and even the small European traders. They therefore enjoyed a monopoly of the trade between the interior and the coast, and until the 1870s, some of them acquired considerable wealth.

However, during the 1880s, this period of commercial prosperity came to an end. This was during the 'scramble for Africa', when there was not only a world-wide economic depression, but a growing rivalry among Europeans in West Africa. European steamships gradually pushed aside the small boats of the Americo-Liberian traders. Liberia became a poor country incapable of generating the capital to develop her economy. Though Liberia is a small country, it is fairly richly endowed with natural resources, especially forest and mineral resources. But these resources remained mostly unexplored until about the middle of this century principally because of Liberia's lack of capital.

The national poverty was worsened by a corrupt and wasteful political tradition; much of the money borrowed from abroad for economic projects ended up in the pockets of government officials. By the end of the nineteenth century, the original Americo-Liberians had, through intermarriage, evolved into large family groups, which exhibited all the characteristics of dynasties and endlessly rivalled one another for government appointments. The civil service became heavily overstaffed and, therefore, a big burden on the nation's weak economy.

On top of all this, Liberia's economic life was being constantly undermined by the persistent hostility and intrigues of the European powers and European companies.

Another dark page in the history of Liberia concerns the relationship between the Americo-Liberians and the indigenous African peoples. From the beginning, it was not very different from the relationship of European settlers in South and East Africa with the African peoples in those places. Like the European settlers, the Americo-Liberians were arrogant and looked down on the cultures of the indigenous peoples as primitive. In many instances, their method of acquiring land from the owners was fraudulent.

In the coastal areas where Americo-Liberian social, legal and political institutions were fully established, an African could only acquire civil rights by losing his culture, and becoming assimilated. This meant that the African must give up his language and speak English, learn to live and dress like an Americo-Liberian, give up his indigenous religion or Islam and become a Christian, renounce his rights to his rightful share in the communal land in the indigenous society, and give up his loyalty to his chief or king and accept loyalty only to the Americo-Liberian Government in Monrovia. The usual way of doing all this and thereby becoming acceptable into Americo-Liberian society was through the system of apprenticeship which the Americo-Liberians established. An Americo-Liberian family would take an African child into their home, and the African child would live and work there as a servant and thereby become familiar with the way of life of Americo-Liberians, adopt Americo-Liberian names and usually end up by marrying an Americo-Liberian. Needless to say, the Africans regarded this system as a humiliation and resented it.

In the politics of the Americo-Liberian state, only the few assimilated Africans were allowed to participate. By the beginning of this century, a few assimilated Africans had managed to rise to high positions in the state. One became Secretary of State (i.e. Minister) for education in 1915, and another Vice-President in 1925. But the non-assimilated Africans were regarded by the Americo-Liberians as too primitive to take part in the political process. Among the African peoples in the interior territories, the policy of the Americo-Liberian Government was one of indirect rule. The chiefdoms were treated as protectorates in which the traditional rulers ruled under the supervision of commissioners appointed by the Monrovia Government, and with the support of the frontier army. Traditional courts were established in which the chiefs administered traditional law. The commissioner was the court of appeal to these chiefs' courts. The Americo-Liberian commissioners usually exercised their authority very oppressively. The people were compelled to pay taxes, to surrender their land, to render service to the government, especially in road construction, and to enrol in the government's frontier forces.

Economically, the indigenous Africans suffered many disabilities and discrimination. They were gradually excluded from the trade of the Liberian coast, and ultimately were prevented by government authority from competing commercially with the Americo-Liberians. For instance, the government declared six Americo-Liberian towns along the coast as international trading ports, thereby compelling all the coastal trade to be diverted to such towns. As a result, the indigenous towns along the coast (especially the towns of the Kru people) quickly lost their trade and degenerated into poor villages. Appeals to the government by the Kru that at least one of their towns should be declared an international port achieved no result. Moreover, to ensure that the Africans would not obtain the right type of education for entry into the government services, only technical education was provided for them, whereas it was literary education that was required for public service employments. Even the few who had literary education were discriminated against in civil service appointments. In addition, since Liberia was not an industrialised country, there were few job opportunities for the people with technical education.

Revolts by the indigenous Africans against Americo-Liberian authority were frequent, and were brutally crushed by the Liberian Government's police and army.

The era of economic troubles which began in the 1880s continued until the 1940s. Throughout this period, successive Liberian governments tried unsuccessfully to generate economic development by raising loan after loan from Europe or from America. Usually, the country ended up with no development to show for these loans. Almost invariably, each loan became a big debt, and the country would have to raise another loan to pay for it. This process recurred and recurred until the 1940s.

From 1944, many changes began to occur in the political and economic history of Liberia. The man who was responsible was William Tubman, who became President of Liberia in 1944 and held that office until 1971.

Tubman's economic revolution was achieved mainly by opening the doors of Liberia to foreign businesses and especially by bringing Liberia into very close ties with the USA. One of his first acts was to make the American dollar the official currency of Liberia. Then, in order to show that Liberia had become a solid friend of America, he declared war on Germany and Japan who were the enemies of America in the Second World War. As a result of this, Liberia received much American financial aid. For instance, she received 22 million dollars in 1945 to build the port of Monrovia, and 40 million dollars in 1949 for other public constructions, and other aids and loans in the following years. Under Tubman, Liberia received almost 200 million dollars in American aid.

American companies were encouraged to bring in capital to develop the mineral and agricultural resources of Liberia. Liberia is particularly rich in good quality iron ore, and during the 1950s American companies invested heavily in mining the iron. By 1961 iron ore had become the greatest Liberian export, and Liberia had become one of the greatest producers of iron ore in Africa. Liberia is also rich in other minerals like diamonds, gold, manganese and columbite, but only diamonds and gold were yet being mined on a small scale by 1970.

In agriculture, the most important development was the establishment of rubber plantations, also with foreign capital. The Firestone Rubber Company of America had invested heavily in Liberian rubber before Tubman; but rubber production was expanded a lot as a result of Tubman's open door policy. Tubman encouraged Liberians also to establish small rubber plantations of their own.

All these policies enabled Liberia to rise out of poverty. Not only did Tubman pay the debts he inherited; under him the national budget multiplied about twelve times between 1944 and 1963. This meant more income for the average Liberian and more government funds to spend on education, health services and communication. Tubman showed particular interest in developing education and health. For instance in 1962 he made 2 million dollars available for the provision of health facilities, and in 1963 about 3 million dollars for education. Between 1944 and 1962, the number of Liberians attending different types of school grew from about 10,000 to about 80,000. By 1965 Liberia had three institutions of university level, the biggest of which was the University of Liberia.

Politically and socially, Tubman did more than any other Liberian leader before him to make the indigenous peoples of Liberia feel like citizens of the country. He always declared that his greatest ambition was to unify all Liberians into one happy nation, and his record shows that he was sincere. He took steps to stop the practice of coercing and repressing the indigenous peoples, and he began to extend liberally to the interior peoples the educational and health facilities provided by the government. It should be remembered that Tubman persevered in these efforts against the determined opposition of a good proportion of his Americo-Liberian people. Especially during his early years as President, many leading Americo-Liberians were violently opposed to both his economic policy and his policy towards the indigenous peoples. More than once, his opponents plotted to assassinate him. In spite of such opposition, however, Tubman pursued his policies with single-minded resolve. Although his efforts to integrate the indigenous people into the Liberian society were not entirely successful, there is no doubt that their position was very different in 1971 from what it had been in 1944.

William Tubman is the greatest president yet in the history of Liberia. No doubt there were certain flaws in his leadership. He was a great politician and a natural leader of men, but his unparalleled political skill was often mixed with a certain measure of ruthlessness towards his opponents. Indeed, in spite of his praises for democracy, Tubman could not tolerate opposition. Under him, the freedom of the press was stifled. The presidential elections became a one-man affair in which William Tubman repeatedly competed against himself and repeatedly won more than 90% of the votes. He has also been criticised for the way he managed his 'open-door' policy towards foreign investors, which gave foreign businesses virtually complete freedom to exploit the country. Yet, all things considered, William Tubman deserves to be regarded as the maker of modern Liberia.

William Tubman died in July 1971 after twenty-seven years as president of Liberia. He was succeeded by his vice-president, William R. Tolbert.

15 Ivory Coast

Like most African states the Ivory Coast is a small country, covering an area of about 123,000 square miles and with a population of 4,000,000 by 1970. It is, however, a country blessed with natural resources: abundant forest and mineral wealth. Since it became independent in 1960 its economy has grown faster than that of most other African countries. The Ivory Coast was generally believed by 1974 to be the richest of the French-speaking African countries south of the Sahara.

From the late 1950s, when the people of Ivory Coast began to take some part in the affairs of their country, the man responsible for shaping its policies has been Félix Houphouët-Boigny. Houphouët-Boigny came into the political limelight after the Second World War. When the French Government called a Constituent Assembly in Paris in 1945 to discuss the future of the French Empire, Houphouët-Boigny narrowly won the election to represent Ivory Coast. For the African people in the French Empire, the most important consequence of the Paris meetings was the law by which the French Government agreed to abolish forced labour in their colonies. This was something dear to the Africans, something for which they had long agitated. As the man mostly responsible for the achievement, Houphouët-Boigny became the virtually undisputed leader of Ivory Coast, and the most influential politician in French West Africa.

In April 1946, Houphouët-Boigny founded the Democratic Party of Ivory Coast (PDCI) – the party that was later to lead the country to independence. In October 1946, he called a meeting of leading nationalists from all the colonies of French West Africa. The meeting met in Bamako, and the nationalist leaders, at the suggestion of Houphouët-Boigny, agreed to found a common political movement to co-ordinate all their various nationalist struggles. This was the African Democratic Rally (RDA). As its leader, Houphouët-Boigny became perhaps the most influential nationalist leader in the whole of Africa. The PDCI became the Ivory Coast branch of the RDA.

In the forties Houphouët-Boigny's political ideas were radical and in advance of his time. While most nationalist leaders of French West Africa were thinking only of achieving more rights for Africans as French citizens within the French Empire, Houphouët-Boigny was daring to talk about independence. The RDA, for instance, declared that its goal was the 'emancipation of Africa from the colonial yoke', and in pursuit of this goal, affiliated with the Communist Party of France which showed much sympathy for the desires of colonial peoples. Representatives of the colonies were being elected to the French parliament in Paris at this time, and the alliance with the French Communist Party gave the RDA bloc considerable influence in the French parliament.

However, Houphouët-Boigny's radicalism was short-lived. From about 1948, the French Government became determined to stamp out all traces of radicalism in the colonies. Very reactionary governors were sent to the colonies, and in Ivory Coast, Houphouët-Boigny's party came under intense official pressure. The colonial administration openly supported its opponents and did everything to destroy it. By 1950 the PDCI was beginning to show signs of strain. The party continued to enjoy the support of the masses and this support was expressed in many places by popular riots resulting in clashes with the colonial authorities, the death and wounding of hundreds of Africans and the imprisonment of thousands. Nevertheless the pressure was beginning to wear down the leaders of the party, who began to advocate abandoning their radical stance. In spite of the alliance with the French Communist Party, most of the leaders of the RDA-PDCI were not communists anyway. Houphouët-Boigny himself had always said that his alliance with the French Communist Party was only tactical. In answer to French allegations that he was a dangerous communist he had once said, 'Can it be said of me, Houphouët, a traditional chief, a doctor, a big landowner, a Catholic, that I am a communist?' The view that the party should give up its radical stand won the day; in September 1950, Houphouët-Boigny broke off the alliance with the French Communist Party.

From then on, his policy was to make himself a good friend of the French Government. He became a great defender of French colonial policies. Between 1957 and 1959 he was Minister of State in Paris, and in that position he defended French colonialism, even on the floor of the United Nations. When General de Gaulle offered the French colonies in 1958 the choice of voting to remain in the French Community or becoming independent, Houphouët-Boigny was the most ardent campaigner for remaining in the French Community. He argued that remaining with their colonial masters was the only way in which African countries could make economic progress. It was also the only way in which each African country could prevent its many ethnic groups from fighting among themselves. Of all African leaders, Houphouët-Boigny was the only one unimpressed by the independence of Ghana in 1957. He regarded Ghana's achieving independence as a foolish step.

As a result of Houphouët-Boigny's vigorous campaign and use of government power, the Ivory Coast voted 'Yes' almost unanimously in 1958 to remain within the French Community. But this did not mean that the common people of the Ivory Coast did not want independence. In fact, they wanted it as much as the people of other African countries. The example of Guinea became attractive to all those countries which had rejected independence in 1958. In Ivory Coast, Senegal, Upper Volta and Dahomey, the masses of the people began to ask for independence. Houphouët-Boigny discovered that if he did not change his mind, he would lose the leadership of the people of Ivory Coast, especially after even the French Government itself, owing to the demands of the other colonies, had reluctantly agreed to the idea of independence. Houphouët-Boigny therefore bowed to the inevitable and in November 1960 Ivory Coast became independent.

Economic development

Even before independence, Houphouët-Boigny's over-riding interest as leader had been the economic development of his country. Indeed, this was the chief reason for his growing conservatism in the 1950s. As he saw it, close co-operation with France was essential for the economic development of his country. To him, other considerations were secondary. He would rather work quietly under France to develop the economy of the Ivory Coast than fight for independence, which to him was a fanciful goal with uncertain benefits.

The attainment of independence did not change these views much. Ivory Coast, he told his countrymen as soon as independence was attained, had achieved some economic development under the French. The economic progress of the future would be achieved by developing quietly along the capitalist lines already established under colonialism. There would be no wandering from this path, no adventures or fundamental changes of approach. In agriculture, far from expelling the French settler farmers, Ivory Coast would encourage them to expand their plantations, and would even attract more settlers. Great emphasis would be placed upon agriculture to expand the volume and variety of export crops, and to increase the food supply for the population. Agricultural development would be entirely in the hands of individual farmers, whether citizens or foreigners. 'We do not need an agrarian revolution in the Ivory Coast,' he once said. 'Some choose African socialism; we prefer a policy of realistic peasants.'

To industrialise quickly, everything would be done to attract foreign investment. And there would be nothing like nationalisation. 'We have no factories to nationalise but to create,' he said, 'no trade to control but to better organise; no land to distribute but to better utilise.' The country would first establish those industries which would make use of the country's agricultural and mineral products. Later, perhaps in the 1970s, bigger industries could be embarked upon.

The government would, however, lay down the general guidelines for economic development and guide the economy along such lines. Since there were no Ivorians with the capital to take part in industrialisation, the government would become a capitalist by investing part of its income and by borrowing money to invest. While doing this, the government would gradually help the rise of an indigenous class of businessmen by providing vocational training and making some credits available. Moreover, at some future time, the government would sell its investments in certain businesses to private Ivorian businessmen.

These, then, are the ideas that guided the Ivory Coast's economic development after 1960. Immediately after independence, an interministerial Committee for Development was set up, as well as a General Administration for Planning, to see to the problem of economic planning. Soon, a plan, 'Ten-Year Perspectives for Economic Development, 1960–69', was published. This was not a well integrated plan but a series of general guidelines and statements of the goals aimed at in various fields.

In agriculture, the French settlers were encouraged to expand their plantations. More Frenchmen came as settler farmers, many of them settlers fleeing from Algeria after its independence in 1962. An increasing number of Ivorians also began to go into cash-crop farming. The government encouraged the indigenous farmers to improve their methods – for instance, to change from shifting cultivation to crop rotation, and to begin to grow a wider variety of crops. In 1961, a system called the 'Civic Service' was established under which young farmers from the villages were given short courses in modern farming methods and then sent back to their villages. A similar system was later established for young women to teach them housekeeping and other skills that would make them efficient wives for the young modern farmers. Trained agricultural extension workers were sent to the rural areas to help and advise the farmers. Encouragement was also given to farmers to start voluntary co-operatives whenever feasible. If the government found it necessary, it went to the aid of certain crops by offering to buy them at a stable price or even by subsidising their prices. By a land code of 1963, the government acquired control over uncultivated land and so was enabled to attract farming populations to the sparsely populated south-western districts. In this way, the area under cultivation was considerably increased.

The two main cash crops which Ivory Coast was producing at independence were cocoa and coffee. As well as increasing production of these crops, new crops – bananas, pineapples, sugar cane, rice, oil palm and rubber – were introduced.

As a result, Ivory Coast has been one of the very few African countries in which agriculture did very well in the years after independence. Indeed, the rates of growth aimed at in the 'Perspectives' were almost consistently exceeded throughout the 1960s. The growth of cash-crop production did better than that of food-crop production. The volume of cocoa and coffee exports increased, but these crops ceased to be the only cash crops exported by Ivory Coast. Indeed, as the other export crops increased in volume, the percentage of cocoa and coffee in the total exports fell. Between 1960 and 1965, the volume of banana exports doubled, and the volume of pineapple tripled. The volume of exports of palm produce, rubber and timber increased steadily throughout the decade. Coffee and cocoa remained the leading cash crops, but by 1970, the old dependence on them as the *only* cash crops was a thing of the past. By 1970, Ivory Coast was still importing some food, although throughout the 1960s food production had steadily increased. Between 1960 and 1965 alone, the volume of rice production increased by 140%. The national aim was that some time between 1970 and 1975, rice importation would become unnecessary.

To encourage the growth of industries, the government not only invested capital but offered many attractions to foreign investors: low tax on profits, protection for capital, permission to transfer capital and repatriate profits freely. During the 1960s, therefore, there was rapid industrialisation. In the first ten years of independence, industry was growing at an average rate of about 18% per annum; between 1960 and 1965 the total volume of industrial production doubled. Industries using locally produced raw materials were given particular attention. These included factories for making cigarettes and cigars from tobacco, textile mills using local and imported cotton, coffee mills, rice mills, factories for canning fruits, fish and vegetable oils. But factories for making fertilisers and assembling cars were also built. By the end of 1967, there were 284 private companies in the country with a total investment of about 52,000 million francs, and about 26,000 Ivorians were employed in industries.

Mining has not done so well, but after independence much attention was given to surveying the mineral resources of the country. The production of manganese and diamonds increased; indeed diamond production doubled between 1960 and 1964. However, the total quantities of these minerals have not been very large. Some gold, iron and tantalite mining was started in the late sixties, while the search for petroleum was also initiated.

Commerce has grown. The large French trading companies came to open shops in Abidjan, the national capital, and some of the bigger cities. The Syrians and Lebanese expanded their trading businesses from the large towns to the small towns. There has been some expansion of indigenous trading activities also, especially on the very small scale and in the villages.

To foreigners visiting the Ivory Coast, the most spectacular development since independence has been the rapid rate at which public buildings and construction works have been springing up all over the country. Between 1960 and 1970, Abidjan grew from a comparatively small town into an impressive city of beautiful streets, skyscrapers and hotels. A state housing corporation, set up soon after independence, established a number of low-cost housing projects.

Some attempt has even been made to improve the native quarters of Abidjan and the shanty settlements on the outskirts of the city, all of which were slums in 1960. While main roads were being constructed, special feeder roads were also built to products from the farms. In order to encourage the agricultural opening up of the sparsely populated south-west, a huge port was built on the coast at San Pedro. In the central region, a huge dam was built at Kossou to provide water for irrigation, electricity and inland fishing.

The economic history of independent Ivory Coast, then, has been a success story. From independence to 1970, the gross national product grew by an average annual rate of between 8% and 9%, making the economy of Ivory Coast one of the fastest growing in the world during that decade. A five-year plan for 1971–5, introduced in 1970, envisaged that the rate of growth of about 8% annually would be maintained.

Two major criticisms, however, have been levelled against this economic progress. The first is that President Houphouët-Boigny has interpreted progress too narrowly as meaning simply the rapid expansion of production. As a result, national resources have been devoted mainly to encouraging the expansion of production, at the expense of human development. For instance, the rate of the growth of education was slow throughout the 1960s. Houphouët-Boigny's view was that a poor country like Ivory Coast should first concentrate on expanding production and thereby creating wealth. After that there would be enough money to spend on education. Enabling huge numbers of school pupils to be educated from the beginning would only mean diverting money away too early from production to consumption. The opposing view is that educating people and helping them to improve their lives should be one of the first aims of development.

In accordance with Houphouët-Boigny's principles, the 'Perspectives' of 1960 set down the goal of providing schools for only 50% of school-age children by 1970. As a result, education expanded relatively slowly. Primary and secondary schools were built, but mostly in the south, while the most remote areas of the north continued to have little or no educational facilities. The most important educational development of the first decade of independence, the founding of the University of Abidjan in 1964, was only accomplished with French financial aid.

The second criticism of Houphouët-Boigny's economic policies is that they have benefited most not the Ivorians but foreigners. The door was kept completely open to foreign investors in all spheres of the national economy, and Ivory Coast simply became a country open to foreign exploitation, a country free only in name. Not all the profits have gone to the foreigners. A growing number of Ivorians have been employed, and the foreign businesses have paid taxes to the Ivorian Government, which has also taken part in the industrialisation by investing some capital. The economic expansion has made possible a lot of public works which benefit the Ivorian people, the agricultural policies have greatly benefited Ivorian farmers and improved their incomes and standard of living, while the new factories which make use of local farm products have expanded the market for the goods produced by Ivorian farmers. However, it still remains true that the economic policies have resulted in too strong a foreign control of the economy. Though the French settler farmers are few, their role in the agricultural economy has been very important. In commerce and industry, it has been impossible, even with government encouragement, for any class of indigenous businessman to compete with the foreign companies. What has resulted from Houphouët-Boigny's economic policies is not Ivorian capitalism but foreign (mostly French) capitalism in the Ivory Coast.

Foreign policy

President Houphouët-Boigny's foreign policy abroad has consistently been conservative. Believing that co-operation with France is essential for the economic progress of Ivory Coast, he has kept very close to France in foreign affairs and maintained strong French influence over his country. In Africa, his policy has followed the same lines. Believing that without strong attachment to Europe African countries cannot survive, he has been a strong opponent of the radical type of nationalism. Believing that Africans cannot maintain wider political unions, he opposed from the beginning any attempt to transform the Pan-African movement into a political union of African states (or United States of Africa). The OAU, being a loose league of sovereign states, has agreed more with his own idea of what Africa should be trying to build. He was also from the beginning one of the leading members of the Monrovia Group, the conservative wing of the Pan-African movement.

Thus, his first major action abroad around the time of independence was to foil attempts to create an independent federation of French West Africa. During the colonial era, France had established a federal administration for all her West African colonies, with its headquarters based in Senegal, under a High Commissioner. As independence approached, many leaders of French West Africa hoped to transform this colonial federation into a federation of independent states, for the economic and political benefit of the members. It would have greatly reduced their economic dependence on France. However, both France and Houphouët-Boigny opposed the plan. Houphouët-Boigny did not wish to share the wealth of comparatively richer Ivory Coast with the poorer countries of French West Africa. Having successfully blocked the creation of the federation, he opposed any other attempt to form any other federation. Thus, when Soudan (now Mali), Senegal, Upper Volta and Dahomey announced in 1959 that they had formed a federation, Houphouët-Boigny used his influence to persuade Upper Volta and Dahomey to withdraw.

Houphouët-Boigny has, however, always been ready to support the looser type of organisation of sovereign states. He was the brain behind the creation of the 'Conseil d'Entente', an organisation for some economic co-operation among a number of small French-speaking West African countries. He was also the chief promoter of the Brazzaville Group and of the Common Organisation of African and Malagasy States (OCAM).

Domestic politics
At independence, Houphouët-Boigny's PDCI was the only political party in the Ivory Coast. All the other parties which had grown up in the post-World War years had faded out during the 1950s and their leaders had either joined the PDCI or withdrawn from politics. Although Houphouët-Boigny was not responsible for the rise of a one-party state, he was glad of it and determined to preserve it. As he told his countrymen, he was not against the idea of opposition parties, but he believed that a young country like Ivory Coast struggling for economic progress could not afford to have more than one party. Educated Ivorians were so few anyway, he said, that it did not make sense for them to divide themselves among many parties. Everybody should stay within the one national party and there make his contribution to the national growth. Within the national party, there would be room for the expression of differences of opinion, since anybody who disagreed with the leaders would be free to speak up within the party.

The one-party state has survived in Ivory Coast ever since. Indeed the country has enjoyed considerable political stability, and there has been comparatively little organised opposition to the leadership of President Houphouët-Boigny. Very little ethnic trouble has been experienced either. Though the country has about sixty main ethnic groups, some of them quite antagonistic to one another, tribalism has not been a major factor in Ivorian national life. The most serious sign of tribalism occurred just before independence when the Agni of the south-eastern areas of Ivory Coast, a very proud people, rejected Houphouët-Boigny's leadership and tried to secede from the country by petitioning the French Government to grant separate autonomy to their small kingdom of Sanwi. The French, however, turned down the request, and thereafter the government was able to deal successfully with this local threat to national unity.

From the traditional rulers, also, the national leadership has experienced practically no difficulty. For one thing, very few of the chiefs emerged from colonialism with any authority or influence. For another, as a traditional chief himself, Houphouët-Boigny has treated the chiefs with care and consideration. Under his leadership, the chiefs have been generally satisfied with their lot and shown a great willingness to support the government.

The only quarter from which Houphouët-Boigny has experienced opposition, therefore, has been from among the more radical elements of society – the younger elite, the students and workers. Even before independence, they had begun to criticise his conservative approach. They felt that Houphouët-Boigny's economic policy was not in the true interests of the nation, and doomed the country to neo-colonialist economic exploitation; and that his foreign policy made Ivory Coast a tool in the hands of France.

As early as 1958 a confrontation developed between Houphouët-Boigny and the Ivory Coast Works Union (UTCI). While Houphouët-Boigny was enthusiastic about the French Community, the workers demanded full independence. The workers were also opposed to his policy of retaining Frenchmen in many important positions in the civil service. In support of their demands, the workers began to strike. When the government made a law in August 1959 to limit the right of the workers to organise themselves and to strike, the workers replied by going on a big strike and marching on the President's residence. The government brought out the army, arrested many of the strikers and dismissed many from their jobs. The strike collapsed. The government then followed this up in 1960 by systematically bringing the workers under the control of the party. As the economic progress of the years after independence provided more jobs for the workers and improved their standard of living, the workers gradually reconciled themselves to being members of the party. Many of them were elected into parliament, and one was even appointed Minister of Labour and Social Affairs.

The growing class of young intellectuals, however, proved more difficult to deal with. In the late fifties, Houphouët-Boigny began to attract them into the party. Then in 1958, in deference to their demand, he allowed them to form a distinct youth wing within the party. Branches of the youth wing sprang up all over the country, its leaders being the young graduates returning home from French universities. As might be expected, co-operation between these well educated and very nationalistic young people and the conservative leadership of the PDCI proved difficult. Many leaders of the youth wing began to demand that it should constitute itself into a completely separate movement. And although this did not happen, the youth wing did, from 1959 on, become very independent of the party leadership by setting up its own constitution, electing its own executive, selling its own membership cards. This alarmed the party leadership, and steps were taken to destroy the independence of the youth wing. The sale of its membership card was prohibited, and its local branches were brought under the control of the local party secretaries. Some of its leaders were co-opted into the party leadership, and some even to parliament. Like the workers, the leaders of the youth wing gradually reconciled themselves to their role as loyal members of the party.

However, the Ivorian students in France and Senegal refused to compromise. Indeed their criticisms of the conservatism and the capitalist policies of the government increased. So troublesome did they become that the government had to order the arrest of one of their leaders. The government then followed this up by destroying the unity among the students. A government-supported students' union was sponsored, and within a short time most of the students were attracted into it.

By the end of 1961, then, it seemed as if the party had successfully destroyed all pockets of radical criticism and dissent. But this proved deceptive. In mid-1962 the government suddenly became aware that some young people within the party, some of them holding important party and national positions, were plotting to topple the President. In January 1963, after spending months carefully setting a trap for the plotters, the government took action. While a party meeting was being held at the President's home in Yamoussoukro, the police came in and began to pick up the plotters. Hundreds of people, including ministers, parliamentarians and top officials, were arrested all over the country. The leading plotters were tried in secret, and fifty were sentenced to prison and thirteen to death.

Before the tension caused by these developments had died down, another, and much more serious, plot to carry out a *coup d'état* was discovered. In August 1963, the country was plunged into fear as a new wave of arrests began. The makers of the new plot included highly placed persons like the President of the Supreme Court, six ministers, many members of the national executive including some of the party's foundation members, and many members of parliament. There were also some leaders of former rival parties and ethnic opponents of the President. After the arrests came trials, imprisonments and purges.

These plots shocked Houphouët-Boigny and produced serious consequences for the country. In the arrests and the party purges that followed, the radical elements and all suspected enemies of the government were eliminated from politics, and their places in the party machinery, parliament and government were filled with people known to be reliable supporters of the party's policies. Secondly, it was decided that from then on, civil servants had to become politically committed to the party's policies. Steps were therefore taken to indoctrinate civil servants in the party's philosophy. The non-involvement of the civil service in partisan politics was swept away. Thirdly, it was decided to build a special party militia which the party could call upon in times of danger. For this party militia, which was to remain independent of the army and police, only persons known to be unflinchingly loyal to the party were recruited and given military training. The party thus acquired its own army which was soon to number up to 6,000. If the national army dared to organise a coup, the party's army was there to defend the government. Finally, the party was reorganised, its local branches were strengthened and made more subservient to the central party leadership, the youth wing was dissolved, and the workers' unions were brought more closely under party control.

The plots thus led to the elimination of all opposition and to immense strengthening of the control of the party and the President over the country. Since then, Houphouët-Boigny's leadership has encountered no serious challenge. This has been due not only to his enormous powers of repression but also to his popularity because of the benefits the people derive from the country's economic progress.

16 Senegal

Until 1957 the French West African colonies were linked together by a federal colonial administration with its headquarters in Senegal. This gave Senegal considerable importance among the French West African colonies. It also made Senegal the most developed and educationally advanced French colony in West Africa by 1960, and Dakar, the capital of Senegal, the finest city in tropical Africa.

As independence approached, however, the federal arrangement gradually broke down. By 1957 each colony attained a certain measure of internal self-government and its leaders focused their attention on affairs of their own country. By the time of the referendum on the constitution of the French Community in 1958, each colony had struck out on its own separate road. And when independence finally came, the French West African colonies became independent not as a federation but as separate countries.

The only exception to this was the federation created by Soudan (now Mali) and Senegal just before their independence in 1960. Léopold Sedar Senghor, the leading political figure in Senegal, had suggested to the leaders of the other colonies that French West Africa should go into independence as a federation. He believed that such a federation, with a total population of over twenty million, would make for faster economic development and enjoy greater political influence than would the separate small countries. As the leader of Senegal, moreover, he wished to preserve the federal arrangements, under which Senegal had been the heart of French West Africa, a position from which she had derived many advantages. Many other leaders of French West Africa, with the notable exception of Houphouët-Boigny of Ivory Coast, shared Senghor's views on federation.

Therefore, as soon as they had voted 'Yes' in the 1958 referendum, the leaders of Senegal, Soudan, Upper Volta and Dahomey called a meeting to work out a federation. On 17 January 1959, they announced that they had formed a federation with the name Mali Federation. Houphouët-Boigny, however, was bitterly opposed to the formation of the Mali Federation, and used his great influence to persuade Upper Volta and Dahomey to withdraw from it. But Senegal and Soudan refused to break up. And so in June 1960, Senegal and Soudan achieved independence under the name of the Mali Federation.

The Mali Federation was, however, short-lived. First, Soudan was larger in area and population than Senegal, but Senegal was much richer. Therefore, while Senegal contributed more financially to the federation, Soudan enjoyed greater political power because of her bigger population. This situation made many well-meaning Senegalese unhappy. From the beginning there was fear of being dominated by Soudan.

Secondly, the party in power in Soudan, the RDA-Soudan (the Soudanese branch of the old African Democratic Rally) was a more radical nationalist party than the party in power in Senegal, the Senegalese Progressive Union (UPS). The RDA-Soudan leaned towards a radical socialist philosophy. Its leaders were much more opposed to French influence than the leaders of the UPS. Finally, the RDA-Soudan had developed a very detailed organisation which made it possible for it to control Soudan very firmly. Its tentacles reached deep into every village in the country. The leaders of the UPS saw this all-pervading organisation of the RDA as a threat to the freedom of the people of Soudan, and were generally worried about the radicalism of the RDA.

Thirdly, even before independence, Senegal and Soudan had disagreed on the nature of the constitution for the federation. The Soudanese leaders had suggested a unitary constitution. Having only one government for the whole federation, they had argued, would be much cheaper than having a federal government, and one government each for Soudan and Senegal. They had also suggested that the single government should be headed by an executive president controlling wide powers. The Senegalese had refused to accept these suggestions which they saw as a means of establishing Soudanese domination over Senegal. The constitution that was ultimately adopted agreed more with the views of the Senegalese – a provincial government each for Soudan and Senegal, and a federal government headed by a President with a Vice-President. But the suspicion persisted that the Soudanese leaders would try to destroy this constitution and attempt to replace it with one more to their liking.

Things quickly came to a head after independence. The President of the federation was Modibo Keita of Soudan. His Vice-President, Mamadou Dia, a leading Senegalese politician, was also Minister of Federal Security and Armed Forces. Léopold Sedar Senghor was head of the provincial government of Senegal. A few weeks after independence, Modibo Keita tried to remove Mamadou Dia from his control of Federal Security and Armed Forces. The Senegalese saw this as a threat to them. Consequently, on 20 August, the Government of Senegal under Senghor used local forces to arrest Modibo Keita and other ministers of the federal government and sent them off to Bamako, the capital of Soudan. This was the end of the Mali Federation. Later, Soudan adopted the name Mali, the name it has borne ever since. The government of Senegal then settled down to face the problems of nation-building – with Senghor as President and Mamadou Dia as Prime Minister.

The general picture since independence
Léopold Sedar Senghor, the man who led Senegal to independence and has remained its President, is one of the most famous leaders of independent Africa. Apart from being a statesman, he is also a dis-

tinguished scholar, philosopher and poet. Senghor is in the forefront of African intellectuals of our times who have projected African culture through their writings. Acknowledging that modern African culture is a product of the interactions of traditional African culture with European traits imported through colonialism, Senghor has done a lot to define the authentic African culture. According to him, it is Africa's original contribution to the universal civilisation of the human race. In spite of observable cultural differences between the peoples of Africa, he says, there are certain fundamental cultural characteristics common to all of Africa which distinguished Africans from the rest of mankind. These elements constitute the distinctive African contribution to human civilisation. The African must ensure, he says, that in his modern culture the distinctive and authentic African elements predominate over the acquired European traits. This is not a racist doctrine, or a doctrine seeking to make Africans separate from the rest of mankind. Senghor sees all cultures as part of, and contributions to, the single universal culture of mankind. But he insists that, to be able to make a recognisable contribution to this universal human culture, Africans must preserve the authentic elements of their culture. This in brief, is Senghor's philosophy of Negritude.

Thus Senghor has often said that as leader of Senegal, his concern is to find authentic African solutions to the problems of Senegal. And most of these solutions are to be provided through the pursuit of 'African Socialism'. Senghor is believed to have been the first man to use the term and has done more than most African leaders to define it. According to Senghor, it is based not on the alien doctrine of class warfare but on the communal spirit and organisation of traditional African society.

There has, however, been considerable difference between Senghor's pronouncements and his actual policies and actions as the ruler of Senegal. In contrast to his statements about 'decolonisation', 'Africanisation' and 'African Socialism', French influence has been much more obvious in Senegal than in any other independent French-speaking African country. Moreover, Senegal has been more dependent on France economically than most other former French colonies.

There are two reasons for this. In the first place, Senegal is a small country with limited human resources (about $3\frac{1}{2}$ million at independence) and limited natural resources. Its main source of wealth at independence was its groundnuts. Ten years after independence, groundnuts still constituted its chief export crop and foreign exchange earner. As a result, Senegal was compelled to depend heavily on France after independence. In the second place, Senghor is in prac-

tice a very cautious man. In spite of his grand philosophical pronouncements, he does not involve himself in any adventures or take
any steps about whose results he is not sure. For instance, although he
advocates Africanisation, he has said that he will not Africanise
whenever Africanisation will lead to the lowering of standards and of
performance. To the type of Africanisation which leads to a fall in
standards he has given the name 'Africanisation at a discount' or
'cut-rate Africanisation'. For him, Africanisation is justified and good
only when it is absolutely certain that Africans are available who can
maintain the high level of efficiency which the French officials had
established during the colonial era.

Thus, economically Senegal has been very far from free. By 1964,
about 79% of her exports went to France and about 58% of her
imports came from France. There have been considerable attempts to
trade with other countries since; but even by 1970 most of Senegal's
foreign trade was still with France and with France's partners in the
European Common Market. Indeed, Senegal's associate membership
of the European Common Market ties its economy to those of the
members of the Common Market. For many years after independence,
Senegal depended heavily upon the subsidised prices France was
paying for its groundnuts. Practically all the capital invested in Senegal,
practically all the funds needed to carry out her Development Plans,
have come from France. French businesses enjoy enormous freedom
in Senegal and exercise considerable influence on Senegalese politics.
For many years after independence, Senegal was still occupied by the
French army. President Senghor permitted this, not only because he
felt that the presence of the French army provided security for his
government, but also because the French army brought Senegal certain economic advantages. Until about 1964, nearly 10% of Senegal's
total external income was derived from the presence of the French
army. Even after 1965, when a serious reduction was made in the
French forces in Senegal, some French troops remained.

Even though Senegal was so educationally developed at independence that she could easily have manned her own services and also
helped her less fortunate neighbours with educated personnel, the
Senegalese Government preferred to keep the Frenchmen who had
been employed in Senegal by the colonial government. In 1959, the
year before independence, Senghor had entered into a 'technical assistance' agreement with France for the provision of French personnel to
man Senegal's civil service. Under this agreement, the number of
French personnel employed by Senegal even increased in the years
after independence. By 1963 the number was 1,380; by 1966 it had

increased to 1,523. By 1971 it had come down to 1,209, but even then Senegal had perhaps the highest concentration of French employees in French-speaking Africa.

Senghor's explanation is that he does not want administrative efficiency to be lowered: to engage in 'cut-rate Africanisation'. From about 1961, the government began to attempt to shift the French personnel from the purely administrative jobs to the more technical ones – to education and the ministries of economic planning, industry and commerce. But in practice, the distinction between the so-called purely technical and purely administrative jobs have proved impossible to establish. And the total result of this policy of French technical assistance is that French citizens have continued to play an important role in Senegal's decision-making and administrative processes. Needless to say, this has greatly enhanced France's influence on Senegal's national policies. It has also enhanced the freedom of French businesses in Senegal and the amount of influence they wield on the country's affairs.

Not infrequently, African nationalists inside and outside Senegal blame France for this policy, describing it as a French neo-colonialist manoeuvre to continue to enslave Senegal. But the truth is that it is not so much France as Senghor who has been responsible for the policy. There have been times when the number of 'technical assistants' demanded by the Senegalese Government has been larger than France has been willing to supply.

In education too, the Senegalese Government has preserved the classical French system almost completely unchanged, with the intention of ensuring that Senegal's educational qualifications remain acceptable in France. They are not, however, always suited to the needs of Senegal. Very little scientific and technical education has been introduced into the secondary schools and university. As a result, Senegal has continued to produce an over-abundance of secondary school leavers and university graduates who are suitable only for employment in administrative positions. It was not until very close to the end of the 1960s that subjects like agriculture, agronomy and development economics were introduced in the University of Dakar.

Another effect of this educational policy is that it has made the school system very heavily dependent upon the importation of French teachers. Senegalese teachers with the qualifications to maintain the colonial standards and traditions of French instruction have been few, especially at the higher level. By 1971, the academic staff of the University of Dakar was the least Africanised university staff in the whole of Africa outside the Republic of South Africa. Until 1967 the

176

University of Dakar had no African professor and only a few African lecturers. Its administration too was manned almost completely by Frenchmen. Senegal has produced many men qualified to teach in a university; but the complete control of the University of Dakar by the French has made that university unattractive as a career for Senegalese intellectuals.

Economic development

Although President Senghor has always declared that the direction of Senegal's economic development is determined by African Socialism, in practice much freedom has been allowed to private enterprise – both foreign and indigenous. From 1960 to 1962 some steps were taken towards building a socialist economy. In 1961 the *Office de Commercialisation Agricole* (OCA) or Office of Agricultural Commerce, was created to market Senegal's groundnuts. Produce marketing co-operatives were established all over the country to buy the groundnuts from the farmers. The collection and marketing of groundnuts, the most important crop, was thus nationalised. As a result, the private French and Lebanese companies which had always purchased the groundnuts from the producers were thrown out of this sector of the national economy.

The man who was mostly responsible for this socialist measure was the Prime Minister, Mamadou Dia. Within the ruling party, the UPS, Mamadou Dia belonged to the radical wing which advocated a far more radical socialist programme than Senghor was ready to accept. In 1962 their disagreements finally led to a crisis which ended with the removal and imprisonment of Dia. After the removal of Dia, Senghor pursued a very liberal policy towards foreign businesses. Again and again he has declared that Senegal would not nationalise foreign businesses. Nationalisation, he says, is outdated as a means of achieving socialism. Moreover, for nationalisation to be beneficial, he says, a country would need to have abundant capital to pay off the foreign businesses, and large numbers of citizens qualified to manage state enterprises, neither of which Senegal has. Therefore, although the co-operative programme has been continued in agriculture, Senegal has pursued a predominantly liberal capitalist policy.

Unlike the Development Plans of most African countries, Senegal's Development Plans have placed more emphasis on the development of agriculture than on industrialisation. The government's aim is to ensure that the improvement of the standard of living of the rural population keeps pace with that of the urban population. The First Development Plan, adopted in 1961, stated that agricultural development would be achieved in two ways – first through the establishment of co-operatives, and second through 'rural animation'. 'Rural animation' was defined as the process of awakening the sensitivity of the Senegalese masses to the problems of development, a process of making them aware of the great developments that they could achieve if only they would co-operate with the government to realise its plans. One of the ways in which 'rural animation' would be achieved was the training of rural 'cadres' or militants who would go back to the villages to lead and enlighten the rural population.

These policies have ensured considerable agricultural development in Senegal since independence. The production of groundnuts has been expanded. But at the same time, encouragement has been given to other crops, principally cotton, to diversify agricultural production. Because of this diversification, groundnuts accounted, by 1971, for only about 50% of total agricultural production. The production of rice, the main food crop, has also been expanded. Other important food crops are millet and sorghum. Fishing has been greatly expanded, and Senegal also produces some cattle, sheep and goats. On the whole, however, the total food production has proved inadequate for the nation's food needs, and as a result Senegal has continued to import food, especially rice.

By independence Senegal already had many industries – mostly because of being the centre of French West Africa during the colonial times. Since independence, its liberal policies towards foreign businesses have led to a fairly rapid pace of industrialisation, and by 1971, Senegal was one of the most industrialised countries in West Africa. Among its major industries are the making of groundnut oil and the canning of fish. Between 1960 and 1970, the production of phosphates, Senegal's principal mineral, more than tripled.

Transportation and communication facilities have been improved since independence. By 1971, Senegal had a good network of roads and railways. The railways link with those of neighbouring Mali and serve as the main route for Mali's exports and imports.

Political developments
Senghor's party, the UPS, has ruled Senegal since independence virtually without opposition in the parliament, while Senghor himself has encountered virtually no opposition in the presidential elections. On the whole, too, in a continent in which most other countries have experienced violent political changes, Senegal has enjoyed remarkable political stability.

A very important reason for this political stability is that, although

Senegal is made up of many ethnic groups, she has been fortunate to experience little or no inter-ethnic strife. Whatever opposition there has been to the UPS has arisen from ideological disagreements with Senghor's ideas and policies.

Another reason is that Senghor himself has been a very skilful politician indeed. Unlike most other African leaders, he has dealt with opposition not by trying to crush it, but by trying to persuade it to accept his point of view and eventually come over to his party. Although his party has consistently won all the elections, he has never tried to eliminate all opposition and establish a one-party state. He has always allowed some token opposition to exist, while making sure that it cannot grow to such an extent as to threaten his position. Within his own party, the UPS, he has played the same sort of skilful politics. The UPS has never been a tightly united party. It has always been divided into factions separated from one another by differences of ideas on how to approach national problems. But Senghor has always stayed outside and above these factions and thereby always acted as the arbiter between them. In that way he has been able to prevent the party from breaking up. Moreover, the position of arbiter has given him immense authority within the party.

As a result, although Senghor's Government has experienced a number of crises, he has been able to handle each one successfully. The first occurred two years after independence within the UPS, when the radical faction, led by the Prime Minister Mamadou Dia, advocated far-reaching measures to build a socialist economy, and gradually became dissatisfied with Senghor's more moderate policies after independence. At the end of 1962, this faction tried to carry out a *coup d'état*. But, with the aid of the army, Senghor foiled the attempt. Mamadou Dia was imprisoned, but many of his followers were allowed to keep their positions in the party and the government.

By 1965, disagreements between the factions had again grown so strong that the party was almost beginning to break up. Once more, however, Senghor managed to prevent disaster. He called for a spirit of unity not only within the party but in the whole nation. And to achieve this, he persuaded the main opposition party, the PRA (Parti du Regroupement Africain) to join the UPS. This action created a new atmosphere of national unity. By 1968 only a tiny communist party existed in opposition to the UPS.

By the middle of 1968, however, the government was confronted by a new sort of opposition – from the students of Dakar University. The students had always been critical of President Senghor's economic and foreign policies which they regarded as conservative. In May

1968 the students went on strike, and serious students' riots occurred in Dakar. The general workers' union also went on a general strike. The situation became so serious that the government ordered the army to occupy the university campus. Early in 1969, the students rioted again. Although the government ultimately granted many of the demands of the students and workers, the spirit of resistance to Senghor's policies continued to exist among the students.

17 Guinea

Guinea was the only French colony which voted 'No' against de Gaulle's constitution for the French Community in 1958. As a result of that vote, Guinea became independent on 2 October 1958. France immediately withdrew all economic and technical assistance, and Guinea found itself, overnight, without financial experts, engineers, doctors and administrators. Even government records were taken away by the French officials. France also cut off all trade with Guinea. And since almost all the trade of Guinea had been with France, Guinea was very hard hit. Guinea's export products piled up at the ports as the French refused to accept them. At the same time, imported goods quickly ran out in the shops.

Even if Guinea had not received this savage treatment from France, it would still have found things difficult economically. Guinea is a small country with very limited resources. Its land area is only about 94,560 square miles, and its population at independence only about 3 million. Only a very small percentage of this population was literate in 1958. Indeed, in education and economic development, Guinea was one of the least developed of the French colonies by 1958.

The man who persuaded the people of Guinea to vote 'No' and who therefore led the country into independence was Ahmed Sekou Toure. Sekou Toure had first entered politics as a trade unionist. In 1947 he founded his Democratic Party of Guinea (PDG) as a branch of the African Democratic Rally (RDA) founded in 1946 as a movement of French West African nationalists, under the leadership of Houphouët-Boigny of Ivory Coast. In the course of the 1950s, the PDG gradually became the dominant party in Guinea. In the elections held to the Guinea Territorial Assembly which was established in 1957, the PDG won 58 out of 60 contested seats. And by 1958 the party had practically no organised opposition in the country. Guinea therefore embarked upon independence as a one-party state, a condition which has been maintained since.

Economic developments

The economic history of independent Guinea is a story of a brave little country struggling against enormous odds to expand its economy and improve the living conditions of all its citizens. As spelled out by President Sekou Toure at independence, there were two goals for the country's economic development: firstly to break the foreign hold on the economy, and secondly to establish a state-planned and state-controlled economy. Since his days as a trade unionist, Sekou Toure had always been a socialist, and since Guinea's independence he has been one of the leading exponents of African socialism. His European and American critics often called him a communist, but Sekou Toure replied that the communist concept of class warfare is not applicable to Africa since Africa has no classes. His concern has always been to organise the economy of his country in such a way that its economic development would benefit all the people, not just a few.

In a sense, the angry and total withdrawal by France was a blessing in disguise. It taught the people of Guinea the important lesson that they had to take their destiny into their own hands. They were left completely free to manage their own affairs as they saw fit, to destroy the structure of the colonial economy and erect in its place a new economic structure more in accord with their own desires and needs. No other African country was so quickly Africanised after independence as Guinea.

The quick change from the colonial economy is perhaps best illustrated by the statistics of Guinea's foreign trade. In 1958, 69% of Guinea's exports went to France and 78% of its imports came from France. By 1961 only 17.8% of Guinea's exports went to France and only 12.2% of her imports came from France. Meanwhile, Guinea had established trade relations with many other countries all over the world, and although France changed its mind not long after Guinea's independence and began to trade actively with Guinea again, the new picture of Guinea's foreign trade did not seriously change. By 1970, the leading trade partners of Guinea were the Soviet Union, Czechoslovakia, Poland, the United States, then France and Britain. No other African country can boast such a rapid loosening of commercial ties with former colonial overlords.

When France withdrew all her economic and technical assistance, Guinea had to look elsewhere for assistance. The United States, as an ally of France, refused to help at first. However, the Soviet Union and other European countries as well as Ghana and China were eager to help. The Soviet Union and the Eastern European countries offered money, arms and technicians. Within a short time, the Soviet Union and the Eastern European countries gave Guinea a loan of about 35 million dollars (i.e. about £12 million) and sent about 1,500 technicians and advisers. Ghana gave an interest-free loan of £10 million. China helped to start a rice-development project which brought hundreds of Chinese technicians to the country. In addition, many Guinean students were given scholarships by Eastern European countries to study in their universities.

Guinea, however, did not tie itself to. the apron strings of any country. Although most of its immediate assistance came from the communist countries, it left itself free to receive offers of assistance from any other sources. Thus, when the United States at last changed its mind, Guinea was free to accept its help, and within two years of independence, a small American aid programme was under way.

Meanwhile, the campaign to socialise the economy had been embarked upon as soon as independence was won. To take the trade of the country away from the European and Lebanese merchants, a national External Trade Office was created and state trading monopolies set up to handle all the export and import business and the sale of goods in the country. Eventually all banking and insurance businesses were nationalised, and regulations established for all aspects of economic activity.

The government also initiated an ambitious programme of economic growth involving the rapid mechanisation of agriculture, the establishment of new industries, the expansion of mining, the expansion of schools, health services and road transportation. The Development Plan envisaged that the capital for these programmes would come from two main sources: first foreign loans and aids, and second the 'human investment' of the Guinean people themselves. 'Human investment' meant free labour; the underemployed people all over Guinea would be mobilised to build roads, schools, dispensaries, public buildings and other projects.

To mechanise agriculture, large quantities of farming machinery were imported from the Soviet Union, and many farm projects were begun. A start was also made with industrialisation. A tobacco factory, a dairy and a printing plant were established, and the Guinea Airlines was inaugurated with aeroplanes bought from the Soviet Union. The mining of bauxite and diamonds was steadily expanded. A very ambitious programme of educational expansion was initiated, with schools springing up in all parts of the country. Health services also expanded rapidly, most villages being provided with dispensaries. The country also witnessed a boom in state construction projects: offices, official residential quarters, roads, a sports stadium and a beautiful hotel in Conakry, the national capital.

In spite of all this economic and social progress, by 1961 Guinea was in serious economic difficulties, mainly due to the very low standard of education which caused a drastic shortage of qualified administrators, technicians, accountants and teachers, to bear all the rapidly increased burden of planning and management called for by the development projects. As a result, many of the projects suffered from inefficient management. For instance, the management of the Conakry port was so inefficient that perishable export goods like bananas were kept waiting at the port until they rotted. The state trading monopolies often over-imported goods not usually required by the people while under-importing other goods urgently needed. The circulation of goods in the country was inefficient, resulting in shortages in some parts of the country and glut in other parts. The same was true of food crops. As a result, while the villages had a lot of food, food shortages made life difficult in the urban centres.

Also, because of the dearth of qualified Guinean administrators, managers and planners, a lot of the foreign aid was poorly administered, so that the country did not derive much benefit from it. For instance, the types of agricultural equipment bought from the Soviet Union were not suitable for African conditions. The ordering of such machinery and their spare parts was so poorly managed that when they broke down the spare parts were usually not available for a very long time. Many of the other imports from the Soviet Union were fancy goods not particularly important to the lives of the common people. And all these were paid for from the Soviet loans.

Unfortunately too, there were some serious mistakes in the arrangement of priorities. Thus, too much of the early loans was expended on showy projects like the sports stadium rather than on productive enterprises.

'Human investment' contributed far less than was hoped. Because it resembled too vividly the forced labour of the colonial era, it was not easy to get the people's enthusiastic participation. Moreover, many of the projects on which the people were asked to give their free labour (like the building of residential quarters for government officials) could not be easily shown to be advantageous to the common people and, therefore, could not excite their enthusiasm.

Finally, many corrupt practices developed which worsened the whole situation. Although the President himself lived in simple style and appealed repeatedly to other leaders to do the same, many leading citizens sabotaged the national efforts by engaging in smuggling and black market practices. Rice and cattle were smuggled across the border to obtain foreign exchange, and the foreign exchange was then used to import various luxury goods.

By 1961, therefore, the country was in trouble. Since most of the foreign aid had come in the form of loans, the nation had accumulated a huge foreign debt. National production was falling; so was the volume of the main agricultural exports – bananas, palm produce, coffee and cocoa. Growth was recorded only in mining. Though the masses of the people remained loyal, secret criticisms of the government grew among the better educated elements in society. At the end of 1961 a plot against the government was discovered among the secondary school teachers.

Although pursuing its socialist policies, the government began to make some changes in order to adapt to the situation. For instance, to make the state-run commerce more efficient, the big slow-moving state commercial monopolies were broken up into smaller corporations. Planning too was considerably decentralised so that the provincial administrations began to play a more significant role in making and executing development plans. It had always been the government's policy to allow participation by private capital in certain areas of the economy – especially in developing the mining and processing industries. From 1962 more deliberate efforts were made to increase foreign investment. In April 1962 a private investment law was passed whose objective was to attract foreign capital. After that a sizeable amount of private foreign capital came into the country, especially into her rich mineral industry. However, the government continued to regulate the operation of such foreign investment, and having itself provided capital for investment, now owns shares in most businesses in the country. Finally, relations with France gradually improved. A settlement was reached between the two countries in May 1963, with the important advantage that France agreed to release certain moneys which had been owing to Guinea. Trade with France also began to improve. Trade with the USA, as well as the volume of American aid, increased. On the whole, although no spectacular economic development took place in Guinea, the country survived the difficulties of its first few years of independence and began to make progress from about 1963.

Guinea's greatest source of wealth is its minerals. It has perhaps the largest known deposit of high quality bauxite in the world, as well as considerable deposits of iron ore, gold and diamonds. Bauxite mining, begun in colonial times, grew rapidly after independence, the capital for such growth coming from the USA, Germany, Switzerland and other foreign countries. An American company by 1971 owned the largest number of shares in the biggest bauxite mining company in the country. In 1968 a group of foreign companies was given extensive bauxite concessions at Boke near the coast. Three years later, an agreement was reached to expand the project to raise bauxite production at Boke to nine million tons annually. Under these agreements, it was envisaged that total investment in the Boke project – by the foreign companies, the Guinea Government and the World Bank – would amount to $250 million (or about £85 million).

Alumina, made from bauxite, was Guinea's main export and foreign exchange earner by 1972. But the production of iron ore also increased. Between 1958 and 1962 alone, the volume of iron ore export doubled. Some gold and diamonds were also being mined. The volume of diamonds exported increased sharply immediately after 1958, but later declined.

Guinea's agricultural products are bananas, palm oil and kernels, cocoa, coffe, corn, cassava and rice. Of these, bananas, palm produce, cocoa and coffee are exported. The volume of rice production gradually increased after 1958. But on the whole Guinea's agricultural production did not increase as fast as the population. As a result, Guinea had to import more food.

Guinea has huge resources of hydro-electric power. A project was embarked upon in the late sixties to build two dams on the Konkoure River, which would be among the greatest suppliers of hydro-electric power in West Africa.

Much progress was made in social development during the 1960s, most spectacularly in education. Within the first five years of independence, school enrolment tripled. The problem of shortage of teachers was solved with a programme of teacher training coupled with the hiring of teachers from abroad. The United States aid programme included after 1962 the provision of American teachers through the Peace Corps. For the training of high level manpower, Guinean youths were sent to universities in the Soviet Union, France, America, and many Eastern European countries. Many of these went on government scholarships, but some scholarships were also provided by the countries to which the students were sent.

On the whole, the level of economic and social development in Guinea was still low by 1970. By 1969 gross national product was only $280 million (or about £95 million), and per capita income was only $80 (about £27) – one of the lowest in Africa. The living standards of the people were still low; about 90% still lived on subsistence agriculture. Food production was still lower than the food needs of the population. However, in the light of the condition and circumstances of Guinea at independence, the first fifteen years of independence were years of considerable progress.

Domestic and foreign politics

As conceived by President Sekou Toure, independence was to be not merely the removal of European colonialism but the total destruction of 'the habits, conceptions and ways of conduct of colonialism' and their replacement with 'forms that are Guinean forms, conceived by the people of Guinea'. The duty of the ruling party, the PDG, was to lead the nation to achieve this revolution. The PDG was therefore the 'motor of the Revolution', the 'guardian of the will of the people'. It was the duty of the party to formulate the national goals and the means of attaining them, and the government was to be the people's instrument for carrying things out. But the party was not to be a party of the elite but of all the people, a party whose will was dictated by the people. Through the party, the people would control the leading citizens who, in the government, the civil service and the army, were carrying out the national programmes.

The PDG was therefore organised as a truly people's party. A party branch with a party committee was set up in every village. By 1963, practically all the adult population of Guinea belonged to the party. The national leadership of the party was the National Political Bureau of which Sekou Toure was the secretary. The party leadership frequently urged the people to participate actively in the affairs of their local branches and to make their views and wishes known through the local party channels. Participation by all was the party's watchword. Only by participating actively in the local branches could the ordinary individual influence national policies. Each local branch met weekly, and full attendance at these meetings was frequently urged. Special encouragement was given to youths and women by reserving for them special numbers of seats on the local party committees, and by appointing them into important national positions.

In addition, the Guinea Government did more than most African governments to foster national unity. Like other African countries, Guinea is a conglomeration of many peoples, the three largest ethnic groups being the Foulah, the Malinke and the Soussou. At independence, the party experienced some opposition from the Foulah. In the referendum on the French Community in September 1958, more people among the Foulah than among any other ethnic group had rejected Sekou Toure's appeals and had voted 'Yes'. As soon as the country became independent, however, Sekou Toure set about winning over the Foulah. The most prominent of his Foulah opponents was appointed into the cabinet. Other leading Foulah elements rose to very important positions in the country. In fact, the next in rank to Sekou Toure himself in the cabinet was a Foulah. These conciliatory methods paid off. By 1962, Foulah opposition had vanished. Moreover, in the year before independence, Sekou Toure had abolished chieftaincies in Guinea, thereby eliminating the commonest force of local sectionalism. In general, the party employed its great influence among the people to encourage the feeling of oneness. A number of practices and conventions were also designed to encourage close contacts between peoples of different ethnic origins and to inculcate broad nationalist awareness among the educated elements in society. Thus it was made national policy that secondary school students should go to school, and government officials should serve, outside their own ethnic regions.

Guinea benefited immensely from all these political policies. A society gradually evolved in which the ordinary people in their villages are well informed about the policies and actions of their government, a society in which the ordinary man can feel that his participation in national affairs is welcomed and respected. Moreover, a very strong feeling of national solidarity has been nurtured. In spite of her economic troubles, Guinea has enjoyed more political stability than most other African countries. Unlike most other government leaders, Sekou Toure could drive or even walk about among the people without a bodyguard – even in the late sixties when political assassinations and military *coups d'état* had become a common occurrence in Africa.

It is not, of course, that the regime had no enemies at home or that the country's stability was never threatened. Indeed the regime passed through a number of political crises. In November 1961, the government became aware that the secondary school teachers were secretly circulating some documents which were highly critical of the whole political and economic system. It is not known whether the teachers did plan to overthrow the government. However the government reacted by arresting the leaders of the teachers' union. Thereupon, the secondary school students went on strike and demonstrated against the government. The resulting political tension was fairly easily brought under control, especially because the government was massively supported by the illiterate and semi-literate masses. The leaders of the plot were sentenced to death.

In November 1965, a more serious threat to the government was unearthed in the form of a plot by some civilians and military men to carry out a *coup d'état*. One of the leading figures among the plotters was Mamadou Toure, a distant cousin of President Sekou Toure.

Then in November 1970 came the most serious threat that the regime had ever encountered. By then quite a sizeable number of Guinean opponents of the regime were living in voluntary exile abroad. Moreover, next door was Guinea (Bissau) where the people had been fighting the liberation war against Portugal since 1963. Sekou Toure's Government had always given assistance to the liberation force of Guinea (Bissau), much to the annoyance of Portugal. In November 1970, a combination of Portuguese forces, Guinean exiles and other mercenary elements suddenly invaded Guinea. Conakry, the capital city, was attacked. For a few days bitter fighting occurred between the invaders and the Guinean forces. The invaders were driven out. Though the invasion failed, it stunned the nation, and it was followed in 1971 by the arrest, trial and imprisonment or execution of persons suspected of collaborating with the invaders.

None of these crises, however, weakened the government's control or influence. Indeed, each of them tended ultimately to strengthen the sympathy of the common people for the regime.

On the international scene, Guinea has had one of the most stormy careers of the independent states of Africa. Guinea's defiance of France in 1958 made Sekou Toure second only to Dr Nkrumah as the most popular nationalist leader, and he has always remained on the more radical wing of Pan-Africanism. Like Dr Nkrumah, he has consistently advocated the use of radical means to end all colonialism in Africa; he has also advocated the creation of larger political unions in Africa. He was one of the leading members of the group of African leaders who, early in the sixties, formed the Casablanca Group.

Sekou Toure's belief in larger political unions led him to form a union with Ghana, which was to be a nucleus of an all-West African Federation. When Mali agreed to join the union, it looked as if the dream of a West African Federation was to be fulfilled. But the members of the union failed to get the neighbouring countries to join. And since Ghana, Guinea and Mali are not a continuous block of territory, it was impossible to give any constitutional and practical form to the union. However, Sekou Toure has never ceased to express his belief in larger political unions in Africa.

With some of Guinea's close neighbours, Sekou Toure's radical nationalism and Pan-Africanism have sometimes led to trouble. Although he and Houphouët-Boigny of Ivory Coast were close colleagues in the RDA in the late forties, their relationship deteriorated quickly in the fifties. Toure has often said that Houphouët-Boigny is too French for his liking. On a number of occasions, Houphouët-Boigny has accused Sekou Toure of trying to engineer radicals to start trouble in Ivory Coast. Sekou Toure too has accused Houphouët-

Boigny, as well as President Léopold Senghor of Senegal, of aiding French plots against him. Sekou Toure has always criticised such organisations as the Conseil d'Entente, the Brazzaville Group and OCAM as being tools of French neo-colonialist influence in Africa. With the overthrow of Dr Nkrumah in Ghana in 1966, hostile feelings developed between Sekou Toure and the military rulers of Ghana because he gave shelter to Dr Nkrumah in Guinea. When Dr Nkrumah died in 1972, Guinea's relationship with Ghana once more became tense, because Sekou Toure attempted to dictate to the Government of Ghana the conditions under which Dr Nkrumah's body should be buried. He would not release the body, he said, unless the Ghana Government agreed to bury it in Accra and to accord Dr Nkrumah the recognition he deserved as Ghana's national hero. The tension was short-lived, but before it was finally ironed out, it involved almost all of Africa in feverish negotiations between Ghana and Guinea.

In the wider world, Sekou Toure's policy has been one of strict non-alignment. His defiance of France in 1958 and his socialist policies at home have always made him rather unpopular with the Western powers. Indeed in the first few years of independence, his relationship with the Western powers was very tense. For some time, the United States even refused to accord Guinea any official recognition, and none of the Western powers would give Guinea economic aid in the first few years of independence. In contrast, the Eastern powers were ready to come to her aid. And so, a very close relationship developed between Guinea on the one hand and the Soviet Union, China and many Eastern European countries on the other.

Sekou Toure, however, never allowed aid to become a means of establishing any foreign political influence over his country. Thus, when he had reason to believe, during the 'teachers' plot' of 1961, that the Soviet representatives in Guinea were meddling in the affairs of Guinea, he expelled the Soviet ambassador from the country. This led to a considerable deterioration in his relationship with the Soviet Union for some time. In 1962 a major crisis developed between the United States and the Soviet Union over Cuba. The Soviet Union asked Sekou Toure to allow them to use Conakry airport as a stopping base for their aeroplanes on the long journey to Cuba. But Sekou Toure refused, on the grounds that to grant that permission would be to involve Guinea in the cold war between the Eastern and Western powers.

As soon as the Western powers got over their early emotional reaction to Guinea's independence and socialist policies, Sekou Toure was ready to enter into normal relationships with them. Regular air communication was established between Guinea and the United States, and Guinea received aid from the United States and encouraged American capital to come into Guinea's mining industry. Relationships were normalised even with France. But just as he had done to the Soviet Union, Sekou Toure prevented the United States or France from establishing any influence over his country. He also would not commit himself to them in their cold war moves. Moreover, his relationship with the Soviet Union improved once the 1961 'teachers' plot' crisis was over, while he continued to maintain good relationships with the other Eastern powers, especially China.

18　Zaire

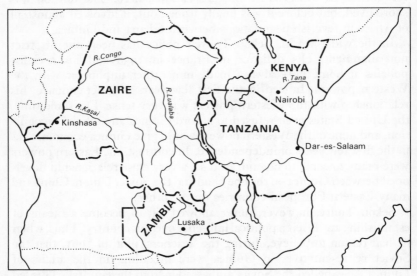

Independent East and Central African states

The Republic of Zaire, formerly Congo (Kinshasa), became independent on 30 June 1960 in very inauspicious circumstances. The colonial power, Belgium, had ruled the country on the assumption that it would never become independent. Consequently they had done practically nothing to prepare its people to manage their own affairs. For instance, they had deliberately made the primary school the highest level of education, with the result that when Zaire became independent, only very few of its citizens had any education above the primary level. Most of these were the products of the church seminaries; of university graduates, Zaire had only about thirty. Moreover, the literate Zaireans had been given no chance to participate in any aspect of the country's central government and so had acquired no experience in tackling national issues. Until one year before independence, they had been denied the right to form political parties and associations or publish nationalist newspapers. They had been prevented from travelling outside their country or becoming acquainted with the methods of nationalist politics in the rest of Africa. Until 1958, probably not more than two or three of the future leaders of Zaire had ever travelled beyond the country.

At independence, in place of broad national parties, political parties emerged representing particular regions and ethnic groups. No less than twenty-seven parties won seats in the pre-independence general elections. The literate leaders had had little or no contacts with one another, each being confined in experience to his own province. In fact, probably most of them had never met.

Almost all responsible positions in the civil service, the police, the army and the judiciary were occupied by Belgians and with no trained Zaireans to take their place. This was particularly serious since the loyalty of these Belgian officials to the young nation was doubtful. For instance, some top Belgians in the army had been opposed to the Belgian Government's granting independence to Zaire and had thought of using force to prevent it. Some of these military officers were in collaboration with the more extreme members of the Belgian civilian population in Zaire who would have liked to seize power for themselves in the way the white settlers later did in Rhodesia.

At independence, the army was in a dangerous mood. Owing to the wave of nationalism sweeping the country, the Zairean soldiers could no longer respect their Belgian officers. In fact, they expected that indigenous officers would immediately replace them. However, the political leaders were aware that it would take time to train the Zairean soldiers to take over as officers. This created resentment among the soldiers who accused the political leaders of reluctance to extend the benefits of independence to the Zaireans serving in the army. Here then was the spectacle of an African army resentful both of its foreign officers and of its own compatriots who were leading the country.

These are some of the main elements behind the great tragedy which the books refer to as 'The Congo Crisis'. The newly independent nation was a very fragile structure indeed, and within a week of independence it began to break down.

Six days after independence, on 5 July 1960, the collapse began in the army. Zairean soldiers of the national army, the Force Publique, mutinied against their Belgian officers in Kinshasa and within four days, the mutiny spread to the rest of the country. In a few places, the soldiers killed white civilians. As a result, Belgium flew in Belgian forces to protect Belgian lives and property. The Zairean Government permitted the presence of the Belgian troops, provided they were used only for protecting Belgian lives and property, and for some time, the situation showed some improvement.

However, two events occurred on 11 July which led to a total collapse of order. First, the Belgian navy unleashed an altogether unnecessary bombardment on the coastal city of Matadi and the news quickly spread all over the country that the bombardment had caused the deaths of hundreds of the people of that city. In answer, Zairean soldiers in various parts of the country set out to avenge the Matadi massacre on the white population. This in turn led to widespread intervention by Belgian troops. The second incident was the declaration by Katanga province, under the leadership of Moise Tshombe, that it seceded from Zaire and became a separate independent state. It soon became clear that the Belgians were behind the secessionist movement. Belgian troops helped Tshombe to disarm and expel Zairean troops who opposed the secession and also to build an army to defend Katanga.

These incidents confirmed many people's fears that Belgium was out to reconquer the country. As a result, the Zairean Government of Patrice Lumumba as Premier and Joseph Kasavubu as President broke off relations with Belgium and accused Belgium and her Western allies of attempting to destroy the sovereignty of Zaire. The masses of the people reacted with widespread attacks on the white population. The white civil servants, police officers and military officers fled and within a short time Zaire had one of the most Africanised bureaucracies in the whole of Africa. Meanwhile, Belgium was flying in more troops to various parts of the country.

The Zairean Government now tried to tackle the two major problems facing it – to end the secession of Katanga and to establish order and stable authority. But it was handicapped by the fact that its civil service was drastically inexperienced and its army leaderless and disorderly. Consequently, on 12 July President Kasavubu and Prime Minister Lumumba invited the United Nations Organisation to send forces to help in expelling the Belgians and in keeping order. The following day, the UNO agreed, and also offered to send technical advisers to help the Zairean Government organise its own civil service and army. On 15 July, the first UN troops began to arrive. By 4 September official Belgian troops had been forced to withdraw from all parts of Zaire, including Katanga. There were still, however, hundreds of Belgian and other foreign mercenaries helping Katanga.

Katanga's secession proved more difficult to tackle. Lacking adequate forces of his own for that task, Lumumba expected that it was part of the assignment of the UN forces. However, the UN forces refused to be so used, insisting that they were not supposed to interfere in the country's internal politics. On 8 August disintegration advanced further when South Kasai followed the example of Katanga and announced its secession.

Lumumba tried to raise military aid from other African states and from the Soviet Union. By 26 August his forces had stamped out the secession of Kasai and by early September they were poised for the invasion of Katanga. By early September too, some military assistance had arrived from the Soviet Union. However, before the invasion of Katanga had got under way, the government itself collapsed.

Between Kasavubu and Lumumba, there had never been very close association. The arrangement whereby one was made President and the other Prime Minister just before independence was only a political compromise, and it was very shaky indeed. Within Kasavubu's own party, there were persons who remained strongly opposed to Lumumba, while Kasavubu himself could not always reconcile himself to the radicalism and the flamboyant ways of Lumumba. These differences gradually built up towards a crisis, and on 5 September 1960, Kasavubu broadcast a statement announcing his removal of Lumumba from the Prime Ministership. Lumumba replied with a statement deposing Kasavubu as President.

The chaotic power contest thus unleashed reached its climax with the arrest of Lumumba in December 1960 and his assassination in January 1961. The confusion enabled Katanga to strengthen its secession and South Kasai to re-establish its secession. Having lost the contest in Kinshasa, the national capital, Lumumba's chief supporters moved to the province of Orientale which was more friendly to them and there at Kisangani in December 1960, they established the base of their own government which they claimed to be the legitimate government of the whole country. In short, by December 1960, Zaire had broken down into four separate entities – Katanga, South Kasai, the areas under Kasavubu's Government based at Kinshasa, and the areas under the Lumumbist Government based at Kisangani in Orientale province.

Each government had an army of its own and some fighting occurred in various parts of the country. Each government also won some support abroad. However, since the presence of the UN forces ruled out an outright military solution, negotiations ultimately took place.

And the end result of these negotiations was the agreement to convene a meeting of the independence parliament on the campus of Lovanium University in July 1961. All groups, with the exception of Katanga, were represented at this meeting of parliament. The meeting arrived at the compromise of setting up a new government under the Prime Ministership of Cyrille Adoula, a man reasonably acceptable to all sides. The government which Adoula formed comprised ministers from all the camps represented at the Lovanium meeting. Antoine Gizenga, Lumumba's leading follower, was made Vice-Premier. And so the constitutional chaos which had begun with Kasavubu's sacking of Lumumba in September 1960 now appeared to have come to an end.

However, among some of Lumumba's followers, there persisted a strong suspicion of the new government, especially because it was feared to be too much under Belgian and Western influence. By October 1961 Gizenga was back in Orientale trying to reorganise the Lumumbist forces against the Adoula Government. But other leading Lumumbists refused to join him in this rebellion, and so in January 1962 he was arrested and imprisoned. Thus, though with difficulty, the compromise unity established at the Lovanium meeting managed to survive.

This establishment of a legitimate government for the rest of the country made it possible to concentrate efforts on the destruction of Katanga's secession. Fortunately, too, the UN had meanwhile become prepared to use force to expel foreign mercenaries and political agents from Katanga. From August 1961, the UN forces embarked upon this project, meeting stiff resistance from the Katangese forces. However, by December, Katangese resistance had more or less collapsed and Tshombe agreed to meet Adoula. At their first meeting, Tshombe accepted almost all the terms laid down by Adoula for reintegration of Katanga into the nation. But, no sooner did the meeting come to an end than Tshombe began to question the agreement. From March to June 1962, negotiation went on intermittently. It soon became clear that Tshombe had no intention of giving up Katanga's independence and that he was only playing for time to reorganise his forces and consolidate Katanga's secession. Tshombe therefore gradually lost prestige with most members of the world community and, at the UN, most members became agreeable to drastic plans for ending Katanga's secession. Consequently, when the new Secretary General of the UN, U. Thant, proposed a plan to this end, the UN accepted it. The plan provided for the preparation of a new federal constitution for Zaire (including Katanga) and the application of economic sanctions against Katanga if she should refuse to accept this plan. Once more, Tshombe announced that he accepted the plan, but once more it became clear that this acceptance was insincere. Consequently, the UN became agreeable to the use of force against Katanga, and on 28 December 1962 the final thrust of UN forces into Katanga began. On 14 January 1963 Tshombe announced the termination of Katanga's secession. Zaire had become one country again.

The Adoula Government now turned its attention to the task of creating a constitution acceptable to the whole country. However, it was not allowed to do so in peace. Many pockets of opposition to Adoula had persisted, and in parliament, pro-Lumumba groups tried again and again to destroy him. From October 1963 the opposition became violent and began to use force in attempts to seize various parts of the country. Moreover, the trade unions were always hostile. They were always criticising the high salaries earned by the politicians and in 1962 they had organised nation-wide strikes. Finally, in various parts of the country, there were factional troubles as each ethnic group sought to establish some separate administrative unit of its own. As a result, the provinces began to disintegrate into mutually hostile units.

In spite of these troubles, a constitutional framework gradually emerged. In the place of the six provinces of the time of independence, twenty-one new provinces were created. In January 1964, the government set up a commission to draft a new constitution for the country, which was completed in April. Zaire became a federation with twenty-one provinces.

In June 1964, Adoula's Prime Ministership came to an end. To strengthen the national reconciliation, President Kasavubu invited Moise Tshombe back from exile and appointed him Prime Minister. The appointment was very unpopular with radical nationalist leaders in the rest of Africa. In Zaire itself, trouble soon began with pro-Lumumba elements. Two of Lumumba's former friends, Christopher Gbenye and Pierre Mulele, started a rebellion in the north-eastern parts of the country. They captured the city of Kisangani, and on 7 September 1964 they announced there the formation of what they called the 'People's Republic of the Congo'. War then ensued between the government of Tshombe and the government of the rebels. In this war, Tshombe received considerable assistance from Belgian forces flown in for the announced purpose of saving the lives of Europeans trapped in Kisangani. Consequently, the rebels were defeated within four months.

Even then, opposition to Tshombe remained strong and, therefore, on 3 October 1965, Kasavubu forced him to resign. Evariste Kimba, a former close associate of Tshombe, was appointed Prime Minister.

But by then, the army had come to the conclusion that the civilians were incapable of establishing good stable government. Therefore, on 25 November 1965, General Joseph Mobutu, the commander of the army, peacefully took over the government, declared himself President and announced that he would rule for five years.

Gradually Mobutu took full control of the country. He stripped parliament of its powers, took over control of the police force, and assumed the authority of both President and Prime Minister. He then ruled the country very firmly. At times, his early actions appeared very harsh. For instance, in June 1966 he had four top politicians publicly hanged for plotting to assassinate him. However, Mobutu's actions did not come out of cruelty. If he did harsh things in his first months as ruler, it was because he believed that Zaire would never know peace until it had a firm government which would tolerate no factious wranglings.

Mobutu's most important constitutional reform was the abolition of the federal system to enable a single strong government at the centre to manage the affairs of the country. He nationalised the police forces of the provinces and placed them under the control of the Ministry of Interior. Convinced that the existing system of 21 provinces was too expensive and difficult to manage, he reduced the number of provinces to eight. He also lowered the status of the provincial Assemblies by reducing them from legislative bodies to mere consultative bodies. The President was given the power to nullify the decisions of the provincial authorities if such decisions did not agree with the central government's policies. The provincial governors became civil servants who were employed by the central government, were under the supervision of the Ministry of Interior, and could be transferred or sacked by the central government.

In 1967 to create a popular base for his government, Mobutu founded a national political party, the Popular Movement of the Revolution (MPR). Although an opposition party was legally possible, none emerged. And in 1969 the President announced that the MPR would be the single national party of all Zaireans – a party of national unity. The effect of the founding of this party is that it made it possible for civilians to be brought into the task of leading the nation, all under the umbrella of Mobutu. Most prominent Zairean civilians welcomed this. Both at the national and local levels, the MPR propaganda was geared towards encouraging citizens to take an active part in political affairs and to accept civic responsibilities. The objectives of the party were stated to be the fostering of national unity, economic progress and economic independence, the restoration of the people's confidence in government, and the revival of the nation's international prestige. The army was made to stay out of politics, but as a readily available source of support to the President.

As part of his efforts to foster the growth of national consciousness, President Mobutu began a campaign to encourage his countrymen to do away with European names and return to indigenous ones. Starting with the country itself, he changed its name from Congo to Zaire, the name of its capital from Leopoldville to Kinshasa, and revived many old indigenous place names all over the country. He changed his own name from Joseph Mobutu to Mobutu Sesse Seko, and called upon all prominent citizens to change their names also. On 30 June 1966, the sixth anniversary of Zaire's independence, President Mobutu proclaimed the late Patrice Lumumba a national hero, named a major street in Kinshasa after him, and announced that a statue would be erected in his honour.

As ruler of Zaire, Mobutu proved a dedicated fighter for national unity and national consciousness. In the ten years after his coming to power, Zaire enjoyed considerable political stability. His government experienced only two serious political challenges. In the summer of 1966, Katangese military units mutinied in Kisangani and for about two months resisted the national forces. In mid-1967 some mercenary forces employed by the Zairean Government revolted and attempted to bring the government down. Some units of the national army even joined them. The rebels held the cities of Bukavu and Kisangani for some time but they were eventually driven out of the country.

The political troubles of 1960–65 took a huge toll in human life. But, on the whole, the country continued to do fairly well economically. Except in the brief periods of very intense commotion, the roads, railways, river transport, and schools were maintained; the large plantations in places like Kwilu were maintained by the foreign companies which owned them. In spite of the withdrawal of all Belgian doctors, the medical services were kept running, thanks especially to the assistance rendered by the World Health Organisation. On the whole, only scattered areas of the country suffered drastic economic dislocation, and such areas included those districts through which the conflicting armies moved or where inter-ethnic antagonisms led to serious communal violence. Mining, the most important industry of Zaire at independence, was, on the whole, continued. Copper mining in Katanga did not decrease, gold production in Orientale and tin production in Maniema and North Katanga were sometimes interrupted, but they did not stop. However, most of the diamonds mined during the years of trouble were exported fraudulently, with the result that the country could derive no income from them. Production of consumer goods like cement, sugar and beer increased remarkably.

The secret of this economic well-being is that Zaire is very richly endowed by nature; in mineral, forest and agricultural resources, perhaps the richest country in Africa. After General Mobutu took over power in 1965 and established orderly government, the country's economic fortunes greatly improved. A great deal of resources was then devoted to developing education, especially post-primary education, and particular attention was paid to the training of teachers. Zaire's position was fully re-established as one of the world's largest producers of copper, diamonds, gold, silver, tin, cobalt, uranium, radium, zinc and iron.

In 1966, Zaire began to establish stronger control over the great foreign companies which had long exploited the country. A government decree made it compulsory for all these companies to move their headquarters to Zaire. Most of the companies obeyed, except Union Minière, the great mining company which controlled the huge copper resources of Katanga. As a result, the Government of Zaire took over its assets and handed them over to a new state-owned company, the General Congolese Ores Company. In 1967–68, the government continued to try to increase its participation in the country's rich mining industry by becoming a partner in the other mining companies. The matter was finally settled late in 1969 to the satisfaction of the government and the companies.

19 Kenya

Kenya became independent on 12 December 1963, under the Prime Ministership of Jomo Kenyatta, one of the most famous African nationalist leaders. One year later, the country became a republic, with Kenyatta as President and another prominent leader, Oginga Odinga, as Vice-President. These two men were the President and Vice-President of the Kenya African National Union (KANU), the political party which led Kenya into independence.

Kenya entered independent nationhood with a constitution which considerably weakened the authority of its central government, thanks to the antagonisms among the ethnic groups in the country. Of these ethnic groups, the largest and most advanced in Western education at independence were the Kikuyu. Next to them were the Luo. These two peoples, usually referred to as the majority peoples, had co-operated in founding the KANU in 1960 and they constituted the base of KANU's power. However, a host of smaller ethnic groups, worried about domination by the Kikuyu-Luo alliance, organised themselves into the Kenya African Democratic Union (KADU) which constituted the official opposition to the KANU Government at independence. In the three years preceding independence, the fears of the smaller peoples grew very high. As a result, KADU demanded from the British a quasi-federal set-up which would give each province considerable authority over its own affairs. Though opposed to this arrangement, KANU finally accepted it so as not to delay independence. Kenya therefore became a quasi-federal country with seven provinces each with its own authority.

No sooner was independence achieved than KANU began to take steps to destroy the quasi-federal set-up. In August 1964, they proposed its abolition to the Kenya parliament. While this proposal was being debated, they toured the country intensively, trying to persuade the masses of the people. They also wooed members of KADU, and some of them began to 'cross the carpet' and join the KANU. So successful was the government in these campaigns that the members of the KADU finally agreed voluntarily to dissolve their party in November 1964. Consequently, the constitutional proposals of the government were passed unanimously, and so, in December 1964, Kenya became a unitary state, a one-party state, and a republic.

The Kenya parliament at independence was made up of two chambers – a lower chamber called the House of Representatives, and an upper chamber called the Senate. A constitutional amendment in 1967 merged the two chambers into one, called the National Assembly.

In general, one of the greatest ambitions of Jomo Kenyatta was to weld the peoples of Kenya into a united, harmonious nation. Kenyatta himself was widely accepted as the father of the nation, and his hatred of inter-ethnic bitterness was well known. He coined the slogan, 'Harambee' meaning 'Let us all pull together'. So successful was he immediately after independence that Kenya became universally acknowledged as one of the most stable countries in Africa.

However, below the surface, there were signs of trouble which eventually became apparent. Even among the Kikuyu, there were various kinds of antagonism – between some districts and others, between the landless men and the growing class of landed gentry produced by the colonial government's policy of land consolidation in the 1950s, between those who had taken part in the Mau Mau revolt against the colonial government in the early fifties, and those who had not. Also, though the Kikuyu and Luo were now allies, there were strong memories of hostility between them. For instance, during the 1940s, Kikuyu-Luo rivalries had led to violent conflicts between the two peoples in urban centres like Nairobi, and the memories of these incidents were still alive in the 1960s. Finally, even though the smaller ethnic groups found a common cause in resisting Kikuyu-Luo domination, there were various types of rivalry and suspicion among them, principally conflicting claims to land.

As a result, before independence every locality had certain interests to protect against its neighbours, and every locality therefore used its educated sons as its champions. The arena in which the rivalries were fought out was the District Councils, because after the Mau Mau revolt, the colonial government had prohibited all countrywide political organisations. The district had therefore become the focus of all political activity, and district politics was dominated by the endless disputes between contending groups. Many of the future political leaders of Kenya were products of these district politics.

When in 1960 the colonial government at last allowed Kenyans to form political organisations, both KANU and KADU were in reality alliances of district politicians, although very much less was usually said about this than about the broader inter-ethnic antagonisms and rivalries in the country at large. In many districts, leaders who had long fought each other as champions of opposing interests now became members of the same political party, particularly of KANU.

This weakened KANU's efforts to unify the country. It was not often easy for the party to control local bosses, and the assertion of local and personal interest was often strong within both party and government. Also the party was often faced with the problem of reconciling its leading members who had long opposed each other at the district level. At election time, it was very common to find many KANU members standing as independent candidates against official party candidates. Finally, even in parliament, KANU often could not discipline its own members to support the party policies.

After independence, disagreements among leaders of the party over national policies became more and more open. Of the personal rivalries, that between Oginga Odinga and Tom Mboya, secretary of the party, became the most violent. In general, the leaders of the party gradually split into a 'radical group', advocating such policies as nationalisation of parts of the economy and considerable economic reforms, and a 'conservative group' opposing any nationalisation. Odinga became identified as the leader of the radicals. From the conservative side, accusations began to be voiced that the radicals were communists and that they were receiving money from foreign communist countries to plan a violent overthrow of the government. Side by side with this, tribalism grew stronger in parliament and in the country at large. Talk of Kikuyu domination began to be frequently heard, and the alliance between the Kikuyu and Luo became visibly weakened. In 1964 a mutiny occurred in the Kenyan army. Though it was easily suppressed, its very occurrence contributed greatly to the poisoning of the national atmosphere. Meanwhile, Kenyatta continued to act as a force for unity, though circumstances eventually identified him with the so-called conservative group.

Finally, in 1966, the breaking point was reached. In April Odinga and his supporters resigned from KANU to found a new opposition party, the Kenya People's Union. Kenya thus became a two-party state again.

KANU immediately moved to destroy the new party. Its first measure was to push through parliament a proposal that any parliamentarian who resigned from his party must resign from parliament and seek re-election. This led to the mini-election of June 1966 in the 29 constituencies whose members had resigned from KANU and joined the new KPU. The election campaign generated a lot of bitterness and, in a few places, violence. When it was all over, KANU won 20 of the 29 seats and KPU was thus reduced to only nine members in parliament. In the Luo areas, Odinga's home area, the KPU did extremely well. This meant the virtual collapse of the Kikuyu-Luo alliance.

The KANU Government now used all its power to try to wipe out the KPU. Victimisation was freely used, and leading members of the KPU, including Odinga himself, spent some months in detention or imprisonment. All this produced greater and greater bitterness in the country, with consequent outbursts of violence. The situation was not helped by the fact that within the KANU itself, indiscipline and rivalries did not cease. Then, on 5 July 1969, Tom Mboya was assassinated, by a Kikuyu. Since Mboya was a Luo who had remained loyal to Kenyatta and had been widely regarded as perhaps the best man to succeed Kenyatta, the Luo now regarded his assassination as a Kikuyu plot to make it impossible for even a loyal Luo to lead KANU and rule the country. For a while, inter-ethnic war looked likely, but thanks especially to Kenyatta's personal magic, the danger passed.

The assassination and the threat of national collapse which followed seem to have demonstrated to all sides the dangers that could result from continuation of bitter politics. As a result, under the leadership of Kenyatta, some sort of national reconciliation was worked out, and on 8 September 1971 Odinga returned to KANU.

Side by side with these troubles, Kenya was confronted in the first four years of independence by trouble with the neighbouring Republic of Somalia. Just before Kenya became independent, Somalia had made a claim to the north-eastern province of Kenya, on the grounds that its inhabitants were Somalis. Border clashes began to occur between the Somali and Kenyan armies, and in the province itself, terrorist organisations sprang up determined to achieve the merger by force. These troubles continued until 1967 when the Somali and Kenyan Governments at last agreed to begin negotiations instead of continuing to fight.

At independence, the economic life of Kenya was controlled mostly by foreigners. European companies owned the big commercial and industrial establishments. European settler farmers held the best agricultural lands on the Kenyan highlands. Practically all the small-scale trading was in the hands of Indians. Indians also made up most of the non-European professionals like lawyers and doctors.

Therefore, one of the most important objectives of independent Kenya was to increase Kenyan participation in the economy. A vigorous programme of education soon made enough Kenyans available to replace foreigners almost completely in the civil service and other government establishments. In the field of private business also, Kenyanisation was conscientiously pursued. Both in government service and private business, Kenyanisation did not mean discrimination against Indians but deliberate encouragement of Kenyans. After independence, the Indians (about 137,000) were offered full Kenyan citizenship, with all the benefits and responsibilities. By 1970 only about 60,000 had taken up Kenyan citizenship. The others preferred to opt for British citizenship and carry British passports, thus remaining aliens in Kenya. Even against such aliens the Kenyan Government took no drastic steps, in sharp contrast to neighbouring Uganda where President Idi Amin summarily expelled alien Indians in 1972. The Kenyan Government made laws aimed at increasing Kenyan participation in small-scale trade and businesses. As a result Kenyanisation began to make considerable progress in business, though not as much progress as it made in the civil service.

Similar policies were pursued towards agriculture. At independence, many of the European settler farmers fled in panic to England, Rhodesia and South Africa. But their fear that they would be persecuted by independent Kenya soon proved unjustified. After independence, the Kenyan Government did not confiscate the farms of the white settlers but offered to buy them. Many of the farms were bought and the government was therefore able to throw much of the Kenyan highlands open to Kenyan farmers.

The main export crops of Kenya are coffee, tea and animal products. Of these, coffee is the greatest foreign exchange earner. Kenya also produces cattle, maize, wheat, sisal and sugar.

Since independence, Kenya's expanding industrialisation has been in oil refining, textiles, cement, paper making, tyre manufacturing and the bottling of soft drinks. Kenya is a very attractive country to tourists, and the Kenyan Government greatly expanded the tourist trade, especially during the second half of the 1960s. Income from tourism in 1969 was £16.7 million; by 1970 it had jumped to £21 million. By the latter date, tourism had become the largest foreign exchange earner after coffee.

Nairobi, the capital of Kenya, became the communications centre for the whole of East Africa as well as East Africa's foremost international city, marketing and banking centre.

Every year after independence, the Kenyan Government spent many times more money on education than the colonial government ever did. It encouraged towns, villages and other communities to build their own primary schools. Such communally built schools, called 'Harambee' schools, expanded education to very remote places. In 1970, the University of East Africa was broken up into three autonomous universities and the University of Kenya thereby came into being.

The policy of the Kenyan Government was to tap capital from all available sources to industrialise the country. The goal of Kenya's economic development was defined as 'African socialism', which Kenyan leaders explain as a policy of careful governmental supervision of economic development so as to prevent the enrichment of the few at the expense of the many. The government would actively encourage private enterprises, both foreign and indigenous, but all enterprises would be under careful governmental guidance and supervision. In addition, the government would invest capital in certain areas of industry. Except for a few specified cases, the government would not nationalise businesses already established. The government's view on nationalisation was that nationalisation is not often a wise step. It means spending its limited capital on buying up enterprises already established by private capital, a step which does not increase the number of industries in the country. Rather than use its capital to nationalise what already exists, the government should spend it to create new industries. Kenya's 'African socialism' also aims to encourage co-operative enterprises among the people. After independence, considerable encouragement was given to co-operative farms and a whole series of self-help ('Harambee') schemes.

Almost all the foreign investment and foreign aid which has come to Kenya has come from America and the countries of Western Europe. Although the Kenyan Government officially professes a policy of non-alignment, it has generally leaned towards the West and has experienced occasional frictions with the countries of the Eastern bloc. During her conflicts with Somalia, Kenya became very nervous because Somalia was receiving arms from the communist countries. Also, after Oginga Odinga's formation of the KPU in 1966, the Kenyan authorities became suspicious that the communist countries were giving secret encouragement to the opposition to start violent trouble against the government. These experiences poisoned the relationship between Kenya and the communist powers.

20 Tanzania

The Republic of Tanzania comprises two parts – Tanganyika on the East African mainland and the neighbouring island of Zanzibar. Both were British colonies until the early 1960s. Tanganyika became independent in December 1961 and Zanzibar in December 1963. Tanganyika entered independence under the leadership of a nationally popular party, the Tanganyika African National Union (TANU) led by Julius Nyerere. In Zanzibar, on the other hand, the independence government was controlled by the Zanzibar National Party (ZNP) which represented the wealthy Arab minority. The Africans, who constitute the majority of the inhabitants of the island, were represented by the Afro-Shirazi Party (ASP). At the pre-independence elections, the British had so arranged things that while the ASP won more of the popular votes, the ZNP won more seats in parliament and therefore formed the government. Within a month of Zanzibar's independence, the racial and economic antagonisms between the few, wealthy Arab landowners and businessmen and the masses of poor Africans exploded in a successsful revolution by the Africans which took place on 11–12 January 1964. A revolutionary council was formed to govern the island, under the leadership of Sheik Abeid Karume, leader of the ASP. On 22 April 1964 Tanganyika and Zanzibar united under the new name of Tanzania.

In the two and a half years between the independence of Tanganyika and the formation of Tanzania, very important developments took place in Tanganyika. Nyerere and his party had always said that independence was to be only the first step in revolutionising the country. With independence achieved, the government and the party proceeded with single-minded resolve to initiate change and progress in all aspects of the national life. Within one year, local government and administration had been reorganised and Africanised. In the place of the colonial provinces and districts, the country was divided into new 'regions' and 'areas'. The colonial local civil servants – the provincial and district commissioners – were replaced by African regional and area commissioners. These were political appointees who were known for their loyalty to the party and for their local popularity. Each regional or area commissioner was assisted in his administrative duties by a high civil servant called secretary. He was also responsible for organising the party, assisted by an official called the deputy party secretary.

In this way, the government and party were unified, in each region and area, in the person of the commissioner, a man who was clearly a part of the people and who spoke their language. In a predominantly illiterate country, there could hardly have been a more graphic way of demonstrating to the people some of the meaning of independence. By the arrangement also, some of the national talent was kept in the local areas instead of being drafted to the capital, Dar es Salaam.

At first, the system showed weaknesses. Owing to the very low level of education of the country at independence, many of the commissioners were men appointed not so much because of their sound education or administrative ability, but because of their loyalty to the party. Also, many commissioners took their party duties more seriously than their administrative duties. Nevertheless, the system proved, on the whole, very suitable for the Tanganyikan situation and, in the years that followed, showed considerable improvement in quality.

Other changes in the local government system were the institution of an elected council for each district and the abolition of chiefs as local government functionaries. In many parts of Tanganyika, chiefs were very unpopular because of their association with the colonial authorities during the independence struggle. During 1962 the chiefs were asked to resign and an executive officer was appointed to take charge of the administration of each council.

One of the main aims of the Government of Tanzania has been to ensure that the people participate fully in the planning and execution of development programmes. So regional, district and village development committees were set up to formulate and implement development plans for their respective areas of authority. Through them the people of each local area were encouraged to plan and embark upon various types of development projects by themselves. And in each area, the local party encouraged enthusiasm for these projects.

The Government of Tanzania also devoted a lot of energy to evolving a new constitution suitable for the needs and circumstances of the country. Though TANU was the overwhelmingly popular party in mainland Tanzania, there were nevertheless some small opposition parties – the African National Congress, (ANC) and the People's Democratic Party (PDP) – which, during 1962 made some advances in certain parts of Tanzania. The inevitable failures of the new TANU-controlled local administration had alienated local feelings in some areas; many people resented the financial burdens which the new government had imposed as the price of development; and many educated people believed that for democracy to survive there had to be two or more parties. It was all these fragments of anti-TANU sentiment that made the opposition parties considerably influential during 1962.

However, opposition to TANU was never a very serious challenge, and in the first presidential election in October 1962, Nyerere's opponent, Zuberi Mtemvu, the ANC leader, got only a few thousand votes. This victory convinced most people that Tanzania was in reality a one-party state. From then on TANU became committed to the policy of making this true in law.

TANU's first step was to welcome all its opponents, whether African, Asiatic or White, into its ranks. As a result, by January 1963, many former non-members of TANU had willingly come within its fold. The PDP died a natural death.

The second step was to frame a constitution setting out the details of a democratic one-party state. While this matter was still being considered, an army mutiny occurred in Dar es Salaam in January 1964. The mutiny was essentially a protest over the soldiers' low pay and the continued retention of expatriate officers; it was also fairly easily suppressed. Nevertheless, it shook Nyerere profoundly and demonstrated to all the possible dangers of national disunity. Therefore, the goal of national unity through the democratic one-party state was now urgently pursued.

A week later, Nyerere appointed a commission – the One-Party State Commission – to make suggestions for the new constitution, which became law in 1965. According to this constitution TANU became the only party on mainland Tanzania and the ASP in Zanzibar. All candidates in parliamentary elections must be members of the legal party. To ensure that elections would still have some meaning for the people it was laid down that the party must approve two candidates for each constituency. The election of September 1965 demonstrated that though Tanzania was a one-party state, the people's democratic right to choose their representatives was still preserved. Many prominent TANU leaders and ministers from the first independence government were defeated. This successful establishment of a democratic one-party state is now regarded by Tanzanian leaders as one of Tanzania's greatest contributions to the ideas about solving the problems of independent African states.

Economically and educationally, Tanzania was one of the most backward of British possessions by 1961. Since independence, Tanzania's economic development has been tremendous. Its leaders have pursued more seriously and more successfully than the leaders of probably any other African country policies aimed at achieving a society of equal opportunities for all. The declared policy of Julius Nyerere is to build 'a true socialist state . . . in which all people are workers and in which neither Capitalism nor Feudalism exist'. This policy of development was spelled out in full in the famous Arusha Declaration in 1967, in which Tanzania was committed to the building and maintaining of a socialist state by vesting ownership of all means of production in the people of Tanzania through their government and their co-operatives. The ruling party would become a party of the peasants and workers.

As a result, the government nationalised all commercial banks, all insurance companies, many other commercial and processing enterprises, and acquired controlling shares in all other enterprises. Because Tanzanians were neither very well educated nor very experienced in business, many of the state enterprises have not done as well as was hoped. But the government has courageously continued to pursue its socialist policies.

For purposes of rural development, the government set itself the task of reviving the traditional spirit on which pre-colonial Tanzanian society was based – common family ownership of land and crops, respect for the needs of one another within the family, and the consequent security of members within the family. This spirit, called Ujamaa or familyhood, is now the watchword of Tanzania's rural economic and social programmes. In practice, it has meant the establishment of co-operatives (called Ujamaa villages), owning the land and crops in common, taking all decisions in members' meetings and sharing the products of the farm equitably. Not only does this system ensure that the land belongs to the people, it enables the country to get the benefit of modern agricultural methods and tools.

In general, Tanzania tries to rely on its own resources and hard work, and not foreign aid, as sound foundations for economic development. Vigorous educational programmes quickly made it possible for Tanzanians to oust foreigners from their dominant positions in the national economy and administration. Tanzania also took the bold step of starting to develop an indigenous language as its official language. Swahili is now the language of education, of politics and business, and serious efforts are being made to develop this language to the level where it can be used for all purposes – technical and scientific. The growth of this *lingua franca* is contributing a lot to the growth of national unity and national consciousness.

To encourage national self-reliance, Tanzania places a great emphasis on austerity and sensible frugal living among its citizens. The tendency towards ostentatious and wasteful living, so common among the well-to-do classes of independent Africa, has been firmly suppressed in Tanzania. Moreover, the party policy following the Arusha Declaration laid it down that every party leader, minister, parliamentarian or other public official must be either a worker or peasant and should neither be associated with capitalism nor be seen to live a life of luxury. In this, Julius Nyerere himself serves as the leading national example. In his dress and private life, Nyerere has continued to be the simple and humble man that he was before he became a public figure. Not surprisingly, he has not always found it easy to carry his immediate lieutenants with him in this matter, and some of them have tried to cling tenaciously to the businesses they had established, the houses which they had built for rent, and the expensive cars which they had bought before the new party ideas were adopted. However, Nyerere's sincerity and simplicity are so disarming that he has succeeded in carrying the vast majority of the people with him.

21 Zambia

Zambia is a small country with an area of about 290,000 square miles and a population of about four million. It became independent on 24 October 1964 under the Prime Ministership of Dr Kenneth Kaunda. Before independence, it was known as Northern Rhodesia.

The history of independent Zambia has been very greatly influenced by its geographical location. Immediately to its south is Rhodesia, south of Rhodesia is South Africa, and to the south-west Zambia actually shares a border with Namibia which the apartheid government of South Africa controls as a colony. To the east and west of Zambia respectively are Mozambique and Angola where the people were already fighting for freedom from Portuguese imperialism before Zambia's independence.

Now, in the first years of Zambia's independence, the rest of independent Africa saw Zambia as the ideal base from which to organise the liberation struggle against the white minority governments of Rhodesia and South Africa and through which to send assistance to the freedom fighters in Mozambique and Angola. In short, Zambia was to be Africa's spearhead against white domination. The leader of

Zambia, Dr Kaunda, himself a staunch Pan-African nationalist, willingly accepted this role for his country.

However, this hopeful vision did not last long. The series of military coups in Africa from about 1965 tended to weaken Pan-African unity since almost every country became preoccupied with its own internal troubles. The removal in 1966 of Dr Kwame Nkrumah, the most radical advocate of Pan-Africanism, was particularly damaging. Now and again, quarrels broke out between African countries, the settlement of which absorbed the energies of the Organisation of African Unity (OAU). Many countries did not pay their contributions to the liberation fund which the OAU had established. In short, as the years passed, the hope of a united African march on Southern Africa gradually vanished.

Moreover, Zambia had its own problems and suffered from its own weaknesses. In the first place, within its own territory lived about 10,000 whites, most of whom were of Rhodesian and South African origin. These men were very important to the economy of the country, especially to the copper mining industry which was its principal source of wealth. In spite of his political ideals, President Kaunda had to accept that the continued presence of these whites was necessary for the economic well-being of Zambia. In short, he had to continue to shelter within his country large numbers of people who shared the aspirations of the white minority dictators of Rhodesia and South Africa.

Secondly, Zambia's former colonial masters had always tied it politically and economically to her southern neighbours. As a result, practically all Zambia's communications with the outside world were through Rhodesia and South Africa since Zambia itself is landlocked. Zambia could not export copper or import goods from abroad without depending greatly on Rhodesian roads. Also, nearly half of Zambia's imports at independence and for years afterwards came from Rhodesia and South Africa. Consequently, when the whole world employed economic sanctions against Rhodesia from 1965 on in the hope of forcing the white minority government to renounce its unilateral declaration of independence, Zambia too was seriously affected.

Consequently Zambia has concentrated a lot of effort on redirecting its economy. Fortunately its northern neighbour is Tanzania, another independent country whose leaders are seriously committed to the anti-imperialist struggle. It is towards Tanzania, therefore, that Zambia has been gradually turning. Particularly towards this end, a railway project was embarked upon, with a loan from China, to connect the Zambian copperbelt with the Tanzanian port of Dar es Salaam.

Surveying of the route for this 1,000-mile railway line, called the Tan-Zam railway, began in 1968 and construction began in 1970. It was nearing completion by 1975. By then, though the efforts at redirecting the Zambian economy had shown considerable success, fairly important economic connections still remained with Rhodesia and, to a lesser extent, with South Africa.

Finally, Zambia has suffered from internal divisions. As in most of colonial Africa, Zambia, while a colony, was one country only in name. Between the Bemba country of northern Zambia and peoples of the southern province, there was very little communication. Until the late fifties, reasonable unity was achieved by the nationalist leaders because of their common fight against British policies, especially the British creation of a federation comprising Zambia, Malawi and Rhodesia in 1953. In those years, the leading nationalists were Harry Nkumbula from the south and Kenneth Kaunda from the north. Nkumbula was leader of the main nationalist party, the African National Congress of which Kaunda was a member. But a split occurred in the late fifties when the younger politicians followed Kaunda to found another party. 'Tribalism' has played an important part in Zambian politics ever since. By the time of independence, Kaunda's party, the United National Independence Party (UNIP), had its main stronghold in the north but enjoyed some support elsewhere, while Nkumbula's African National Congress (usually called Congress) controlled much of the south, especially the Bantu Botatwe area.

Kaunda's UNIP won the pre-independence elections and led Zambia into independence, but Congress continued to be strong in the south. Kaunda always claimed that UNIP was above ethnic loyalties; he also believed that it would be better for national progress if Zambia could become a one-party state. However, he refused to create a one-party state by legislation, preferring to achieve the same goal through democratic elections and gentle wooing of Congress members. While this wooing was going on, government appointments were manipulated to show to all that it paid to belong to UNIP. The posts of provincial resident officials and the assistant district commissioners or secretaries – all went to members of UNIP only, even in areas where UNIP had little or no following. UNIP men warned in their speeches that only known members of the party could get government loans to start co-operatives. In spite of all these tactics, Congress continued to be the party of many ethnic groups of the south, as was amply demonstrated in 1968 when Congress won clearly all four seats in a by-election held in the south. The government resorted to bringing various types of charges against Congress leaders and getting some of them sent to jail, but even this did not crush Congress. Southern ethnic loyalties to Congress and opposition to UNIP remained very strong.

Moreover, in 1967, a third political party had arisen which also based its strength on a particular ethnic group. This was the United Party, founded by Nalumino Mundia, a former leading member of UNIP. Mundia was a Lozi, and his party was committed largely to the protection of the interests of the Lozi ethnic group.

Worst of all, even UNIP itself was not above being disturbed internally by the clash of ethnic interests. The party early developed the policy of sharing ministerial and other important appointments fairly equally between its leaders from north and south. But this did not prevent the growth of ethnic rivalries within the party, which reached a climax in 1967–8, with the election of a Vice-President for UNIP and the government. When it was all over and Simon Kapwepwe, a Bemba, had won, most of the other ethnic groups began to talk of the aggressiveness and over-ambition of the Bemba. The situation grew worse and worse until early 1968 when, at a meeting of the party's national council, some party leaders came to blows. This incident so stunned Kaunda that he angrily left the meeting, returned to State House and began to pack his belongings. 'I am returning to my farm in Chinsali,' he said. 'I am leaving public life for good.' He added that he would not remain as leader and watch 'tribalism, the wasting disease of Africa' take its course in Zambia. With considerable difficulty, the leaders of the party persuaded him to change his mind, and promised him to work together in harmony. But ethnic antagonisms within the UNIP lingered. The rivalry between the UNIP and United Party also came to a head in 1968, producing widespread violence between the Bemba and the Lozi in the copperbelt. As a result, the United Party was banned as a 'threat to security and peace' and its leaders were sent into restriction. At the same time, a revolt was brewing among the Barotse, a people who had, two years before independence, tried to secede from Zambia. Partly as a result of the Barotse reaction against UNIP, Congress emerged from the 1969 election as a strong parliamentary opposition. This produced a new wave of repressive actions against Congress members. Leading members of UNIP began insistently to ask the government to declare Zambia a one-party state. In February 1970, following a spate of political violence, Congress was banned in the Livingstone district of the southern province. Not long afterwards, Kaunda announced that Zambia would soon become a one-party state as a cure to tribalism.

In August 1971, the situation took a turn for the worse when Simon Kapwepwe, who had been Vice-President from 1967 to 1969, resigned from UNIP, accused the Kaunda Government of corruption and inefficiency, and declared the formation of his own party, the United Progressive Party (UPP). Although Kapwepwe insisted that he was not a tribalist, it was obvious that his chief source of confidence was the expectation that he would be supported by his Bemba people, the largest ethnic group in Zambia. Some members of UNIP, including a few parliamentarians, joined the new UPP.

Kaunda reacted sharply to this new development. Many members of UPP were arrested and violence between UNIP and UPP supporters flared up in many parts of the country. As a result, 116 members of UPP were detained in October 1971. All the UNIP parliamentarians who joined the UPP lost their seats in parliament and by-elections were held in their constituencies. Although UNIP recaptured almost all the seats, Kapwepwe managed to retain his own seat. Therefore, President Kaunda took more severe action. In February 1972, he banned the UPP, explaining that it was not a party with any programme for the development of Zambia, but simply one committed to the attainment of power through the use of violence. Kapwepwe and one hundred more of his followers were detained.

During the same month, President Kaunda announced his final decision that Zambia was to become a one-party state. He then set up a commission to advise the nation on the form the constitution of the Zambian one-party state should take. The main opposition party, Congress, was invited to appoint some men to rèpresent it on this commission. Congress, however, denounced the President's decision to convert the country into a one-party state and refused to have anything to do with the commission. Nevertheless, the commission, under the chairmanship of Dr Kaunda's Vice-President, Mainza Chona, began its work in March 1972.

All this however is not to say that Zambia has had no cohesive force. The personality of Kaunda has continued, even in the worst of times, to enjoy much respect and love among the majority of Zambians. Also, the threat represented by Zambia's neighbours has strengthened the spirit of patriotism and nationalism among Zambians. These neighbours have many times violated Zambian territory to attack border villages, and Portugal on occasions imposed economic blockade on Zambia by preventing her exports and imports from passing through the ports of Mozambique and Angola. Moreover, South Africa has been conducting a persistent propaganda war aimed at disrupting Zambia and destroying Kaunda. The fact that Zambia successfully resisted these attacks, and continued to support the cause of the African nationalists of Rhodesia, South Africa, Mozambique and

Angola, is proof of her overall internal strength.

In December 1972 Zambia became a one-party state, with a constitution similar to that of Tanzania. By New Year's Day 1973, most prominent political detainees, including Kapwepwe, had been released.

Economic development

At independence, the economy of Zambia depended chiefly on copper, and has continued to do so. Zambia is the third largest producer of copper in the world (after the USA and the Soviet Union). By 1970 copper constituted 50% of Zambia's gross national product and 96% of her exports, and provided up to 60% of her government's revenue. Therefore, the pace of economic growth has been dictated almost entirely by the performance of the copper export. Thus, in 1969 and 1970 when the world price of copper was particularly good, the Zambian economy did very well. The rate of growth of the gross national product was a very high 10% per annum for both years, and the country recorded very big surplusses in foreign trade. But in 1971 when the volume of Zambia's copper production fell and the world price of copper also fell, Zambia was plunged into serious economic difficulties.

Because of her enormous copper wealth, Zambia has, on the whole, been economically better off than many other African states. But the leaders of independent Zambia realised that no matter how much wealth was derived from copper, an economy dependent almost entirely on only one commodity was a very weak economy. After independence, therefore, one of the chief aims of Zambia's economic programmes was to diversify the economy – i.e. to increase the volume and variety of agricultural production as well as of industrial production. The objective of such economic growth, however, has been stated again and again to be not merely an increase in production, but the total development of the common people of Zambia. According to Dr Kaunda, the philosophy of Zambia's economic development is one of humanism or humanistic socialism. 'This,' said Dr Kaunda in 1970, 'means that everything undertaken in Zambia is done with the interests of the common man uppermost in mind.' In accordance with this philosophy the objectives of Zambia's successive Development Plans have been the expansion of education, the Zambianisation of the economy, the expansion of housing, social welfare and health, the expansion of communication and transportation facilities, the diversification of the economy, the expansion of employment opportunities and of incomes, and the narrowing of the gap between the incomes of the rural and urban populations. The Development Plans envisaged that funds for the programmes would be provided by copper.

On the whole, considerable progress has been made along these lines. Zambia has witnessed a fairly fast rate of industrialisation, leading to an ever-growing range of 'made-in-Zambia' goods – cement, building materials, furniture, textiles, electronic appliances, plastics, etc. A car assembly plant was in the plans by 1971. These new industries have greatly expanded job opportunities for Zambians. By 1971, more than 500,000 Zambians were employed in wage-earning jobs. However by that date the total number of jobs was considerably lower than the target which the government had set, and urban unemployment had become a big national problem as more and more people poured from the rural areas to the towns in search of jobs.

While welcoming foreign investment, the government itself has provided much of the capital for industrialisation. In the late sixties, the government adopted the policy of acquiring 51% shares in industrial enterprises. In 1970, it acquired 51% shares in the largest mining companies. Between 1970 and 1971, all insurance business was nationalised.

Through its Zambianisation policy, the government has greatly increased the employment of Zambians into top jobs in business by controlling the rate of employment of expatriates into such positions. Zambianisation has also meant increasing the share of Zambians in the nation's commercial life by limiting the commercial activities of foreign companies to the sale of certain specified commodities and reserving the sale of other commodities to Zambians. The government has also given encouragement to indigenous Zambian businesses.

Much emphasis has been given to the diversification of agricultural crops. At independence, the two major crops were maize and tobacco. Many new crops – cotton, sugar cane, citrus – have been introduced since independence. Of these, cotton and sugar cane have done quite well. Poultry was expanded to such an extent that by 1971 it had become second to maize as Zambia's second largest agricultural enterprise. On the whole, however, agricultural production has been expanding too slowly for the increase in population. Indeed the production of maize, the nation's main staple food, fell almost consistently after independence, compelling Zambia in 1971 to begin to buy greatly increased quantities of maize from Rhodesia, much against her wish. The main reason for this situation is that the European settler farmers, whose plantations produced most of Zambia's corn before independence, began to leave the country in the years after independence.

After independence, the government decided that the best and fastest way to revolutionise Zambian agriculture was to embark upon

214

the establishment of agricultural co-operatives. By 1971 there were about 1,200 farm co-operatives in the country.

At independence, Zambia's education was one of the least developed in English-speaking Africa. Since 1964, a substantial part of national resources has been poured into the development of education. By 1971, nearly 50% of all school-age children were attending schools, and primary education was free. In 1964 Zambia had only about 100 university graduates. But by 1970, the University of Zambia, established in 1965, had 1,500 students and had already produced hundreds of graduates in all fields. In addition, Zambia is reputed to have had by 1971 one of the most ambitious adult education programmes on the continent.

Impressive progress has also been made in the field of health services. Many hospitals and health centres have been built since independence, the largest of them being the University Teaching Hospital in Lusaka, the national capital. Government estimates show that between 1963 and 1971, the number of hospital beds in the country more than tripled.

22 Ethiopia

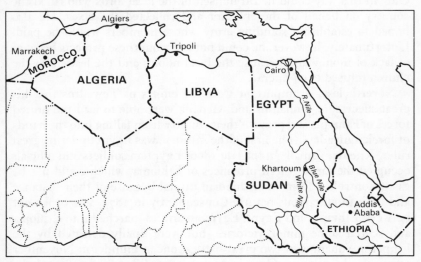

Independent North African states

Until the events of September 1974 Ethiopia was the oldest surviving kingdom not only in Africa but in the whole world. This kingdom or empire with its Christian church and its line of emperors had an unbroken history going back for about 2,000 years. However, Ethiopia has witnessed so many changes since the middle of the nineteenth century that it is now customary to say that the creation of modern Ethiopia began with the reign of the Emperor Tewedros II who ruled Ethiopia between 1855 and 1868. Much was done for Ethiopia by this emperor and his successors – especially Yohannis IV (1871–89), Menelik II (1889–1913) and Haile Selassie I (1930–74). These great rulers expanded the borders of the empire especially to the south, successfully worked for national unity and guided their country to grow into a great and famous modern state in the world.

When Tewedros II came to the throne in 1855, Ethiopia had gone through a whole century of disunity and weakness. The emperor had no power and the whole country was divided among many provincial kings. Even the church was disunited. It looked as if the country was going to disintegrate.

Tewedros stopped the growing disunity. He declared war against the petty provincial kings and defeated them one after the other. Having thus unified the whole country under his own leadership, Tewedros aspired to turn Ethiopia into a country not only with one ruler but also with a proper civil service whose officers were paid. Only in this way could he rid himself of the local lords who ruled the country on behalf of the emperor and collected the taxes. He also hoped to establish a standing army whose members would be paid. Unfortunately, however, he could not carry out these projects because of lack of money and because the local nobles and the leaders in the church refused to co-operate.

Nevertheless, so important were the efforts of Tewedros that his great successors, Yohannis and Menelik were able to lead the united forces of Ethiopia and prevent their country from falling into the hands of foreign invaders. The first of the invaders was Egypt under its great ruler, Khedive Ismail. In the late 1860s Egyptian soldiers and officials occupied the far northern provinces of Ethiopia, which could not be easily controlled from the Ethiopian capital because of their distance and their mountainous nature. Consequently in 1875, war broke out between Ethiopia and Egypt. Egyptian armies marched into Ethiopia and scored some minor victories, but were finally defeated by the Emperor Yohannis in two great battles, one at Gundet in November 1875 and the other at Gura in March 1876. The defeats forced the Egyptians to withdraw from most of Ethiopian territory. However, Egypt still controlled the Red Sea ports through which Yohannis was anxious to obtain free access to the sea. By the Treaty of Adowa of 3 June 1884, Egypt withdrew its forces from the rest of Ethiopian soil and also granted free access to Ethiopia to the Red Sea through the port of Massawa.

These victories enabled Yohannis to strengthen further the unity of the country. Realising that his government did not have the machinery for ruling the whole country effectively from the capital, he recreated the provincial kings, but he made sure that each one of them would henceforth be appointed by the emperor and would hold office at his pleasure. He also banned certain religious sects which threatened the unity of the Ethiopian Orthodox Church, and made it compulsory for Muslim and other non-Christian Ethiopians to accept Christianity and become members of the Orthodox Church.

It was very fortunate for Ethiopia that these things had happened. For, not long after the Treaty of Adowa with Egypt in 1884, the scramble of the European powers for Africa became intense. The European power which now attempted to take control of Ethiopia was Italy. So strong was the Italian pressure that the Emperor Menelik had to make a treaty with the Italians soon after he became emperor in 1889. However, Menelik had no intention of giving his country to anybody. Therefore, when the Italians marched their army into Ethiopia he soundly defeated them at the battle of Adowa in that year. This victory preserved the independence of Ethiopia when the rest of Africa became colonies and protectorates of various European powers.

In addition to preserving Ethiopia's independence, Menelik also expanded its frontiers into the territories towards the south. The old province of Shoa which used to be the southernmost province of Ethiopia became its central province. Among the new peoples thus added to the empire, the Gallas were the most numerous. Ethiopia's borders today are more or less the same borders established by Emperor Menelik.

While all these things had been occurring, the rulers of Ethiopia had gradually adopted new instruments and new techniques in order to modernise and strengthen their country. Ethiopian armies were armed with European guns. Emperor Menelik hired foreign advisers, built a school with European teachers at Addis Ababa, and authorised the building of a railway line from the French port of Jibuti on the Red Sea to Addis Ababa. Menelik also began to establish the rudiments of a modern civil service. The modernisation of Ethiopia was quite different from the modernisation going on in other African countries, ruled by European colonial powers. These colonial masters were bringing in new institutions, ideas and techniques in a way suitable to their own designs and goals. In Ethiopia, on the other hand, modernisation was under the firm control of the country's ancient rulers. As a result, Ethiopia preserved its ancient institutions – its emperor, its church, its social institutions – and used the new ideas and developments to modernise them gradually. Ethiopia is the only example in Africa of an authentic African kingdom which modernised itself in its own way.

The ruler under whom this modernisation was most fruitful is the Emperor Haile Selassie. Haile Selassie first acted as Regent from 1916 to 1930. It was in 1930 that he finally became emperor, and he ruled Ethiopia for the next 44 years. Though physically small, he had many qualities of a great leader: a great capacity for work, an excellent memory, a mastery of detail, a quick and inquiring mind, a broad outlook and a fine judgement of men and issues.

From the beginning, Haile Selassie was committed to introducing changes into Ethiopia and turning Ethiopia into a modern state. But he also knew that it would be dangerous to introduce changes in a hurry. He knew that his people were conservative, and that he must always make sure that he took them along with him step by step. His strategy was therefore one of cautiously introducing changes and then making sure that the ground was firm under him before introducing further changes. He took the view that in a country like Ethiopia with traditions dating back centuries, modern progress must be imposed cautiously and not too forcibly. He was what one might call a conservative revolutionary.

First, Haile Selassie took steps to modernise the Ethiopian army and police to make sure that Ethiopia would be able to defend itself against rebellion from within and aggression from outside. Young Ethiopians were sent to train as military and police officers in military and police colleges in Europe. European officers, especially from France, Sweden and Belgium, were hired to train the Ethiopian army, particularly in the use of the most modern weapons. Finally, Haile Selassie established a school for training military officers at Holata just outside Addis Ababa. He began the establishment of an air force by buying several aeroplanes and he established a school of aviation. Within a short time, the Ethiopian army and police, though still not very strong, had become wonderfully transformed. By 1971, of all the commercial airlines established by independent African countries, only the Ethiopian Airline was fully officered by Africans.

Secondly, Haile Selassie began to establish an efficient modern civil service. The first step was the founding of schools to educate Ethiopian children. There was already one government school, Haile Selassie added a second – the Tafari Makonnen School. From these schools, the most promising boys were sent at the emperor's own expense to Europe to study European methods of government. By 1935, he had founded the main ministries of government – the Ministries of War,

Finance, Interior, Foreign Affairs, Commerce, Communications, Health. Foreign advisers were hired to help in seeing these ministries through their first years.

Thirdly, the emperor granted a constitution to his country in 1931, which imposed limitation, though to a very small extent, on his own powers. This constitution provided for a parliament made up of two houses – a lower house and a senate. The members of the senate were to be appointed by the emperor, and the members of the lower house to be elected by the provincial notables and chiefs. The constitution did not yet grant the people 'one man one vote', but its establishment was meant to educate the people gradually towards this end. In the following years, the emperor began to appoint ministers and in 1943 he established a Council of Ministers. Although the ministers still took their orders from the emperor, and although the operations of the Council of Ministers were not really different from the actions of the emperor, this was nevertheless an important constitutional and political change. The provincial administration was also considerably modernised, and educated men were put in charge.

In 1935 the emperor's programme was rudely interrupted by an Italian invasion. Unfortunately, the Ethiopian forces were defeated and Haile Selassie was forced into exile until 1941 when the Italians were expelled and Haile Selassie returned to his task.

He now gave great attention to the building of roads. He had made some beginnings in road-building before 1935; but now built more roads which not only contributed to the economic development of Ethiopia, but also to its unification as well as to the effectiveness of its local government system.

The constitutional progress begun in 1931 was continued with the granting of another constitution in 1955, which provided for a popularly elected lower house. The first parliamentary elections in the history of Ethiopia took place in 1957. In 1966, the emperor surrendered to the Prime Minister the duty of appointing the other ministers. A proper cabinet, with the Prime Minister as its head, thus came into being. In addition, attempts were made to codify the laws of Ethiopia.

Economic and social development under Haile Selassie was creditable. Many primary and secondary schools were built, and in 1951 the University College of Addis Ababa was founded. Haile Selassie encouraged the provision of further health facilities to his people. The Ethiopian branch of the Red Cross was founded in 1935. The first Five Year Development Plan was issued in 1957 and was followed by others.

From the 1950s, the growth of education hastened the pace of progress. University graduates began to occupy most of the important positions in the country. On the whole, the educated people were impatient for more and quicker changes. Though agreeing with the need for progress, the emperor generally tried to hold them in check to ensure that changes would not be embarked upon in too much of a hurry. The impatience of the educated men may have been behind an attempt made in 1960 to topple the emperor from power. While the emperor was abroad, a section of the army carried out a coup with the backing of some civilians. However, the coup was very quickly suppressed by forces loyal to the emperor.

After the unsuccessful 1960 coup impatience became more obvious among the growing class of educated youths. The movement for change expanded to include demands for reforms not only of the political system but of the whole political, economic and social system. The younger generation wanted politics and government processes to be fully democratised, the hold of the church on politics, social life and education to be removed, and the age-old land tenure system (of absentee landlords and tenant farmers) to be swept away. By the late 1960s Ethiopia began to experience civil commotions. In the last months of 1969, riots by the students of Haile Selassie University shook Addis Ababa repeatedly, resulting in clashes between the police and the students in which some students were killed. In May 1971, another series of massive students' riots led to thousands of arrests.

In Africa, as well as in the rest of the world, Emperor Haile Selassie's tact and ingenuity won considerable respect for his country. Perhaps the most outstanding achievement of his foreign policy was his success in making Addis Ababa acceptable to the rest of Africa as the headquarters of the Organisation of African Unity.

But his foreign policy also encountered serious difficulties. Soon after neighbouring Somalia became independent in 1960, it demanded fairly extensive territories in Ethiopia's eastern provinces, claiming that the territories were inhabited by Somalis. The quarrel with Somalia threatened to develop into a major confrontation, and Ethiopia, like Kenya, became seriously worried that Somalia was receiving military assistance from the Soviet Union and China. The quarrel with Somalia, however, soon paled into insignificance beside the troubles Ethiopia ran into from 1962 over developments in Eritrea, Ethiopia's thirteenth province.

From very ancient times, Eritrea on the Red Sea was part of the empire of Ethiopia, but it was an area in which Christian Ethiopia frequently clashed with her Muslim Arab neighbours. It was the scene, for instance, of many conflicts between Egypt and Ethiopia under Yohannis in the late nineteenth century. During the European scramble for Africa, Italy succeeded in seizing Eritrea, which remained an Italian colony until 1941. It was from Eritrea that the Italians invaded and conquered Ethiopia in 1935. In 1947 Britain, who had taken charge of Eritrea since its capture from Italy in 1941, surrendered Eritrea to the United Nations Organisation, which in 1952 decided that Eritrea should be constituted into an autonomous state federated to Ethiopia. This federal arrangement under which Eritrea had its own assembly and government, continued for ten years during which tension grew between the Eritreans who were Christians and those who were Muslims. The neighbouring Arab states began to interfere secretly in this internal trouble. The emperor therefore decided to annex Eritrea and in 1962 he successfully pressurised the Eritrean assembly to agree to the termination of the federal arrangement and the complete annexation of Eritrea by Ethiopia. Eritrea therefore lost its autonomy and became a province of Ethiopia.

To counter the growing threat of annexation by Ethiopia, some Eritreans founded in 1961 the Eritrean Liberation Front (ELF) to fight for the freedom of Eritrea. It won immediate support from the Arab states. Training camps for its guerrillas were set up in Syria, and Radio Damascus regularly beamed its inflammatory propaganda to the people of Eritrea. In the years that followed, the assistance received by the ELF from the Arab states grew in scope and proportions.

In a way, the Arab interference in the Eritrean trouble was a continuation of their ancient conflicts with Ethiopia in Eritrea. But more recently Arab interest has centred on the port of Massawa, which controls an important part of the coast of the Red Sea. In the hostility between the Arabs and Israel, the Arab states and the Muslim states strongly in sympathy with them controlled all the coast of the Red Sea – with the exception of the coast of Ethiopia and Eritrea. Since Ethiopia wished to take no sides in the Arab–Israeli troubles, she allowed the Arabs and Israelis equally to make use of the port of Massawa. The Arabs resented this, and hence their support of the ELF insurgents. The ELF received military and other assistance from Syria, Iraq, Sudan and Libya.

At first, the threat constituted by the ELF was insignificant. But from 1968 on, their guerrilla activities sharply increased. Their first major confrontation with the government forces occurred at Hal-Hal in northern Eritrea in September 1968. The guerrillas were routed. But from 1969, they became better trained, better armed and more daring. Throughout that year, they carried out daring raids inside the province, destroyed petroleum tankers travelling the highway from

Massawa, and destroyed or hijacked planes belonging to the Ethiopian Airlines. In 1970, they became more active still. In November of that year, they wiped out two villages in western Eritrea and, about the same time, ambushed and killed the general commanding the Ethiopian forces in Eritrea. By early 1971, although the ELF guerrillas did not control any part of Eritrea, their activities were spread over more than two-thirds of the Eritrean countryside.

From 1969, therefore, the Ethiopian Government began to take serious steps to control the situation. The full military might of Ethiopia was diverted to Eritrea, and a state of emergency was proclaimed over the province. To deny the guerrillas food in the countryside, government forces began to move the rural population into fortified villages.

All these led to a great deal of suffering for the people of Eritrea. The stern measures adopted by the government caused the guerrilla activities to thin down considerably by late 1971, though the war was far from over.

On the international scene, the Eritrean crisis led Ethiopia into immense complications. Relations with her Arab neighbours became badly strained. Indeed, indirectly, Ethiopia was drawn into the Arab-Israeli war and into the wider cold war surrounding it. Not only did the Arab states support the ELF, a lot of Soviet assistance also reached the ELF through them. It was in fact the sophisticated Soviet weapons that made the ELF so formidable from 1969 on. Of course, this led to a cooling off of relations between Ethiopia and the Soviet Union. Meanwhile, confronted by such enemies, Ethiopia turned more and more for military aid to the United States of America and even to Israel. This compromised Ethiopia's diplomatic position seriously, and some of the Arab leaders began to describe Emperor Haile Selassie as an agent of Israeli aggression and Western imperialism in the Red Sea region, while Arab members of the OAU demanded that the OAU headquarters be removed from Addis Ababa. It also led to more Arab assistance to the ELF. By 1970 it was obvious that some of the extreme ELF leaders and their Arab supporters had come around to desiring, not merely the revival of Eritrean autonomy which had been lost in 1962, but the complete separation of Eritrea from Ethiopia as an independent state.

Towards the end of 1973, however, a major change occurred in the relationship between Ethiopia and the Arab States. After another war between the Arabs and Israel in October of that year, Ethiopia joined the ranks of African countries which supported the demand that Israel should withdraw from Arab territories occupied in recent wars.

Ethiopia even took the unexpected step of breaking off diplomatic relations with Israel on the matter. Naturally, this led to considerably warmer relations between Ethiopia and the Arab States.

Meanwhile, however, discontent with the emperor's conservatism at home was approaching a climax. Ultimately, early in 1974 the army stepped in and, after carefully stripping the emperor of his authority, finally removed him from power in September 1974. On 27 August 1975, the emperor died and was quietly buried.

The 1974 coup was followed by months of crises and anxiety for Ethiopia. The new military rulers made themselves universally unpopular soon after the coup by summarily executing more than sixty leading citizens who had taken part in Haile Selassie's Government. Then the ELF launched a massive revolt to free Eritrea and, as the Ethiopian army was sent in, intense fighting ensued in most parts of the province. At the same time radical elements, especially students, who had urged and welcomed the removal of the emperor, began to show that what they wanted was not a military government. They began to agitate for the establishment of a civilian government and the military rulers had to take firm steps to suppress their agitation. However, by mid-1975, although it was obvious that these troubles had not ended, the military regime appeared to have established its control over the country, including Eritrea.

23 Sudan

The Sudan Republic, the largest country in Africa, became independent in 1956. From then until 1972, her history was dominated by political crises, of which the conflicts between the northern and southern provinces were the most prominent. One can only understand this conflict by tracing its roots in the past history of the Sudan.

The fifteen million people of the Sudan are roughly divisible into the Muslim Arabs of the north, numbering about eleven million at independence, and the black African peoples of the south, numbering some four million. Until the early nineteenth century, the Sudan was made up of many independent kingdoms, chiefdoms and sultanates. Then in 1822, the Egyptians under Mohammed Ali came, conquered and, in the process, unified the country and ruled it until the 1880s. In 1881, a local Muslim leader, called the Mahdi, started a holy war and expelled the Egyptians, and he and his followers then ruled the country until it was reconquered by a combination of British and Egyptian forces in 1898. In 1899, the British and Egyptians entered into an agreement called the condominium agreement, to rule the country jointly. In reality, it was the British that managed the affairs of the Sudan in the years of the condominium, 1899–1956.

One of the major consequences of the Egyptian conquest in the 1820s was the expansion of European and Arab trade into the thickly forested territories of Southern Sudan. From the northern town of Khartoum, destined to become the twentieth century capital of the Sudan, European and Arab traders went on trading expeditions to the south. At first, the main trade was in ivory, but after the traders began to buy slaves in the south and bring them to the north, the slave trade overtook the trade in ivory. By 1870, between 12,000 and 15,000 slaves were taken northwards from the Southern Sudan annually.

This trade was to have terrible consequences for the future of the Sudan. It sowed the seeds of suspicion and hostilities between the Arab north and the black African south. The northerners learned to treat the southerners ruthlessly and scornfully as slaves, and the southerners learned to regard the northerners as unscrupulous people. These attitudes bedevilled Sudan's politics until the 1970s.

From the beginning of the Anglo–Egyptian condominium in 1899, until 1946, the aim of British policy was to keep the north and south apart as much as possible. In the first years of this century, the soldiers used by the British in the south were northerners; but in 1911, the British began to train southerners as soldiers, and by 1918 southerners had entirely replaced northerners in the army in the south. Partly encouraged by the government, missionary bodies began to establish missions and schools in the south, to win the southerners not only from their traditional religions but also from the Islamic influences of the north.

The policy was stated more clearly in 1930 and was afterwards pursued more vigorously. Northern officials serving in the administration in the south were transferred to the north, and northern officers in the colonial army and police in the south were removed. Northern traders were encouraged or forced to leave the south. Southerners were advised to give up Arabic names, Arabic dress and other elements of Arabic culture, and intermarriage between northerners and southerners was banned. Steps were taken to suppress Islam in the south, and southerners who were Muslim found it difficult to practise their religion openly. Christian missionary work was intensified. Southerners living in the border areas with the north were moved to areas farther south.

The aim was to create a self-contained south, free of domination by northerners. But its total effects were unfortunate. Since the south had very few qualified and experienced men to act as administrators, teachers and traders, the policy resulted in inefficient administration in the south and increased the economic and educational backwardness of the south. Most important of all, it prevented the growth of understanding between the northern and southern Sudanese and, therefore, tended to strengthen the traditional attitudes between the two.

From 1946 on, partly because it was realised that the policy had failed, and partly because of northern and Egyptian pressure, the British abandoned the policy in favour of one with the aim of welding north and south together in a union in which educationally and economically, the south would be the equal of the north. In reality, however, it meant that from 1946 on, the south was progressively subjected to the wishes of the north.

In 1948 a Legislative Assembly was inaugurated for the whole of the Sudan, with seventy-six members from the north and thirteen from the south. In the talks leading to the creation of this assembly the southern Sudanese said it would be used by the north to ride rough shod over them. However, the spokesmen of the south were subjected to such canvassing and even threats that many of them abandoned their views. Although the British promised to include in the ordinance creating the assembly safeguards to protect southern interests, the promise was never fulfilled. Naturally, the southerners reacted sharply against the new policy, and continued to charge that the proceedings leading to the creation of the assembly were all a fraud. The fact that, under the new constitutional arrangement, the southerners experienced considerable economic and educational advance, did not remove their fears. The northerners' political methods only increased these fears. For instance, their introduction of Arabic as the language of education in the south was done in such a ruthless way as to strengthen fears of northern domination.

In 1953 internal self-rule was granted to the Sudan. By this date, the north was very far ahead of the south in all spheres of development. Moreover, while the educated elite of the north had formed themselves into political parties, the few educated southerners had no coherent political organisation. No southerner was invited to the historic meetings preceding the granting of self-rule. It was clear that the northerners were anxious to suppress the southern views, which demanded a delay in the coming of independence to enable the south to catch up with the north a little. The northern political parties, the Umma Party and the National Unionist Party, increased the suspicion and consternation of the south by exporting their intense rivalries to the south. To win elections, each promised all sorts of things to southerners and accused the other of working against southern interests. Moreover, many northern administrators in the south were corrupt and boastful and openly despised southerners. A committee set up to recommend steps for Sudanising the civil service ensured that southerners were given only six minor positions in the civil service.

Although the political inexperience of the northern leaders was really to blame, southerners could not help feeling that they were once again being enslaved by the northerners. Feelings ran high. In August 1955, the southern army, the Equatoria Corps, mutinied, and the mutiny quickly developed into widespread uprisings in the south against northern domination. The government rushed police and army in from the north. Hundreds of people died, many villages were destroyed and thousands of people fled into the forests or across the border into Uganda, Zaire, Kenya or the Central African Republic.

In the midst of these troubles, the British granted independence to the Sudan in 1956. The independence government was controlled by the NUP, but a few months later, a split occurred in the NUP and the Umma Party then came into power. None of this had any effect on the southern situation, as the northern politicians were too busy fighting one another to have time to attend to the grave issues of national unity or of economic development. As a result, the situation in the south deteriorated, and the economy of the nation suffered. The growing economic distress threw even the north into political instability. Consequently, in November 1958, the civilian government had to surrender power to the army, under the leadership of General Ibrahim Abboud.

Like the civilian leaders before him, General Abboud had no answer for the nation's economic distress. For the southern situation, he used vastly increased force and repression, to be coupled with intensive spreading of Arabic and Islamic influences in the south, in the unfortunate belief that national unity would be achieved by culturally assimilating the south to the north. Many Koranic schools were established as well as centres for Islamic instruction of adults. All the agencies of government were devoted to the spreading of Islam and the Arabic language. Restrictions were placed on the practice of Christianity. In 1962, all Christian missionaries working in the south were expelled.

The effect of these policies was to increase the alienation of the south. Many southern leaders fled abroad, especially to Uganda and Zaire, and there founded political parties in exile. In the south itself, resistance against Abboud's repression spread to the countryside. In 1963 the various resistance groups in the forests formed a terrorist organisation with the name of Anya-Nya. Southern opinion was far from unanimous. While some wanted regional self-determination for the south in a federal Sudan, others wanted complete secession of the south from the Sudan. However, all agreed in their opposition to northern domination. The Anya-Nya was dedicated to the winning of complete national sovereignty for the south through the use of force. The clashes between the Anya-Nya and the government forces led to widespread destruction of villages and means of livelihood and forced an increasing number of people to flee the country.

In the end, even the northerners became worried by the news from the south and tired of Abboud's corrupt and unproductive dictatorship. Therefore, in October 1964, the northern masses rose up and overthrew the military regime.

The new civilian government showed itself willing to accept southern participation in discussing the future relationship between the north and south and welcomed the suggestions of the southern parties to call a round table conference. This conference met in March 1965 in Khartoum with 18 representatives from the north and 27 from the south, and with observers from a number of African countries. But the conference failed to reach an agreement. With the Anya-Nya refusing to stop fighting in the countryside and insisting on complete sovereignty for the south, the southern leaders at the conference could not readily accept the suggestion by the northerners to turn the country into a federation. Even among the most moderate southern leaders, distrust of the north was too strong to make compromise easy. Furthermore, although all northern political groups had united to oust Abboud in the previous October, the rivalries and intrigues among the northern parties had re-emerged. An election was approaching, and the northern politicians were becoming more anxious to score points over each other than to solve the southern problem.

However, the conference achieved one important result. It gave the northern and southern leaders a chance to meet and talk face to face. For the first time, many northerners began to appreciate the grievances of the south and the depth of hatred and distrust which existed in the south towards the north.

The new civilian government introduced other measures to conciliate the south, such as starting to southernise the southern administration considerably and releasing many political prisoners. However, in the south itself, so strong was the tradition of hostility between northerners and southerners that the situation remained always explosive, and on 8 July 1965, violence erupted in the southern town of Juba. A quarrel and fight between a northern soldier and a southern hospital worker triggered off the explosion. The northern soldiers went wild, and by the next morning almost all the houses in the southerners' sectors of the town had been burnt and their owners were either dead or in hiding. More than 1,000 people died. Three days later, in the town of Wau, northern soldiers attacked a southern crowd gathered at a wedding reception, and seventy-six people were killed.

These incidents shattered all hope of reconciliation, at least for the immediate future. Most southerners concluded that these massacres represented the true intentions of all northerners. From then on, the south became consumed in endless attacks and retaliations between northerners and southerners, with the Anya-Nya serving as the best armed champions of southerners. As usual in such situations, it was the common people who suffered most. An endless stream of refugees crossed the borders to neighbouring countries. The economy of the nation deteriorated drastically, producing widespread discontent. On 25 May 1969, therefore, a group of army officers led by Colonel Jaafar al-Nimiery overthrew the government in a bloodless coup.

Nimiery's Government soon became very popular with the masses. In July 1971, an attempt was made by some military elements in alliance with the Communist Party of Sudan to overthrow him, but mostly because of the support of the masses, Nimiery triumphed. The coup attempt led to the execution of twelve military officers and three leaders of the Communist Party.

From the moment it came to power in 1969, the Nimiery Government declared that it would pursue the policy of turning the Sudan into a socialist state. It also announced that it would solve the southern problem by granting regional self-determination to the south. It created a Ministry of Southern Affairs, under a southern Minister, to work out the details of the policy, appointed several southerners to important positions, and set aside money for reconstruction in the south. These policies gradually won over the people of the south. Even the leaders of the Anya-Nya became prepared to negotiate and ultimately dropped their extreme demands.

Finally, in the first months of 1972, the Sudan Government announced to the whole world that it had reached an agreement with the southerners, by which the south was to have a regional government of its own. Steps were immediately taken to begin implementation of the agreement. The Anya-Nya guerrilla fighters finally gave up the fight and surrendered their arms. After that, much of the national effort was devoted to reconstruction, especially in the south.

228

24 Egypt

Although Britain occupied Egypt in 1882 by force, its position in Egypt remained undefined for thirty years. French hostility to the British occupation compelled Britain to declare repeatedly that it was temporary. With the outbreak of the First World War in 1914, Britain declared Egypt a British protectorate, to ensure that Turkey, which had entered into an alliance with Germany, would not be able to take Egypt along with her. Moreover, Egypt's new status would enable Britain to use Egypt's resources freely for prosecuting the war.

The Egyptians, however, resented the conversion of their country to a British protectorate. Moreover, Egyptians suffered considerable loss of personal freedom owing to the emergency war measures taken by the British Government. Consequently, as soon as the war came to an end and the emergency was lifted, the Egyptian nationalist movement became very active under the leadership of Said Zaghloul. Zaghloul demanded full independence, the withdrawal of all British troops, and the merger of the Sudan with Egypt. Though Zaghloul was exiled, the nationalist movement grew from strength to strength. Then in 1919, rebellion broke out all over Egypt. As a result, in February 1922, the British terminated the protectorate and Egypt was declared independent.

The independence constitution declared Egypt a Muslim kingdom under its own ruler, whose title was henceforth changed from Sultan to King and who was to rule with an elected parliament. However, the independence of Egypt was not complete. The British forced upon Egypt an arrangement whereby British forces would remain in the country and Britain would continue to have advisers in the Egyptian administration, whereby Europeans living in Egypt would continue to have their special courts (called the Mixed Courts) and would continue to be protected by the British, and whereby Britain would be responsible for the protection of the Suez Canal. In the first post-independence elections, Zaghloul's party, the Wafd Party, won an overwhelming majority and Zaghloul became Egypt's first Prime Minister.

The history of Egypt since independence falls into two main periods, the year 1952 being the dividing line. Until 1952, the Wafd remained the most powerful political party. However, the King, who had the constitutional power to appoint Prime Ministers and to dissolve parliament, saw this party as a threat to his own supreme authority. Moreover, the British, with their army still stationed in Egypt, also regarded the great popularity of the Wafd Party as a threat to the continuation of their influence in Egypt, especially as the party continued to demand full independence and the withdrawal of British troops. In short, power in Egypt was divided among a triangle of forces – the King, the British and the Wafd Party. Egyptian politics followed a more or less regular pattern. The Wafd usually won the elections; but soon after each election, the Wafd was usually thrown out of power either by the King or as a result of clashes with the British. The King would then appoint a new Prime Minister from among the small minority parties which were ready to do his bidding. The new government would rule dictatorially, suspend the whole or parts of the independence constitution, and rig elections. Every time this happened, the Wafd could usually use its popularity to make things difficult for the government. It could not, however, organise a total revolution for fear of British intervention. After some time, circumstances would compel the King or the British to try the Wafd again. So, either on his own initiative or under British pressure, the King would call new elections which the Wafd would win. A Wafd Government would then come into power, only to be thrown out in due course – and so the circle would be repeated.

In such circumstances, Egyptian politics became characterised by instability, terrible animosities among the leaders and the growth of political violence. The people gradually lost confidence in the whole political system and in the nation's leadership. Ultimately, even the Wafd were pushed to commit acts which greatly reduced the popular confidence which it had enjoyed since the pre-independence days. While continuing as the champion of the nationalist aspirations, the Wafd gradually came to the conclusion that it needed to conciliate the British in order to be free to fight the King and other internal enemies successfully. In 1936 a Wafd Government entered into an Anglo-Egyptian Treaty which expanded Egyptian independence somewhat by abolishing the Mixed Courts and the special status of foreigners in Egypt; it also provided for an end to the occupation of Egypt by British forces. But the treaty still recognised the right of the British to station troops around the Suez Canal and made the withdrawal of British troops from the rest of Egypt conditional upon the building of roads and installations for the British forces by the Egyptian Government. As this condition could not be met quickly, British troops continued to occupy major Egyptian cities until 1946. The treaty was consequently very unpopular with the people and regarded as a betrayal by the Wafd of the nationalist struggle.

The people's confidence in the Wafd was further damaged six years later, in 1942. Partly because of the hard conditions forced on

Egypt by the Second World War, and partly because of nationalist hatred of continued British domination of Egypt, Egyptian public opinion was sympathetic towards Germany and the Axis powers. In January–February 1942, when the German army in North Africa marched towards Egypt, many Egyptians welcomed their coming as the beginning of the liberation of Egypt. In many Egyptian cities, demonstrations sparked off by the food shortages developed into anti-British demonstrations. Therefore on 4 February, British troops surrounded the palace and forced King Farouk to appoint a government led by Mustafa Nahas, the leader of the Wafd. This was seen by most Egyptians as an attack on Egypt's sovereignty. By accepting the Prime Ministership under this condition, Nahas further damaged public confidence in the leadership of the Wafd. By the 1940s, the Egyptians had lost confidence in all sections of the national leadership, although the Wafd was to continue to be the least unpopular of the existing political parties.

While the leaders of Egypt were busy fighting bitter political battles, the people suffered economically. It is not that Egypt did not make any economic progress. On the whole, there was considerable industrialisation, and in agriculture, the area of crop cultivation was considerably expanded. But all this economic progress was too small to provide jobs and a reasonably decent livelihood for the rapidly expanding population of Egypt. For instance, between 1907 and 1947 the number of Egyptians deriving their living from the land increased from 2.5 million to 7.5 million, while the crop area increased only from 7.7 million acres to about 9.2 million acres. In general, because the population increase was much faster than economic expansion, the income per capita of the nation fell from about 110 dollars in 1907 to about 64 dollars in 1950. The number of people flocking to the urban areas for jobs increased wildly, but the job opportunities were increasing only slowly. As a result, urban unemployment became a great national problem.

The Egyptian leaders did little or nothing to improve the lot of the people. In fact, existing conditions suited the interests of many of them. For those leaders with urban business establishments, the massive urban unemployment provided abundant cheap labour. To the big landowners, the increase in the farming population was welcome, since it made it possible for them to increase the rents on their land and offer low wages to farm labourers. Since it was these big men who dominated politics, the government concerned itself very little with social problems.

The land was very unequally distributed. By 1952, 6% of the land-owners owned 65% of all agricultural land. The biggest 280 landlords together owned about 585,000 acres while about 3,000,000 peasants (*fellahin*) had to share less than 6,000,000 acres. The average individual holding of the great landlords was 3,765 acres while that of the fellahin was 1½ acres. Most of the fellahin rented from the big landlords a large part of the land they cultivated. About one million could neither own nor rent any land and had to make a living as poorly paid agricultural wage labourers. Furthermore, the taxation on land was so arranged that the big landlords paid little tax while the poor peasants bore most of the tax burden. At the centre of this unjust system lived the King, the greatest landlord of all, whose palace was the last word in luxury and extravagance.

The political failure of the Egyptian leadership, then, coupled with the corruption, injustice and oppression of the economic and social system, produced deep discontent among the people which found expression in various ways. For instance, the communist organisations attracted considerable following. The students and workers became very radical, repeatedly bursting out in demonstrations against the British and the national government. Many religious reform movements emerged into which the discontented lower classes channelled their grievances. Of these, the greatest was the Muslim Brotherhood. Founded in 1928 as a movement to protect Islam against the irreligion and moral laxities caused by the modern changes in society and the impact of European influence, the Brotherhood ultimately expanded its activities into politics, demanding the overthrow of the whole political system and the establishment, in its place, of an Islamic theocracy. When the prestige of the Wafd began to wane as a result of the 1936 Treaty, the Muslim Brotherhood waded into the nationalist struggle, demanding British withdrawal from Egypt and the Sudan to free Islam from Christian domination.

Meanwhile, the movement that was destined to topple the whole system was taking shape in the army. In 1945, a young colonel named Gamal Abdel Nasser began to form a group with the name of 'Free Officers', which was determined to free Egypt from foreign domination and wipe out the corrupt and oppressive political, social and economic system of Egypt. In 1947, the United Nations Organisation created the state of Israel in Palestine. Immediately, civil war broke out between the Jews and Arabs there. The rest of the Arab world, notably Egypt, went to the aid of the Palestinian Arabs, but the Jews won. For the Egyptian military men who fought in this war, the shame and humiliation of defeat was worsened by the discovery that their government had supplied them with cheap and defective weapons and that the politicians had lined their pockets from the war. The army became alienated from the leaders of the nation, and the 'Free Officers' became stronger and more resolute.

From the last months of 1951, events began to move quickly. In October 1951, the Wafd, once more in power, tried to recapture the people's affection by demanding the abrogation of the 1936 Treaty and the withdrawal of British troops from the Suez Canal zone. The British made their withdrawal from the Canal Zone conditional upon Egypt's agreeing to join a Middle East defence organisation to be formed under the auspices of Britain and her European and American allies. The Wafd leader, Nahas, rejected the plan and announced the abrogation of the 1936 Treaty. The British sent more troops to the Suez, and Egypt prepared to defend itself. Meanwhile, great national excitement had been whipped up, and on 26 January 1952, known as Black Saturday, the masses rose in violent riots and burned practically all the symbols of British domination in Cairo – shops, hotels, cinemas, clubs, etc.

The King and his henchmen seized the opportunity of this violent popular outburst to try to wipe out all the radical political movements. For the next six months, leaders and members of the radical nationalist forces – the Wafd, the Communist movement, the students and the workers – were arrested for their part in the burning of Cairo, tried, executed or imprisoned. The constitution was suspended, rigid controls were placed on the press, and the concentration camps were filled to overflowing. All efforts were made to make the army subservient to the King and the reactionary forces but these attempts failed in the end. On the morning of 23 July 1952, the leaders of the Free Officers arrested the high command of the army and seized power. Three days later, King Farouk abdicated and left Egypt for ever.

At first, the new military rulers of Egypt proceeded cautiously. They called upon a very senior officer, General Mohamed Neguib, to accept leadership of the nation. In June 1953 they abolished the monarchy and changed Egypt into a Republic with General Neguib as President and Prime Minister and with Colonel Nasser as Deputy Prime Minister. But they did not yet go so far as to abolish political parties.

However, as they gradually gained confidence, they began to show more and more that they were not ready to share power in Egypt with any other group. In 1954 they took decisive steps to take all power into their own hands. In the first months of that year, the various political groups – the Wafd, the Communists, and the Muslim Brotherhood – began a noisy campaign for an end to military rule. When General Neguib associated himself with the Muslim Brotherhood, the revolutionaries removed him from office and arrested him. Nasser then became Prime Minister. Many big politicians of the old regime were arrested, tried before the Revolutionary Court and sentenced to long terms of imprisonment. The politicians' newspapers were banned. In October 1954 a member of the Muslim Brotherhood made an attempt on Nasser's life by shooting at him. The Revolutionary Government seized this opportunity to arrest, try, imprison or execute the leaders of the Brotherhood and to stamp out the movement. Meanwhile, similar tough measures were taken to suppress the communists and to purge reactionary elements from the army. By the end of 1954, the revolutionaries, under the leadership of Nasser, were the sole masters of political power in Egypt. In June 1956 Nasser became the first elected President of Egypt. And finally in 1962, the revolutionaries launched their own political party – the Arab Socialist Union – which became the only political party allowed in the country.

After the revolution, much energy was devoted to reforming the economic and social life of Egypt. In general, the revolutionary government devoted attention to ending those grave social inequalities which characterised pre-1952 Egypt. One of its first major acts was the Agrarian Reform Law of September 1952, by which the big landowners were forced to surrender all their land holdings in excess of 100 acres. Much of the land thus seized was distributed among the poor peasants and the rest was held in trust by the government. The government helped the farmers to form co-operatives in which members could obtain credits for carrying on their farming, co-operate to improve farming methods and to market their products. As a result of the services rendered by these co-operatives, each peasant steadily increased the productivity of each acre of his farm and his income. On the whole, Agrarian Reform resulted in improved standards of life for the farming population, considerable social levelling in the rural areas, improved methods of farming, and generally better productivity. The government spent a lot of money on improving the poor land and on providing water for irrigation. The Aswan High Dam, built by the revolutionary government, is the largest dam in Africa.

Much was also done to improve the lot of the urban working population. Laws were passed laying down minimum wages for workers, instituting a 42-hour working week, providing for insurance against illness, injury, death, and old age, providing for the distribution of 25% of industrial profits to workers, establishing special tribunals for quick settlement of disputes between employers and employees, prohibiting the employment of adolescents and women in night jobs, etc. In industrial disputes, the government generally showed itself to be a friend of workers. It also gave encouragement to trade unions in their task of protecting the interests of workers. Since strikes were believed to be unnecessary in such circumstances, strikes were prohibited. On the whole, the revolution gave considerable power to workers and peasants in Egypt.

An important programme of the revolution was the nationalisation of Egyptian industry. Banks, insurance companies and hundreds of other businesses were nationalised, compensation being paid to the owners. The greatest establishment in Egypt, the Suez Canal, was nationalised in 1956. Some private enterprise was still allowed, but these were made to conform to the general national planning and all efforts were made to ensure that they did not exploit the people.

Education was greatly reformed and made free and compulsory, with special emphasis on training people in all types of skills. A programme of adult education was started to improve the lives and skill of the people.

Under the revolutionary government, Egypt has pursued a determined foreign policy of non-alignment. In the first few years of the revolution, Egypt regarded the Western powers, especially Britain and America, as its best friends and sought economic assistance only from them. However, the Western powers made Egypt's participation in a Middle East defence arrangement sponsored by them a condition for giving economic aid. When Egypt refused, they withdrew economic aid, especially their promises to help Egypt finance the Aswan Dam project. Egypt reacted by nationalising the Suez Canal to find money to build the dam and was at once faced by invasion by the armies of Britain, France and Israel. In this crisis, the Soviet Union came to its aid by threatening to go to war with the invaders if they did not stop the invasion. The threat, coupled with American opposition to the invasion, saved Egypt, and this event was followed by economic and military assistance from the Soviet Union and other Eastern European countries. In particular, the Soviet Union offered financial and technical assistance towards the building of the Aswan Dam. The Soviet assistance was enormous, but Egypt was always careful not to allow aid to turn her into the vassal of any power. Abroad, Egypt remained one of the greatest members of the non-aligned group of nations. At home, the Egyptian communists thought that the Soviet assistance to Egypt would give them influence in the country; but Nasser quickly showed them that no other group was to be allowed to share political power and influence in Egypt with the revolutionary government. More communists found themselves in prison or concentration camps.

Egypt has also played a leading part in the Pan-Africanist movement. Nasser was one of the leading advocates of the more radical type of Pan-African nationalism who finally organised themselves into the Casablanca Group.

However, Egypt's attention has been occupied more by developments in the Arab world than in Africa. Under Nasser, Egypt became acknowledged as the leader of the Arab world, especially in its aspiration to liberate the Arab lands occupied by Israel. Under Nasser's influence, Arab unity came to mean a political union of Arab states. In this Nasser won a major victory when, in February 1958, Egypt and Syria agreed to form a union – the United Arab Republic with Nasser as its President. In March 1958, Yemen joined the Union. But the movement towards Arab union progressed no further; in fact it soon collapsed when, in September 1961, Syria seceded from the Union, and four months later Egypt dissolved the Union with Yemen. But Egypt has retained the title and flag of the UAR and has continued to give leadership to the Arabs in their struggle against Israel. However, because of Israel's military superiority and the lack of unity among the Arab states, the Arabs have had little success in this struggle. In the Six Day War of 1967, they suffered a rout and lost large areas of territory to Israel. Egypt lost the Sinai Peninsula, and the Jews occupied the eastern shore of the Suez Canal. As a result, the Canal was out of use until 1975, a great loss of revenue to Egypt.

In 1971, President Nasser died suddenly. He was succeeded as President by Anwar Sadat, one of his closest colleagues since the days of the 'Free Officers'.

25 Algeria

After eight years of liberation war, Algeria became independent in July 1962 under the leadership of Ahmed Ben Bella. While Algerians were happily celebrating their independence, it was obvious that they were entering into very difficult times. The mark of the eight years of war was upon everything. The guerrilla warfare in the countryside, the bloody demonstrations in the cities, and French acts of repression and terrorism had produced widespread destruction and heavy loss of life. Nearly one million Algerians had been killed; more than two million had been uprooted from their villages by the French army and herded together in concentration camps called 'regroupment villages'; about 8,000 villages and hamlets had been destroyed by French napalm bombs or heavy guns. There were, by 1962, more than 500,000 widows, 300,000 orphans, more than one million jobless, tens of thousands of cripples and beggars, and about 300,000 who had taken refuge in Tunisia and Morocco. Many government offices, hospitals, telephone offices, and factories were in ruins owing to the activities of the Secret Army Organisation, the terrorist organisation of the French settlers.

To resuscitate the national services and to help establish the control of the independence government, Algeria needed administrators, finance experts, clerks. But such jobs had been more or less monopolised by Frenchmen and other European settlers in Algeria, and in the weeks before and after independence, most of these Europeans fled the country. By October 1962, almost one million Europeans had fled Algeria, most of them trying to avoid what they expected would be Algerians' reprisals for the activities of the French terrorists. The result of such mass exodus was that, in the words of Ben Bella himself, the country's administration was a 'vacuum' at independence. The offices of the central government, the provincial administrations, the technical departments (like the highway department) – all were more or less empty. 'When I entered the prefecture in Oran,' said Ben Bella, 'I personally found just seven employees instead of the 500 who had previously worked there.' And, in many cases, the European employees of these offices had burnt or stolen valuable official records before fleeing.

All over Algeria, public security was weak. Many ex-soldiers of the liberation still retained their guns, while guerrilla bands continued to control isolated patches of the country.

But perhaps the most serious problem facing Algeria at independence was the disunity among its leaders. Unlike most other African countries, this disunity was not based on ethnic rivalries. It was one of the legacies of the liberation war itself. To be able to fight a united war against France, the Algerian nationalist leaders had, in 1954, almost all agreed to work together within one political party – the National Liberation Front (FLN). In 1956, these leaders held a meeting at which they worked out a detailed scheme for prosecuting the war. They set up an Army of National Liberation (ALN) with a general staff; they also set up an assembly of leaders, a sort of parliament – the National Council of the Algerian Revolution (CNRA) – which was authorised to make decisions about the country's future. In 1958, in order to ensure effective negotiations with the new government of France under General de Gaulle, the FLN leaders set up a provisional government – the Provisional Government of the Algerian Republic (GPRA).

However, the FLN never developed into a truly united organisation.

Old political affiliations never completely died out among its leading members, and the war forced on the party a highly decentralised management of the independence struggle. Some leaders who were in exile abroad (especially in Morocco, Cairo and Tunisia) prosecuted the diplomatic and armed struggle against France from there. Within the country itself, it was impossible to manage the guerrilla fighters from only one single centre. Therefore, Algeria was divided into six military districts called *wilayas*, each under a guerrilla commander. There was no dominant leader of the party. At its foundation, the leaders had agreed on the principle of collective leadership to prevent the rise of what they called 'personal power'. Among the various groups within and outside the country fighting under the FLN's banner, co-ordination was poor owing to the circumstances in which they lived and operated. Gradually, each isolated group developed a life, a leadership and ideas of its own. From this situation, there ultimately emerged separate groups, made up of men who had fought together in the guerrilla struggle, or men who had worked together in exile, or men who had lived long in the same prison, or men who had risen together in the National Liberation Army, or even men who had belonged to the same political parties before the creation of the FLN.

Early in 1962, France at last agreed to grant Algeria her independence. It was then that the world first became fully aware of the deep divisions in the Algerian leadership. In May 1962 a meeting of the CNRA was called at Tripoli to draw up economic and political guidelines for the independent Algeria that was then in sight. Though this meeting did agree on a programme, it failed in its attempts to elect a supreme leadership for independent Algeria, because of the sharp rivalries among the main groups. Thereafter, the groups gradually regrouped into two major alliances and the struggle for power between them developed from a war of words to actual armed conflict. By July, one of the alliances – that which was grouped around Ben Bella and which included the members of the General Staff of the National Liberation Army – had become victorious. This is how Ben Bella became the first leader of independent Algeria. Even after this, Ben Bella and his supporters faced a stiff challenge from the wilaya commanders who resisted having their forces disbanded. Another round of fighting followed. Finally, on 9 September, Colonel Houari Boumediene, the Commander of the ALN, entered Algiers in triumph and eleven days later general elections were held to the General Assembly. On 26 September, the assembly empowered Ben Bella to form a government, and two days later the assembly approved his cabinet.

Algeria now had a proper independent government, whose tasks were formidable. The machinery of government had to be put in proper shape. Algerians were recruited to man as many as possible of the administrative and technical positions, high and low, which had been vacated by the fleeing Europeans. A coherent police force was created from all available security units. The ALN was converted into the national army. By using the new police and military forces, the government quickly established order in the whole country. In one or two places, however, the suppression of lawless guerrilla bands continued until January 1963.

The fleeing of European farmers, industrialists and store-keepers had left the nation facing economic chaos. Thousands of Algerians had simpy rushed to seize whatever abandoned properties they could lay their hands on – houses, apartments, shops, restaurants and in some cases, farms. The factories and the bigger farms could not be seized in this way because the workers employed in them would not hand them over to just anybody, and because it needed some higher authority to seize such enterprises. At first, the General Union of Algerian Workers (UGTA) attempted to organise the workers to take over and run the enterprises in which they were employed. But the UGTA had neither the funds nor the organisation to do this well and in the end, the government had to step in.

It was obvious that the country would run into very serious economic troubles, or even be faced with starvation, unless the government ensured the proper management of these factories and farms, which had always produced most of Algeria's wealth and food. In fact, because of the stoppage of work on these enterprises, the economy of the nation was fast approaching collapse. Food was drastically short and unemployment reached a dangerous level.

Certain factors determined the government's policies towards the abandoned enterprises as well as towards the ultimate economic organisation of the nation. First, Ben Bella, a socialist, wanted Algeria to opt for state enterprise rather than private enterprise. He believed that state enterprise would ensure social and economic equality in the country, and was convinced that, since the Algerians had no capital, private enterprise could only mean European domination of the Algerian economy. Secondly, the success of the Algerian liberation war had attracted many foreign socialists and intellectuals to Algeria, and these now became Ben Bella's chief economic advisers. Finally, among the masses of Algerians themselves – workers, students and farmers – there was a great deal of enthusiasm for more and more change, now that the nation was in control of its destiny.

After steps had been taken in October 1962 to stop the irregular occupation of abandoned properties and to institute management committees of workers in the enterprises, the government came out in March 1963 with its master plan. Ben Bella placed before the nation a document containing three decrees. The first defined 'vacant' property as any property not occupied by its owner within two months. This gave the French the option of repossessing their properties. The second decree vested the management of the vacant enterprises, which were not repossessed after two months, in the workers employed in them and laid down the institutional details of the workers' management. The third decree established that the profits of the enterprises would be shared among the workers, after they had paid a percentage into the government's national investment fund and employment fund. The self-managed farms came under the National Office for Agrarian Reform which had been set up by an earlier decree. Other agencies were also set up through which the farms marketed their products and obtained credits. As for the 'vacant' factories, they were simply left under the management of their workers, under the supervision of the National Ministry for Economy.

These measures, especially the March decrees, constitute the pillars of what the government began to call the Algerian 'socialist revolution'. Abroad, Ben Bella's Algeria began to be described as the vanguard of socialism on the African continent. In Algeria itself, the masses were consumed by enthusiasm for the 'socialist revolution'. Ben Bella himself was particularly good at whipping up such enthusiasm, addressing huge crowds, spelling out the aims of the revolution and encouraging the people to expect great things to come. Loudspeakers and posters proclaimed the advance of the revolution, which, they claimed, was not a socialist revolution borrowed from any outside sources but a 'purely Algerian' socialist revolution based on the vast peasant majority – 'the fundamental revolutionary mass'.

By 1964, however, many people had started to have doubts. Educated people pointed out, rightly, that it was ridiculous for Ben Bella to be claiming to pursue a socialist revolution without training socialist cadres who would carry the revolution to the masses of the people and without establishing the institutions for the revolution. To most people, too, the huge gaps between promises and achievements had become obvious. In spite of promises of rapid industrialisation and agrarian reform, no economic plans were produced, even as late as 1965. Some new industries were being built with foreign aid, but work on them was often inefficient and slow. Projects for providing un-employment-relief work for the unemployed failed owing to inefficiency. The self-managed farms and industries were doing badly owing to the inexperience and low level of education among the workers, but also owing to lack of government support and too much political interference. Unemployment was increasing steadily. By 1964, over 700,000 Algerians had migrated to Europe (mostly to France) in search of jobs.

Nevertheless, though Ben Bella lost considerable popularity, he was still very popular in the country by 1965. The real danger to him was not popular discontent, but growing disaffection between him and the leading members of the alliance which had brought him to power. In spite of its success in winning the contest for the leadership of the nation at independence, this alliance never became integrated. The groups within it were still more or less distinct, each clinging to its own leader. The inevitable rivalries, clashes of opinion and personal differences among colleagues in any government had, in the case of the Algerian government, the effect of worsening the relationship between the various groups in the alliance. Within a year of independence, Mohamed Khider and Ferhat Abbas (elected Secretary-General of the FLN and President of the National Assembly respectively at independence) were compelled to resign. Ben Bella and Hauari Boumediene, the former commander of the ALN who was now commander of the national army and Minister of Defence, had moved steadily apart. A military man essentially, Boumediene preferred tightly controlled order to Ben Bella's style of constantly causing excitement. It is not easy to describe the differences between their views, as Boumediene was not hostile to socialism as such but to Ben Bella's methods in trying to achieve it.

In June 1965, the split blew right open. For some time, Ben Bella had been trying to find new political friends for himself. He had, in particular, moved very close to the labour federation, the UGTA. Early in June, he decided to remove Abdelaziz Bouteflika from his post as Foreign Minister. Now, Bouteflika was one of Boumediene's closest friends. The belief grew among the groups around Boumediene that Ben Bella had decided to eliminate them – in fact, that he had planned to carry out a *coup d'état*. On 19 June, Boumediene moved in with his army and arrested Ben Bella and some of his leading men. Though actual protest against the coup was small, it was obvious that the nation was surprised and unhappy about it. On 5 July, Boumediene proclaimed the new government – the Revolutionary Council.

The coup brought to power a man very different from Ben Bella. Ben Bella had been a man of the people, a master of brilliant speeches and a lover of mass rallies and deafening ovations. Boumediene hated crowds and noisy rallies, and in his first two years at least, he was an obscure ruler. For months he made no appearance in public, and whenever he did he could excite no enthusiastic welcome. Ben Bella used to arrive at decisions quickly by consulting only his own small group of friends and advisers. Boumediene revived the system of collective leadership laid down in 1954 and, therefore, his government spent most of its time trying to reconcile the claims and aspirations of the various groups around the seat of power – with the result that decisions could not be taken. Abroad, while Ben Bella's Algeria had been widely accepted as a great pillar of Pan-Africanism and Arab unity, Boumediene's Algeria shrank into its shell, isolated from and suspected by most African and Arab leaders.

Within the first year of Boumediene's leadership, Algeria made little or no progress. Boumediene had started by accusing Ben Bella of turning Algeria into a laboratory for irresponsible socialist experiments. But he had neither the public support nor the unity among his own colleagues to feel strong enough to abandon those experiments. In fact, he could offer little more than the continuation of Ben Bella's economic and social programmes and plans.

The year 1967, however, marked a turning point. A few African and Arab leaders began to feel less hostile to Boumediene. Then, when the Arab-Israeli war of June 1967 broke out, he seized the opportunity to project himself as a great Arab nationalist. In fact, for some time, especially after the Israeli victory over Egypt and the other Arab states, Boumediene, by continuing to proclaim an uncompromising anti-Israel stand, looked as if he would supplant Nasser as the leader of the Arab world.

At home too, the Arab-Israeli war aroused violent nationalist sentiment and brought Boumediene into close contact with the people. After this, he gradually established an image for himself, as a serious, responsible leader interested in nothing but the progress of the nation. He would go on long tours of the provinces, sometimes taking the whole cabinet with him, to study the problems of development projects in the provinces at first hand. Though he lacked Ben Bella's magic for attracting and charming the crowds, he nevertheless began to get warm receptions on his tours.

In these circumstances, his confidence grew and a change began to occur in his attitude to the question of power in the nation. The collective leadership which he had created after the coup was, like the alliance which had brought Ben Bella to power, very seriously riddled with divisions. The principal line of division was that between those who advocated considerable decentralisation or even regionalisation of authority and those who opposed it. The former consisted largely of the former *wilaya* commanders whose influence was provincially based and who hoped to gain from decentralisation; the latter included Boumediene himself and his closest friends. But there were other smaller lines of division – the various old groups existed as before. As early as late 1966, the members of the government had started to disagree openly. Between August and October 1966, two ministers fled the country and joined the ranks of Boumediene's enemies abroad. In mid-December 1967, disagreements between Boumediene and Colonel Tahar Zbiri, a former *wilaya* commander and now a member of the Revolutionary Council, led to an armed showdown. Zbiri lost the contest and his friends within the cabinet fled the country or committed suicide. From then on, Boumediene seized all powers into his own hands. He refused to call the Revolutionary Council and proceeded systematically to establish his control over such national bodies as the UGTA, the Students' Union, the Women's Organisation. His opponents retaliated by trying to topple his government or assassinate him – all to no avail.

With all power now controlled by him and his closest friends, Boumediene entered, in 1968, into an era of intense economic activity. A three-year industrial development plan had been issued in 1967. Under the guidance of the energetic Minister of Industry, Belaid Abdesslam, Algeria began to engage in massive industrialisation, with particular emphasis on heavy industries – petroleum, gas, cement, textiles, canning. This industrialisation programme is believed to have been the largest and most ambitious in independent Africa in the last years of the 1960s. With it went a programme of nationalisation of foreign private industries, with a view to eliminating their competition with the state industries. By the end of 1968, over 80% of all foreign industries had been nationalised.

All the new and the nationalised industries were run directly by the state. Boumediene preferred this to the system whereby workers managed their own industries. However, with a few exceptions, he did not destroy self-management in the factories where it already existed. In fact, some reforms were carried out, with a view to improving the efficiency of the self-managed industries and farms.

Index